REFLECTIVE TEACHING,
EFFECTIVE LEARNING

ALA Editions purchases fund advocacy, awareness, and accreditation programs for library professionals worldwide.

REFLECTIVE TEACHING, EFFECTIVE LEARNING

INSTRUCTIONAL LITERACY FOR LIBRARY EDUCATORS

CHAR BOOTH

American Library Association
Chicago   2011

Char Booth is E Learning Librarian at the University of California, Berkeley. A 2007 ALA Emerging Leader and 2008 *Library Journal* Mover and Shaker, Char blogs about library futures, instructional design, and technology literacy at info-mational (www.infomational.com), and tweets @charbooth. She published *Informing Innovation: Tracking Student Interest in Emerging Library Technologies at Ohio University* (ACRL Digital Publications) in 2009, and *Hope, Hype, and VoIP: Riding the Library Technology Cycle* (ALA TechSource) in 2010. Char completed an ME in educational technology at Ohio University in 2008, an MSIS at the University of Texas at Austin's School of Information in 2005, and a BA in history at Reed College in Portland, Oregon, in 2001.

Printed in the United States of America
15 14 13 12 11   5 4 3 2 1

While extensive effort has gone into ensuring the reliability of the information in this book, the publisher makes no warranty, express or implied, with respect to the material contained herein.

ISBN: 978-0-8389-1052-8

Booth, Char.
   Reflective teaching, effective learning : instructional literacy for library educators / Char Booth.
      p. cm.
   Includes bibliographical references and index.
   ISBN 978-0-8389-1052-8 (alk. paper)
   1. Library orientation. 2. Information literacy--Study and teaching. 3. Information services--User education. 4. Library employees--Training of. 5. Teacher-librarians--Training of. 6. Teaching--Methodology. 7. Effective teaching. 8. Reflective teaching. 9. Learning, Psychology of. I. Title.
   Z711.2.B66 2011
   028.7071--dc22

                                                                2010014026

Text design in Minion Pro and Union by Casey Bayer.

♾ This paper meets the requirements of ANSI/NISO Z39.48-1992 (Permanence of Paper).

ALA Editions also publishes its books in a variety of electronic formats. For more information, visit the ALA Store at www.alastore.ala.org and select eEditions.

For my parents, the most gifted teachers I have known.

Thank you, so much, for everything.

Contents

PART I INSTRUCTIONAL LITERACY

PART II THE USER METHOD

Foreword

WE ALL LEARN—every day. Each day, some new part of our mystically infinitely moldable brains rearranges itself to cope with the new data and performance requirements of our lives. If that sounds a bit like the way your laptop works, you're not far off. Our minds take in vast amounts of information, mash it around a bit using the processes we've learned, and mix it with all of the other data already in there from experiences past. The result is that we function day to day, completing tasks, interacting with others, and laying our own personal stamp on this earth.

In this world of constant information, learning, and change, the tradition of the teacher goes back to the earliest human records. We have an intrinsic desire to learn and to teach others what we know. I can think of no other human institution more dedicated to the process of learning and sharing than the library. Libraries are the knowledge centers of our communities. As a result, the responsibility falls to us librarians to engage both our users and ourselves in continuous learning, so that we might remain a crucial resource in our communities' pursuit of learning. Remember that all of this change, all of this rearranging of data in our computer brains, is for the purpose of making life simpler and better. It's all about ease and contentment, and every single class we teach as librarians, every single tutorial we create, every recommended web tool we message about, is all in pursuit of that simple dream for our users—a content, informed, and easy life.

The riddle of how we learn is ever present in the minds of teachers, trainers, and instructors. How can we best help our little computer brains absorb new information? What can we do to allow ourselves the best opportunity to produce something of value with the data we've been given? How do we learn? How do we teach others, using what we know about learning styles and approaches? How do we train successfully? Each of us knows what we do and don't respond to as learners, but it's difficult to translate those ideas into effective instruction.

As one of the many librarians thrust into the teaching limelight early on and without any preparation, I have always been wary of books of instructional models and seminars on learning theory and practice. My brain screams, "Too academic, too theoretical!" and I turn away. I have always been skeptical of the nonpractical. I've learned to train from others in the trenches, those who have been doing it much longer than I have and who have proven track records of a positive impact on learners' lives. Admittedly, I've always wanted to learn about the theory and practice, but in a way that makes sense to those of us who actually have to *use* it.

This is a book for all instructors and trainers. If you teach in any setting and with any group, this book will create a confidence in your abilities and approach that you are unlikely to find anywhere else. Char Booth is one of the most amazing minds in our profession, and her expertise in the area of instructional design will benefit all of us who take the time to listen to her. She has asked and answered questions about how we learn effectively and, equally, how we teach effectively. Her user-centered focus is what sets her apart from many other instructional designers and experts. The text that follows has numerous techniques that other books just gloss over without any explanation of how to do them well—such as how to develop the confidence you need to be an effective instructor, or how to actually design, conduct, and evaluate effective sessions and learning objects.

Many will assume that this type of book is aimed primarily at the academic audience, but they're wrong. Char has effectively bridged the long-standing divide between the two groups who study learning—the academics on one side looking at the theory, and everyone else on the other side teaching and training away endlessly in the trenches with barely enough time to devote thought to the process. She focuses on engaging the learner and following up on learning outcomes in a way that is accessible for everyone. My thirst for practical theory has finally been quenched with Char's approach to instructional literacy and design. If you want to make your life easier when developing learning and training projects, then you need *Reflective Teaching, Effective Learning*.

Commit yourself to reading this book, but don't worry about memorizing every step or idea it contains. Because Char knows what she's doing, you will absorb the information and approaches she presents and integrate them into your future learning designs. Any volume that takes a lot of the hard work out of developing a training style or learning system is well worth its salt, and Char's USER method measures up. Be ready to have your computer brain mashed around in a good way.

Sarah Houghton-Jan
www.librarianinblack.net

Preface

INSPIRATION

Librarians of all stripes design and deliver instruction every day, yet we rarely receive the training, mentorship, and experience it takes to hit the ground teaching. For many of us, instruction becomes the most challenging aspect of what we do; I felt this when I began my career. The notion of teaching anything to anyone in any format was paralyzing, my pedagogical knowledge was limited, and learning technologies mystified me. The extreme discomfort this created gave rise to a personal vendetta: *improve, or else*. Through experimentation, observation, collaboration, research, continuing education, and more trial and error than I care to recall, I have come to understand more about how and why people learn in information-focused contexts, and how librarians can become indispensable knowledge facilitators among the learners and organizations they support. As I build instructional confidence, I find myself more able to connect with users, students, faculty, and colleagues. *Reflective Teaching, Effective Learning* springs from my love of the moments of real insight and skill-building that occur during this process, and the conviction that they neither need be few nor far between. If you engage with this text and reflect on your practice, my hope is that you will face less anxiety, integrate more fully and with greater impact into your communities of practice, and enjoy a more flexible and gratifying teaching experience overall.

CHALLENGE

Being an educator is about laying yourself on the line, opening up to criticism, and accepting vulnerability so that others may gain knowledge; every learning interaction becomes an opportunity to either stretch or flinch. The strongest instructors and trainers use this challenge to consciously adapt to the situations they engage in and create strategic, personalized learning experiences, rather than becoming discouraged or falling back on routine. If teaching is hard, learning to teach well is harder (and, if the past two years of my life are any indication, writing about learning to teach well may be the hardest of all). This book is for anyone who wants to develop stronger design and delivery skills, become more dynamic and self-aware in their instructional approach, and adapt to the changing library, literacy, and information technology landscape. Building our capacity to contribute actively to the knowledge society is paramount, and developing as instructors and designers is integral to demonstrating our evolving value.

APPLICATION

To frame the instructor development process, in part I of this book I present the concept of *instructional literacy*, which consists of reflective practice, educational theory, teaching technologies, and instructional design, to focus less on *what* you should teach than on *how* to engage your learners. Embedded in instructional literacy are transferable strategies that help you choose technologies and activities that support real outcomes, cultivate your instructor identity, and build a personal learning environment for current pedagogical awareness. To guide you from concept to application, in part II I present the USER method, an instructional design approach that steps through *understanding* a learning scenario; *structuring* educational content; *engaging* learners; and *reflecting* on the knowledge that is built. This method can be used to facilitate any type of instruction in any medium. USER provides strategies for rapidly, reliably, and systematically producing teaching tools and information services that make more impact.

Acknowledgments

FIRST AND FOREMOST, endless thanks and boundless love to Lia Friedman, librarian soul mate and perennial editor, for reading this manuscript many times over, fixing whatever was busted, forcibly pulling my chin up when necessary, and being my champion in all things. Undying respect and gratitude to Emily Drabinski, for steering me away from crap and toward credibility with majestic editorial acumen. Much appreciation to Sarah Houghton-Jan, for always offering inspiration (and for nailing this book's foreword with a railroad spike). Heartfelt gratitude to Chris Rhodes at ALA Editions for his insight and patience with my tendency to put the "dead" in deadlines. Fiercest love to my incredible family for everything, and to my friends for supportively tolerating my randomness over the duration of this project. Thanks also to all who submitted their teaching philosophies, and hats off to my Berkeley, Ohio, Austin, and libraryland colleagues for being amazing sounding boards, collaborators, critics, and guinea pigs. My deepest admiration for every teacher, trainer, librarian, performer, professor, designer, artist, student, presenter, writer, and assorted individual from whom I have gleaned a trick or two; know without a doubt that what I know I know because of you. Special appreciation to those who really take time in answering questions and filling out surveys—you send me. Finally, warmest regards to all who love teaching and learning enough to stick with it. May you know how much you matter when all is said and done.

Introduction
In the Trenches

IF I WAS called to librarianship, I was thrown into teaching. When I started my first job in the field, I was asked (as so many are) to assume a heavy instructional load fresh out of graduate school. I had taken one information literacy class, was almost totally inexperienced at public speaking, and knew next to nothing about learning theory or curriculum design. I understood what I wanted to get across, but when facing a room of twenty-five bored undergraduates, my nervousness made it all but impossible. My hope was to present relevant and interesting information strategies to my students, but I could barely hold their attention while I tried. I stuttered, stammered, rambled, and was confident only in the fact that I led overloaded workshops that resulted in little if any transferable knowledge.

Left with the sobering realization that I knew very little about how to do a large part of my job, I sought help from those with more experience. My coworkers came through generously with planning support and practical tips, but following their skillful advice quickly taught me a lesson: When it comes to instruction, one size most certainly does not fit all. Scripts seemed to play out differently in each class, and exercises and handouts that worked beautifully for others fell flat for me. As time passed, more challenges arose; online tutorials, staff training, conference presentations, and more were all teaching moments I felt unprepared for, and emulation was never a reliable escape hatch. I was consistently vexed by the same questions: *Where am I supposed to begin? What strategies are appropriate in this case versus another? How can I tell if my audience is learning?*

Mounting uncertainties motivated me to learn how to educate without relying solely on trial, error, and terror. To feel more in control I needed to develop my own approach to effective instruction, from an overall aim of becoming more engaging down to the way I established rapport with students as they walked in the door. I wanted confidence that I could facilitate learning not only in a live environment but in any setting, using emerging technologies or traditional methods. I wanted to make better use of limited preparation time, shore up short classes, reduce my nervousness, and ultimately come to enjoy what was literally the only aspect of my chosen profession that I dreaded.

While working full time as a librarian at Ohio University, I enrolled in a master's degree program in educational technology. My fellow students were local K–12 instructors facing budget cuts and strict expectations that they "teach to the test," thanks largely to the accreditation and funding strictures created by No Child Left Behind. Studying with seasoned teachers who shared their on-the-ground insights made me realize that I had never considered my convictions and interests as an educator the way I had as a librarian. I experienced a growing awareness that I needed to cultivate all sides of my teaching self if I was going to improve. It was in this context that I first encountered ideas of reflective practice and instructional design, which have helped me become more assured in the knowledge that I can create learning experiences that are not only pedagogically sound, but authentic reflections of my teacher identity.

LEARNING TO TEACH

My story probably sounds familiar. Despite how often information professionals teach, we are not as systematically trained as other types of educators. The integration of information literacy into LIS practice has been ongoing for decades, yet revised 2008 ALA accreditation standards reveal a continued lack of pedagogical emphasis: "The curriculum of library and information studies encompasses information and knowledge creation, communication, identification, selection, acquisition, organization and description, storage and retrieval, preservation, analysis, interpretation, evaluation, synthesis, dissemination, and management."[1] Most of these elements are central to the educational mission of libraries, yet instruction itself is absent from this list. According to survey research I conducted in 2009, (n=398), only about a third of those who regularly teach and train in libraries completed education-related coursework during their MLS studies, only 16 percent of which was required. Strikingly, over two-thirds of these instruction librarians felt that their LIS education underprepared them to teach—less than 5 percent felt strongly that it had. Seventy percent of those in my study indicated that their employers provide some sort of professional development support, but that their development opportunities remain limited. The result

is not surprising: anxiety is common among new and experienced library instructors, a third of my respondents indicated that they always or frequently experience feelings of anxiety in live teaching scenarios, and another third reported that they sometimes did.

INSTRUCTOR DEVELOPMENT (AND DEVELOPMENT, AND DEVELOPMENT...)

Library instruction occurs constantly via a bewildering number of formats and technologies. Whether online or on the ground, staff trainings, workshops, tutorials, one-on-one interactions, and other learning scenarios and objects are ubiquitous in our organizations. Systematic instructor development is a fundamentally recognized aspect of teaching effectiveness, yet it remains comparatively inaccessible to librarians. Other educators follow a standards-based accreditation process or pursue ongoing training for purposes of certification; we rely on personal initiative and external professional engagement for preparation. All of these can be effective skill builders, but they can also be highly subject to availability.

With limited time and resources, we face the daunting task of not only teaching concrete skills but encouraging a mindset of information and technology self-sufficiency in learner populations ranging from patrons, students, researchers, and faculty to ourselves and our colleagues. Many things, therefore, may have brought you to this book. You could be looking for ways to combat your trepidation in the classroom, activities to motivate audiences, perspective on instructional design and technology, or insight into learning itself. Many of us view any teaching scenario—whether large or small, face-to-face, or online—as unfamiliar and intimidating, not unlike a proverbial dark and unfamiliar forest, full of hidden pitfalls. When you first enter a classroom or start planning a digital learning interaction, it is sometimes like being pushed into the trees blindfolded. My goal is simple: to help you find your way using the survival strategies that constitute *instructional literacy*.

INSTRUCTIONAL LITERACY

Instructional literacy is essentially what I wish I had more of when I started teaching: the combination of skills and knowledge that facilitates effective, self-aware, and learner-focused educational practice. To extend the terrible metaphor, to find your way through the instructional forest you need moxie (reflective practice), a compass (educational theory), a flashlight (teaching technologies), and a large machete to hack at obstacles (instructional design). Instructional literacy balances these four elements:

Reflective practice is a process of understanding and shaping your skills and abilities as you teach, not just assessing your performance at the end of an interaction.

Educational theory is research-based insight into instruction. It consists of learning theory (principles of how people synthesize information and build knowledge), instructional theory (the concepts and methods of instruction), and curriculum theory (content knowledge specific to fields, subjects, and audiences).

Teaching technologies are the tools and media that encourage effective learning in face-to-face, online, and blended instruction as well as methods for evaluating and using them effectively.

Instructional design is a systematic and learner-focused method of integrating reflection, theory, and technology as you plan, deliver, and assess learning scenarios and materials.

Working toward an understanding of each component allows you to make stronger and more informed connections between *pedagogy*, the theory of instruction, and *praxis*, its practical application. For the duration of these pages, you are (I hope) signing up to develop skills that will help you confront the challenges inherent to teaching, training, and designing learning materials. That said, no matter what your goals are or how I address them, like any learner (or traveler) you are ultimately responsible for what you take away from this book (or making it out alive). Instructional literacy is an ongoing process; if you find that you don't learn enough this time around, the next step is always to take another step.

CHAPTER BREAKDOWN

Reflective Teaching, Effective Learning is divided into two sections. Part I examines the components of instructional literacy:

Chapter 1 considers instructor development and the qualities of effective educators.

Chapter 2 explores reflective practice, metacognition, and message design.

Chapter 3 suggests approaches to collaboration and cultivating communities of practice.

Chapter 4 presents theories of learning that offer insight into how people process information and form knowledge.

Chapter 5 outlines theories of instruction that can help learning design become more targeted and effective.

Chapter 6 reflects on strategies for integrating teaching technologies in library instruction.

Chapter 7 investigates the process and applications of instructional design.

Part II provides a framework for library instructional design through the USER method:

Chapter 8 outlines the steps and phases of USER.

Chapter 9, "Understand," describes strategies for understanding your audience and analyzing needs around a learning scenario.

Chapter 10, "Structure," presents practical approaches to organizing and developing any type of instructional material.

Chapter 11, "Engage," explores visual literacy and universal principles of design as well as engaging instructional delivery strategies.

Chapter 12, "Reflect," suggests techniques to help you assess learning and revise your approach based on learner feedback, and reuse instructional objects.

Appendix A provides templates for planning instruction and evaluating technology; appendix B lists responses from library educators to the survey on teaching effectiveness mentioned above.

FLEXIBLE INSTRUCTIONAL DESIGN

Library instruction often consists of either a) entering an established learning community, productivity context, or instructional scenario in order to impart practical skills and support research practice (e.g., course-integrated instruction, staff training), or, b) determining an existing performance or information need and addressing it with just-in-time learning objects or opportunities (e.g., drop-in workshops, embedded learning objects in an online catalog). Both require the ability to identify how each scenario is unique in order to create more responsive learning experiences.

Unique learning contexts are not the only variable in this equation; every educator has strengths and weaknesses. You may feel more confident in your ability to design online materials than presenting live, whereas I might excel at classroom management but feel less equipped to assess students. No matter where your comfort zone falls, you can benefit from a methodical approach to instructional planning that builds on your strengths at the same time that it identifies unique learner needs. Instructional design reduces guesswork by helping you systematically focus on both the techniques and characteristics of each new learning scenario. The USER method is a four-phase template for designing reflective and outcomes-focused instruction in a library context (figure 0.1).

A friend and colleague of mine observed that USER could be applied "either as a thought or action model or a hybrid of both." This is an excellent summary of the method's intent. Think of USER not as a rigid, drawn-out process of formal planning, but a strategy for creating adaptable and reusable library instruction that you can draw from to the degree that your educational context requires. The steps and phases of USER help you think through, design, evaluate, and revise any type of learning interaction or object, from the largest curriculum-integrated information literacy program down to the smallest research guide, on the fly or in painstaking detail.

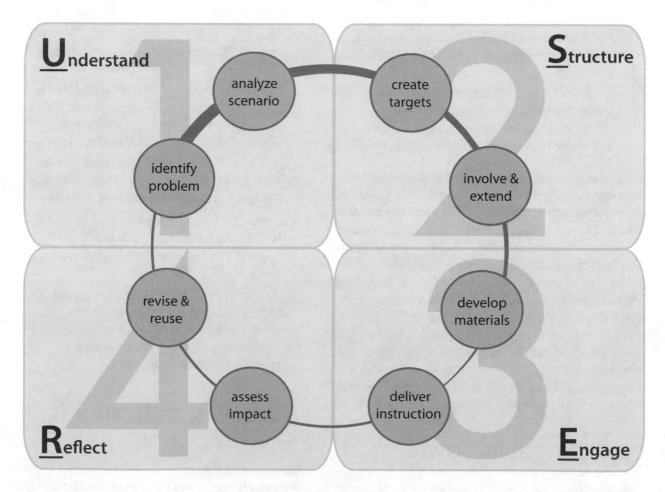

Figure 0.1
USER method

TEACHING TECHNOLOGY: SEEKING STRATEGIES

Pedagogy and praxis are shifting with the information technology climate. Social, mobile, and dynamic tools are expanding active learning and presentation methods, and web-based communication has opened new avenues for interacting and collaborating with audiences. Some librarians deliver instruction using exclusively online platforms; others bring together live and digital teaching methods to create "blended" or "hybrid" learning.[2] Whereas several years ago a static web page was the only means of online instruction, now there are countless alternatives. When it comes to teaching technologies, most instructors are faced with a two-part question: *How can I become familiar with new tools and applications, and how do I use them to enhance learning?*

Because local resources differ and comfort levels range widely, it is important to develop current awareness that helps you experiment with, evaluate, and integrate technology into instruction using a practical, solutions-oriented mentality. Sorting through the options can be difficult, and a common challenge for educators is how to use teaching tools not based on their hype potential, but on their practical affordances—the specific functional qualities they provide that can make a learning interaction more collaborative, active, interesting, and so forth. In *Keeping the User in Mind*, Valeda Dent-Goodman introduces the concept of the "instructional mashup"—combining a variety of tools and approaches to create engaging learning experiences.[3] Throughout this book, I suggest strategies for familiarizing yourself with your options in order to mash together the best applications.

ANTICIPATING YOUR QUESTIONS

Now, to head off a few potential questions at the pass:

Who will benefit from this book?

Any librarian, information professional, or library/information studies student who teaches, trains, or designs can use *Reflective Teaching, Effective Learning*. Librarians in general are being motivated (or forced, depending on your perspective) to change the way we operate and focus more intently on the user experience. In this climate, patron, staff, and self-education are critical to the continued relevance of our organizations. This book invites you to form your own ideas about how to make the learning process more lasting and transferable based on your context and the needs of your community. Some of the concepts I discuss are likely familiar to many readers, such as the importance of appealing to different learning styles and using multimedia presentation formats or social software to increase learner engagement in face-to-face instruction. Other ideas, such as elements of visual literacy and metacognition, may present new ways to think through common problems. The strategies outlined in this book are most directly applicable to those involved in library instruction and staff training, as well as early-career educators. They can also be useful for readers developing online content and applications, creating marketing materials, and deploying public services, all of which have didactic elements. Similarly, anyone who blogs, speaks, writes, or consults in the professional community should understand how to design engaging and learner-centered instructional messages and experiences.

Is instructional design required knowledge?

No, but it is a sound strategy for improving your teaching and gaining a stronger foothold in library practice. Several excellent volumes can supplement your knowledge in this area, such as Bell and Shank's *Academic Librarianship by Design*, Dent-Goodman's *Keeping the User in Mind*, Jerilyn Veldof's *Creating a One-Shot Library Workshop*, and Brian Mathews's experience design-focused *Marketing Today's Academic Library*.[4] I believe that instructional effectiveness is as rooted in cultivating enjoyment of your teaching practice as it is in systematic planning, so my approach to this conversation blends the concept of instructional literacy with the USER design method. Neither approach is about following rules lockstep; each is intended to remind you of important considerations and motivate you to pay attention to areas you might otherwise gloss over.

Instructional design discourages some people because they think it will make their planning process cumbersome. As you read, it is crucial to remember that USER is flexible and scalable, and easily adjustable to suit your needs. I have found that reflecting on design becomes second nature and fosters an attitude of adaptability that keeps the critical elements of engaged learning at the forefront. In my experience,

Activity 0.1 **Targets for Reflective Teaching, Effective Learning**	
Goals (instructor-focused end results)	While reading this book, I will • Challenge myself to _____ • Explore ideas around _____ • Discover useful strategies for _____
Objectives (specific skills acquired)	To reach these goals, I will develop my skills in the following specific areas: • _____ • _____ • _____
Outcomes (learner-focused change)	These goals and objectives will result in the following learner changes: • _____ • _____ • _____

this mindset tends to reduce the anxiety-producing sensation that you, the instructor, are the center of attention. It helps the content, context, and community of instruction—guiding elements in any learning interaction—move into the limelight. In any scenario, instructional design and reflective practice are tools for situating, structuring, presenting, and evaluating information based on how and why people learn best.

How should I use *Reflective Teaching, Effective Learning?*

Cookbooks are without a doubt my favorite type of learning object. The best communicate not only ratios and ingredients but also the gestalt of each dish and the philosophy of the author. They easily fit the needs of different types of people—more experienced cooks may only need recipes to confirm assumptions about measurements or help themselves improvise, whereas novices tend to follow instructions to the letter. I hope that you will use this book in the same way, as a collection of techniques and gestalt you can use to fit your needs and inspire you to try something new. I also hope that it challenges you to think in a different way about what you are teaching. Although education is at least as unpredictable as cooking, my desire is to create a set of theories and rules of thumb that help you confront instruction more confidently.

It helps to read with a pencil in hand and practical goals in mind. The key to learning is personal engagement, and I have tried to practice what I preach by

making *Reflective Teaching, Effective Learning* as interactive as possible. I embed activities in the text and include reflection points at the close of each chapter to help you transfer ideas and engage in discussion with other practitioners. Chapter activities, reflection points, and appendices can also be downloaded from the ALA Editions web extras at www.alaeditions.org/webextras/. I define key terms throughout as well as in the glossary. I encourage you to project your experience onto every page, in order to transfer strategies to your own context. It is useful to have one or several instructional scenarios in mind, such as a class, training session, presentation, or series of tutorials you want to create or revise. Try to challenge yourself to evaluate your own teaching critically, and above all else, reflect as you read—jot down notes, think about your dilemmas and strengths, and record any ideas or questions that come up. Make the content of this book personally meaningful so that you can apply it toward the instructional problems you actually face.

SETTING TARGETS

One way to achieve this is by defining *targets* in the form of goals, objectives, and outcomes. Targets improve the impact of instruction, particularly when participants have had a hand in defining them. During an interaction, clearly communicated targets also double as "advance organizers" that allow participants to understand and prepare for their own learning experience.[5] With this in mind, each chapter begins with a set of goals that provide a template for reflecting on personal outcomes as you finish each chapter.

Take a moment to define a series of targets to help you engage with this text (activity 0.1). At their simplest, goals are your overarching aims, objectives are concrete strategies, and outcomes are the changes that endure after a learning interaction. We haven't delved far into specific theories or approaches, so you should keep your targets broad. In the goals row, you might specify that you want to "challenge myself to gain more confidence in face-to-face instruction." In objectives, you might be interested in "selecting teaching technologies based on learning outcomes." In outcomes, you might imagine any concrete changes in your teaching, such as "more confidence in my teaching persona," "increased collaboration with coworkers," or "a more systematic approach to planning." Don't agonize over phrasing at this point; there is more discussion of targets in chapter 10.

SUMMARY

- **Instructional literacy** consists of four areas that focus your instructor development: **reflective practice, educational theory, teaching technology,** and **instructional design**.
- **Instructional design** and the **USER method** are flexible and systematic approaches to conceptualizing and creating learner-focused education.
- **Targets** are the goals, objectives, and outcomes that allow you to structure measurable learning interactions.

REFLECTION POINTS

1. Think about the four components of instructional literacy—reflective practice, educational theory, teaching technologies, and instructional design—in terms of personal strengths and areas of potential improvement. How would you characterize your relationship (e.g., understanding, experience, comfort level) to each component? Do you already use reflective techniques? Have you only recently heard of instructional design? Try to identify specific high and low points in your own knowledgebase.

2. Take another look at the USER model. Can you identify one phase or step that causes you difficulty during the instructional process, and another that comes more naturally?

NOTES

1. American Library Association, *Standards for Accreditation of Master's Programs in Library and Information Studies* (Chicago: American Library Association, 2008), 12.
2. Hyo-Jeong So, "Designing Interactive and Collaborative E-Learning Environments," in Terry T. Kidd and Holim Song (eds.), *Handbook of Research on Instructional Systems and Technology* (Hershey, PA: Information Science Reference, 2008), 596–613.
3. Valeda Dent-Goodman, *Keeping the User in Mind: Instructional Design and the Modern Library* (Oxford: Chandos, 2009).
4. Steven Bell and John Shank, *Academic Librarianship by Design: A Blended Librarian's Guide to the Tools and Techniques* (Chicago: American Library Association, 2007), quote from p. 9; Brian Mathews, *Marketing Today's Academic Library: A Bold New Approach to Communicating with Students* (Chicago: American Library Association, 2009); Jerilyn Veldof, *Creating a One-Shot Library Workshop: A Step-by-Step Guide* (Chicago: American Library Association, 2006).
5. David Ausubel, *The Psychology of Meaningful Verbal Learning* (New York: Grune and Stratton), 1963.

Part I

Instructional Literacy

Teaching Effectiveness

GOALS

- Discuss the "Curse of Knowledge" and the **SUCCESs approach** to creating streamlined messages.
- Explore the qualities of **effective** (and ineffective) **educators**.
- Develop the concepts of **teacher identity** and **instructional philosophy**.
- Describe the **WIIFM principle** ("What's in it for me?") and how it guides the learning process.
- Describe maintaining current awareness with a **personal learning environment** (PLE).

In this chapter, I explore the qualities of effective instructors, and start things off with a brief note on terminology. Throughout *Reflective Teaching, Effective Learning,* I use several similar-sounding terms to describe different aspects of instruction:

- A *learning object* is any item, lesson, tutorial, text, website, or course created with the purpose of teaching or explaining something.
- An *educational scenario* is the context and environment in which instruction occurs.
- *Instructional messages* engage learners with content and communicate teacher identity.
- *Targets* are the goals, objectives, and outcomes that provide the foundation for objects, scenarios, and messages.
- These elements form a *learning interaction*—the in-person, media-based, or technology-assisted communication between student, instructor, and learning object.

In sum: This book is a learning object, and by reading it you are engaging in an educational scenario. I use instructional messages to focus your attention on a series of targets, all of which combine to create a learning interaction between you, the reader, and me, the author. Ideally, the interplay of these factors results in the formation of useful knowledge by the learner and the accumulation of meaningful experience by the educator. Less ideally, if either party is unable, unmotivated, incapable, or unwilling to create meaning from the interaction, surface-level learning and something that resembles post-traumatic stress occurs instead.

LIBRARIES, NERDS, AND THE "CURSE OF KNOWLEDGE"

If you are currently staring at this learning object, chances are good that you are, like myself, something of a nerd. There are many kinds of nerds: band nerds, book nerds, Twitter nerds, metal nerds, gaming nerds. Under the cat sweaters, Wii controllers, pocket protectors, Androids, or band uniforms, at the core of any nerd you will find an individual with enough passion to let something that interests them take over a bit of their personality. Nerd passion is fueled by a desire to *know*—to be expert, to specialize, and to understand. Since time out of mind, libraries have been sanctuaries for hobbyists, geeks, and nerds, or anyone else who is okay with the fact that they are self-motivated learners. As librarians, we are nerds for knowledge. By making information more findable, usable, and interpretable, we help others in their quest for specialization. This makes us nerd enablers—and therefore more accurately described as *uber-* or *meta*-nerds. Libraries are created for nerds by meta-nerds, so it is not surprising that library educators tend to suffer from an acute case of the "Curse of Knowledge" as we go about instruction.[1] The Curse of Knowledge is the state of being so expert that you have forgotten what it is like to not know something—or, in our case, to not know how to find or evaluate something.

The problem with libraries is that the people who use them are usually not experts, yet we tend to orient ourselves toward expert users. Non-, semi-, and anti-nerds actually make up the vast majority of our patrons. Most people use libraries because they need to do something—finish their taxes, write a paper, research a health problem, or find a quiet place to study. They are there by information necessity and may have much less of a burning desire to know than their nerdier counterparts. I would estimate that, in any given library, four out of five people are on the

path of least resistance, yet our learning objects, information products, and buildings are often directed toward the one remaining self-directed learner—the one who most closely resembles us. This has a way of muddying the waters for typical patrons and preventing them from perceiving how they can use information and productivity technologies more functionally. This is why building our own instructional literacy is important: Every learner could use a few straightforward lessons from us, not only about how to accomplish their information goals with insight and critical thinking, but on what exactly, libraries and librarians can help them *do*.

SINK OR SWIM

Because I was well mentored, my introduction to teaching was relatively painless compared to that of others I know. A few worst-case-scenario examples: After being hired at a public library, one decidedly monolingual friend of mine with no teaching experience found herself tossed into a classroom with thirty nonnative English speakers, many of whom had little experience using a computer. Another was "volunteered" to teach a semester-long, for-credit information literacy class at a large research university on her first day, with only a week to prepare and virtually no guidance. A third began teaching an online course at a community college midsemester, only to discover that half of her students were blithely plagiarizing their assignments the week after a module on information responsibility.

All managed to meet their challenges, but each remembers the sensation of feeling totally unprepared and scrambling for strategies. These examples may be extreme, but they describe a common situation—a librarian staring down an unfamiliar instructional scenario confused, intimidated, or both. Like any other traumatic experience, rushing headlong into teaching can leave lasting scars. Most of us have had "sink or swim" moments as educators, which can occur in any teaching scenario—not just the unfamiliar ones, and not just when you are starting out. Some experience fear or nervousness every time they face a classroom; for others, instructional confidence comes naturally. Although jumping in feet first is an excellent motivator, it can also lead to a situation wherein decisions are made defensively rather than intentionally.

While there are recognized qualities common to strong educators, what makes one teacher "good" is not necessarily universal. Individuality is more important than conforming to a mandated modus operandi, and it is useful to examine how audience and context influences instructional impact. One way of finding common denominators for pedagogical effectiveness among library instructors is to consider our shared challenges:

- Many library educators are involved in instruction on a part-time basis and therefore lack the immersive challenge that allows other educators to develop skills quickly and keep current and engaged.
- Teaching librarians tend to have more limited interactions with learners, meaning that it can be difficult to see immediate or long-term evidence of our interventions.
- Materials and lessons are often repeated, which can generate a sense of redundancy or malaise.
- Library instructors don't follow a mandated program of certification or continuing education, meaning our instructor development is largely self-regulated and context-specific.
- Instructional technologies are constantly changing, and in order to stay current and informed, a strategic evaluation of our own knowledge and abilities is key.
- Our educational contexts and institutional resources vary, making mandated curriculum nearly impossible to achieve (and consequently difficult to train around shared content).

WHAT MAKES A GOOD TEACHER?

Learning is a central aspect of human existence in all but the most dire of situations, and people tend to experience instructor upon instructor throughout their lifetimes. In each phase of my own life as a student, a few educators stand out. In high school I had a garrulous history teacher who would get so lost in his own cowboy yarns that he sometimes forgot to lecture, but who designed such creative assignments that I remember them perfectly. One of my professors at Reed College verged on depression when our papers weren't up to par and would jump on the table and sing show tunes if conversation lagged in seminar.

Another, feared and adored for her telepathic tendency to call on those who hadn't finished the reading, refused to let an idea go before it was fully explored and would rake us over the coals with hilarious, sadistic joy if we didn't talk points through to their logical conclusion. If I put my mind to it I could fill the chapter with mini-profiles of excellent teachers, whom I still meet with wonderful regularity.

What do these individuals have in common, and what inspires me to remember them? Their methods and content differed, but one thing is common: each derived obvious satisfaction from teaching and had high expectations of their students. All went about their jobs with a palpable self-awareness that allowed them to engage, and a personal investment that helped them devote intellectual and emotional energy to their trade. Similar characteristics are true of excellent presenters and designers, who invest in content and engage with audiences to the point that their interest becomes contagious. This is the desired effect: in the case of my best teachers, their motivation made me want to show them what I was made of. Some library educators may feel that our interactions with learners are too limited to achieve this dynamic, which so often requires the time to build real relationships. However, even in the briefest or most virtual of interactions it is possible to channel a sincere enthusiasm and sense of personality that helps participants engage with you and the material more meaningfully. Instructional literacy is in part a process of coming to believe in the value of your own contributions and your ability to be memorable, which simply helps you be more *there*.

Instructors You Remember

Think back on the teachers in your life that stand out. Why do you remember them? Were they exceptionally knowledgeable, funny, or odd? Did they take humdrum subjects and make them interesting, or use unexpected examples or analogies to help you think about things from a different angle? They probably found ways to draw you in no matter how dry their subject matter, or gave you personal attention that made you more interested in performing well. In activity 1.1, list the three strongest instructors or presenters from your own learner experience and identify three characteristics that made them personally effective.

When I create my own list, I notice that each of my bests has variations on the themes of humor, intelligence, and personality. Not surprisingly, there is a

Activity 1.1 **Your Best Teachers**			
Example: Professor X	challenging	insightful	well-spoken
1)			
2)			
3)			

mirror effect in the qualities I strive for in my own instruction and design. Think hard about your own list and draw a lesson from what this signifies that you value in other educators; it is probable that these are the qualities you would most like to possess. Let these characteristics act as benchmarks in the ongoing process of shaping your teaching identity.

Instructors You Have Tried to Forget

By no means do I encourage negativity, but face it—some teachers are worse than others. Imagine my vexation at needing to call out another undergraduate professor for dropping an inconceivably biased remark during class, then dealing with his retaliatory fallout for the rest of the semester. Needless to say, I withdrew from the learning scenario: I retained next to nothing from that point on and resented even having to show up. The flip side of developing an instructional effectiveness strategy is thinking about teacher attributes that have prevented you from learning. From the above experience I came to perceive that it is crucial to strive for cultural sensitivity in speech and action, and to never punish a student for legitimately and respectfully challenging me. In activity 1.2, list three less-than-effective educators (give them code names if this makes you feel guilty) and describe their negative teaching attributes.

Memorable Informal Learning

Because learning takes many forms, teaching effectiveness has to do with more than the traits of individuals. As the information environment becomes increasingly digital, mobile, and social, instructional spaces become more fluid; this expands the potential to apply innovative pedagogies and create less structured learning interactions. Part of what I hope to do in this book is inspire you to think about how effective learning happens outside of the strictures of "traditional" education. Think about it: Maybe you

spent a year obsessing over Dungeons and Dragons as a teenager or saw a nature documentary as a child that you've never forgotten. An example from my own recent experience is Common Craft (www.common craft.com), which has the motto "Our Product Is Explanation." They create simple animated tutorials that translate confusing technological concepts into plain language, some of which I use in training and research education.

Considering what makes nontraditional or informal objects and scenarios hit home can provide some of the best strategic fodder for improving your day-to-day praxis. Examples do not have to be "next-generation" or even contemporary: I personally love the public television children's show *Electric Company,* in both its wildly successful 1970s form and its more recent incarnation (www.pbskids.org/electric company/). This interactive mix of music, dialogue, quick vignettes, and problem-based strategies aligns its message to the needs and characteristics of its audience: You can barely tell that you are learning, which makes you want to keep watching. Another example from public media is WNYC's *RadioLab* (www.wnyc .org/shows/radiolab), which breaks down complex scientific topics using quirky audio production and accessible language. In activity 1.3, list three effective informal instructional objects, interactions, or environments you have experienced and identify the characteristics that made them memorable.

Turning It Around

By reflecting on what makes individual educators and informal learning effective or ineffective, you are creating a mental bank of qualities you either value or want to avoid. For example, while I believe that I am an engaging presenter with a defined design style and sense of personal conviction that I communicate as I teach, I also know that I often rush, experience visible nervousness, and am sometimes less than able to adapt quickly to a situation that requires a major

Activity 1.2 **Your Worst Teachers**			
Example: Instructor Y	arrogant	reactionary	biased
1)			
2)			
3)			

change of plans. Use the previous three activities to consider your own teaching characteristics; be conscious of the positive traits you possess, the concrete ways you would like to improve, and how your learning materials might have more impact. The goal is not to tear yourself down, but to identify things of value you bring to an instructional scenario as well methods for improvement.

DEVELOPING A TEACHING PHILOSOPHY

I am first and foremost a Texan, which means I rely on mottos, slogans, and truisms of all kinds to keep my chin up in the face of adversity. For this reason, some time ago I wrote out my "teaching philosophy" as a way of focusing on what it is that motivates me to help people learn:

> I want to redefine the way people think about librarians, inspire as much critical thought as I do laughter, make sure they come away with something they can actually use, and most important, to never, ever, ever bore anyone to tears.

Learning from other library educators is a ceaselessly useful strategy. I was curious about the teaching philosophies of others, so I asked a number of individuals I personally know to have considerable impact on library education to engage in the same exercise. All I specified was a word limit (75 or less) and the request that they describe "what motivates you to (or as you) teach or present, the characteristics that you aspire to as an instructor or educator, and/or what informs how you encourage learning in others." Here are the responses I received, in no particular order:

> The very first step in learning is simply exposure. Focus on exposure first, find your students' motivation and encourage discovery, and you have a recipe for learning. (Helene Blowers, creator and architect of Learning 2.0: 23 Things)

I want to engage people by challenging their underlying assumptions and then inspire them by providing examples of existing innovative programs. I hope to encourage them to critically assess their current priorities and practices and consider whether they should reconceive their role, taking into account both their professional values and the imperatives of the current technology-oriented environment. (Joan Lippincott, Director, Coalition for Networked Information)

Working in an institution where the students are well prepared and highly motivated, my main goal is to convince them that librarians are 1) welcoming and 2) that we know some stuff. My approach, as it has evolved over the last year or so, is to, believe it or not, throw library jargon at them, thus demystifying advanced research techniques and, by giving a hands-on assignment, helping them put the techniques into practice. (Jenna Freedman, Coordinator of Reference Services and Zine Librarian, Barnard College. www.jenna.openflows.com)

If I am perceived to be a teacher then I have failed. My objective first and foremost is to challenge my students' imaginations and creative capabilities. Real learning is bold and intoxicating and nonlinear. It should be slightly subversive with a tad of radical. I see it as an ongoing transformation that occurs as a series of personal epiphanies. Instruction should flow serendipitously. (Brian Mathews, Assistant University Librarian, Outreach and Academic Services, University of California, Santa Barbara)

I believe that teaching is really about discovery and learning; one of the greatest joys of teaching is the unique story of learning that unfolds for me and

Activity 1.3 **Memorable Learning Objects**			
Example: Electric Company	fast-paced, story-based narrative	visually engaging	contemporary and informal
1)			
2)			
3)			

my students as we explore and experiment together side by side. I try to cultivate a participatory climate that values risk taking and learning experiences that are organic. It is in the messiness and stickiness of learning where real meaning is constructed. (Buffy Hamilton, Media Specialist/Teacher-Librarian, Creekview High School, Canton, Georgia)

My goal in presenting is to help participants create meaning by sharing information clearly, logically, and as simply as possible (but no simpler). Stories, analogies, a "beginner mind," and a nonjudgmental outlook help me foster learning, which happens at that magical intersection between the information being presented and the life experiences and unique perspectives of each learner. My ultimate goal is always to empower participants to make more effective choices. (Peter Bromberg, Assistant Director, South Jersey Regional Library Cooperative, and contributor to www.librarygarden.net)

I strive to convey enthusiasm and passion, to communicate relevance in a way that is both engaging and useful, and to achieve at least one genuine "light bulb" moment. If learners—even a few—have been encouraged to think about something in a way they haven't before, if I have enabled them to become active participants in their own learning, I have succeeded. (Catherine Fraser Riehle, Instructional Outreach Librarian and Assistant Professor of Library Science, Purdue University Libraries)

I strive to always be a student of good pedagogy, to discover and experiment with the latest theory and best practice, and to push myself to be a better teacher. To teach well is to create a permanent change of behavior in the learner. My constant goal is to deliver an outstanding and memorable learning experience, one that leaves students permanently changed for the better even if only in some small way. (Steven

Bell, Associate University Librarian for Research and Instruction, Temple University)

You know what gets me excited? Information. Finding it, thinking about it, critiquing it, wrestling with it, arguing about it, producing it. And I believe every student in my classroom feels the same way, even if they don't know it yet. (Emily Drabinski, Electronic Resources and Instruction Librarian, Long Island University, Brooklyn)

Technology instruction should give everyone a chance to succeed and solve their own real-world problems in a setting that is safe yet challenging. A good instructor facilitates the student's own learning objectives and helps them figure out what their questions are. Learning can be fun and painless. (Jessamyn West, rural librarian, MetaFilter moderator, and owner of www.librarian.net)

Libraries and librarians are faced with a technological and societal wave of change that is ever increasing as we move farther into the 21st century. Preparing new graduates to deal with constant change, use current and emerging technological tools to further the mission of their institutions, and meet the needs of communities of library users while never losing sight of our foundational values and principles is of utmost importance to me as an LIS educator. (Michael Stephens, Assistant Professor, Graduate School of Library and Information Science, Dominican University, River Forest, Illinois)

I want to always remember that when I'm teaching, I'm learning. Part of my job is to embrace the vulnerability inherent in learning something new, critically examine my "authority" and realize what that vulnerability looks and feels like to those in my classrooms. I also think it's my responsibility to point out the flaws and bias inherent in information, both in the ways we gather it and the ways it's presented. (Lia Friedman, Instruction and Outreach Librarian, Head of Public Services, Arts Library, University of California, San Diego)

My role is to help create a community of learners who are responsible and responsive to each other as they build on contextual foundations and extend themselves to acquire new knowledge and skills through innovative connections with communities like those they will serve throughout their profession. (Loriene Roy, ALA past president, and Professor, School of Information, University of Texas, Austin)

I seek to make possible an environment in which inquiry and hands-on learning are encouraged, where information is accessible and usable, and where students learn how to manage the obstacles inherent in the information search process. It is the place of struggle where learning takes root, and fostering an environment that makes it safe for students to struggle productively is a critical part of my teaching practice. (Maria Accardi, Assistant Librarian and Coordinator of Instruction, Indiana University Southeast, New Albany)

My goal is to make students not need me. I was one of those stubborn learners who never asked for help, so I want to help students develop the skills that will allow them to independently find and evaluate information. While I try to show them that the librarians are friendly and useful, I ultimately want them to be able to think critically about how to find information and about what they find without us. (Meredith Farkas, Head of Instructional Initiatives at Norwich University, Vermont, adjunct faculty member at San Jose State University School of Library and Information Science)

What I love about these philosophies is that, in addition to expressing personal conviction and an appropriately fierce learner focus, each pinpoints almost exactly how their authors have motivated me and countless others to become stronger educators and librarians. Not only that, every one contains one or more instructional best practices well worth reiterating:

Me—try not to be boring.

Helene—focus on motivation and discovery.

Joan—challenge assumptions and use real examples.

Jenna—demystify jargon and make things hands-on.

Brian—defy expectations and invite creativity.

Buffy—let learning be organic, even if it's messy.

Peter—teach simply and empower participants.

Catherine—engage people with their own process.

Steven—push yourself to improve.

Emily—be stoked, because it's contagious.

Jessamyn—invite questioning and let learners define their own goals.

Michael—be prepared to adapt.

Lia—question authority in information and in yourself.

Loriene—create a community of learners.

Maria—foster a safe learning environment.

Meredith—make students not need you.

ACHIEVING AUTHENTICITY

Many of the teaching characteristics I identify in this chapter are confirmed by research to be common among successful educators, such as reflectiveness, personal investment, humor, organization, and theoretical knowledge.[2] One quality in particular comes through in every teaching philosophy I received: *authenticity*. Authenticity is the capacity to communicate your self—your personality and sense of identity—during instruction, an overarching concept that covers many qualities of instructional effectiveness. Per Laursen lists seven qualities of authentic teachers,[3] who

- have personal intentions concerning their teaching
- embody their intentions
- have realistic intentions
- relate to students as fellow human beings
- work in contexts fruitful to their intentions
- cooperate intensely with colleagues
- are able to take care of their personal-professional development

Goal orientation, interpersonal connection, and genuine enthusiasm for the task at hand are all aspects of authenticity. In an *In the Library with the Lead Pipe* post, Carrie Donovan gives a convincing defense of authenticity and identity in library education: "A shift in expectations calls for teacher behavior that is purposeful, mindful, and rooted in the self. . . . For those in search of a true teacher identity, authenticity will serve as the best guide."[4] I address the role of authenticity in developing your teaching identity in the next two chapters as well as in chapter 11.

FINDING YOUR SOAPBOX

One of the most important lessons I have learned about authenticity came from Lia Friedman of UC San Diego's Arts Library, who shared her instructional philosophy earlier in the chapter. She is a true example of a teacher-advocate, someone who can captivate an audience and make them care about basically anything. When we discuss presentations we've given or sessions we've taught, she always seems to mention people that approach her afterward with questions or just wanting to chat. In my mind, this is evidence of an ability to first make content interesting enough that it raises questions, and second being approachable enough to generate the equivalent of fans at a library session.

Her strategy is simple. According to Lia, "When I'm up on my soapbox, their eyes get wider." She is describing the infectious interest you can create by communicating with conviction on any topic in which you have knowledge or expertise. Intensity of expression is a key factor in how effectively something captivates our attention, which in turn significantly affects memory and retention of detail.[5] Your soapbox becomes a place of informed sincerity that helps you speak convincingly, a necessary aspect of cultivating a voice or persona you can call upon to engage an audience (an idea I revisit in chapter 11). Your soapbox may be most useful during live teaching interactions, but it can also permeate digital learning objects through a combination of creative visual design and interactivity.

Even content that appears superficially dull can come to life when pitched from a soapbox. What's more, your soapbox can help you challenge, dispel, or leverage learner preconceptions based on your perceived profession, age, gender, ethnicity, and so forth. An example: A subject like integrative biology is not one that would typically stop me in my tracks, yet when I stumbled across an online lecture by renowned UC Berkeley anatomy professor Marian Diamond, I was riveted. Because she communicates with extraordinary conviction, defies countless stereotypes, and uses unconventional strategies to enliven a traditional delivery format, her lectures are among the top instructional videos in YouTube and have been viewed millions of times.

I had the chance fortune to run into Professor Diamond on the Berkeley campus as I was writing this chapter; I introduced myself and asked if she would mind if I used her as an example of teaching effectiveness. After complimenting me on my handshake—hers was a bonecrusher, by the way—she graciously said that she would be delighted, image and all. Even in this brief interaction she communicated infectious enthusiasm and a willingness to engage. While teaching, Professor Diamond constantly drops pithy insights on pedagogy and learning she has picked up from decades of experience, many of which are described in physiological terms that connect deftly to the subject of instruction. Hundreds of comments on my favorite lecture (in which she spends a good five minutes holding a human brain pulled with a flourish from a hat box; see figure 1.1) explode the perennial myth that contemporary students cannot be interested in learning, such as, "This woman is a great teacher, hope my lecturer next sem is half as good as this. . . . she is cool" and "That is a kickass teacher. i need to get her."

Marian Diamond is an individual who has used her soapbox to turn the Curse of Knowledge on its head; she understands exactly how to communicate just enough of what she knows to make people want to learn more. I highly encourage you to watch her unforgettable lectures at www.youtube.com/user/UCBerkeley. For additional examples of the power of the instructional soapbox, view any of the presentations at the Technology, Entertainment, and Design website (www.ted.com), an online mini-lecture clearinghouse that offers "riveting talks from remarkable people, free to the world." Topics with the potential to come across as arcane or esoteric are made captivating and understandable by TED lecturers, such as Hans Rosling's fascinating and visually engaging treatment of international economic development or Oliver Sacks discussing blindness and neural imaging.

BUILD YOUR OWN SOAPBOX

How do you locate the source of infectious interest in yourself? I find that persuasion in general is more natural when you actually believe that the content you share, including your own expertise, is worthwhile and significant. Think about what engages you in what you do; I regularly thank my lucky stars that I belong to a profession that does so much productive good, that gives me insight into the interests and abilities of so many. Do you have similar convictions about being a librarian? If this question draws a blank, think about something you care enough about to soapbox about it. Maybe it's mahjong, or quantum physics, or the Halloween costumes you just made for your three precious ferrets. When you teach, try to channel the enthusiasm you feel for something, *anything* to the task at hand. If you find that the ferrets aren't doing it for you, at least try to convince yourself of the time you can save your students, or how you can be a useful and productive agent in their working and thinking lives. Words of wisdom: if you can't make it, at least try to fake it.

One never-fail strategy is to bring more of who you are into what you teach and design. Half of your soapbox consists of sharing your expertise, but the other half consists of sharing your self; you cannot and will not catalyze knowledge-building if you bleed individuality out of every learning interaction. It pays to show at least some of who you are if you expect people to care, because it is much more difficult to write someone off who is connecting with you personally or who has humanized their own participation in the

process that led them there. Too often, the instruction we encounter is dull and humorless—in Lia's words, "dead words to dead people." An essential aspect of making your content engaging involves making yourself engaging, an *affective* technique that helps create a positive emotional backdrop for your learners (I discuss affective strategies in chapters 4 and 5).[6] The more of myself I put into these pages, the more I invite you to stay with the ideas and approaches as though they were communicated in conversation rather than via a manual or textbook. Consider, for example, figure 1.2. Now that you know I wrote half of this book in a hammock, you might be less likely to dismiss me as a faceless, theory-spitting automaton.

Exposing your self during instruction can also sometimes backfire: you might take me less seriously because of my informal tone or the personal insights I share. That said, this is a strategic pedagogical decision on my part; sacrificing a modicum of my "authority" in order to create a more accessible tone is a risk I have consciously considered and accepted. Some respond well to informality in learning, others find it off-putting (if the latter is your current experience, you might consider detouring to the more abstract and instructional design-oriented chapter 7, or the research-focused chapters 4 and 5). As this parenthetical suggestion implies, it is useful to anticipate as many learner orientations as possible and connect with a

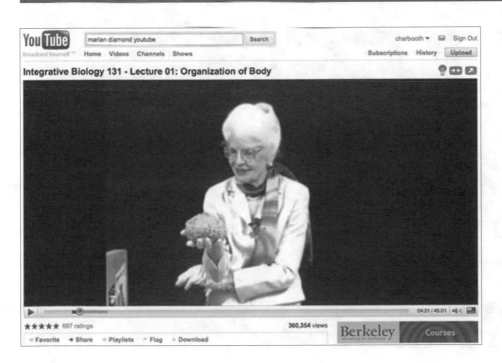

Figure 1.1

Professor Marian Diamond on her soapbox: "I want you to appreciate what you carry in the top of your heads."

works because she is so smart a knows her stuff.

broad range of participants by strategy-switching, processes I explore in greater depth in later chapters.

FINDING THE CORE: YOUR INSTRUCTIONAL MESSAGE

Your soapbox consists of identity and authenticity, but sharing a compelling message is the heart of effective instruction. I mentioned earlier in the chapter that Professor Diamond manages to turn the Curse of Knowledge on its head, encapsulating her content in interesting, accessible terms. Effective educators have an intuitive sense of what captures people's attention and holds it; they find what about their subject matter sparks interest and makes people actually want to learn (known as *intrinsic motivation;* see chapters 4 and 5). In their 2007 best seller *Made to Stick: Why Some Ideas Survive and Others Die,* authors Chip and Dan Heath investigated decades of research in education, business, rhetoric, advertising, and psychology to figure out what makes some ideas last and others fade. According to them, "sticky" ideas are those that are "understandable, memorable, and effective at changing thought or behavior."[7] They argue that how you encapsulate an idea or message is more important than the technology or media you use to convey it; in other words, it is how you get at the "core" of your message that really matters. At the core of any idea that makes people listen, care, and remember are six

factors, which they summarize with a simple acronym: SUCCESs (Simple Unexpected Concrete Credible Emotional Stories).[8] Each letter is a concrete step that helps you communicate messages that "stand on their own merits":

Simple—Find the Core. Share the Core.

Unexpected—Get attention: surprise. Hold attention: interest.

Concrete—Help people understand and remember. Help people coordinate.

Credible—Help people believe. Internal credibility.

Emotional—Make people care. Use the power of association. Appeal to self-interest (and not just base self-interest). Appeal to identity.

Stories—Get people to act. Stories as simulation (tell people how to act). Stories as inspiration (give people energy to act).

These factors are how myths, urban legends, jingles, commercials, parables, and slogans become so persistent. As in marketing, streamlined instructional messages can make the content and purpose of learning clearer and more memorable, both of which are essential for helping participants perceive the value of an interaction and build usable knowledge. Part of my goal in this book is to suggest strategies that help you

Figure 1.2
The author at her "desk"

drill down to the core of any presentation, class, training, tutorial, collaboration, or subject to communicate what is really important about it, why it *matters*, in order to make the most impact.

LEARNER SELF-INTEREST: THE WIIFM PRINCIPLE

Typically, what matters most to people is themselves. When creating an instructional message, it is useful to understand that learners pay more attention, try harder, and understand more clearly when they see the personal benefit of an instructional scenario or object. This is sometimes described as the "What's in it for me?" (WIIFM) principle.[9] Effective educators appeal to the self-interest of their learners by identifying and explicitly communicating this benefit in practical terms during instruction. With any type of teaching, helping your audience see the advantage of an instructional scenario is crucial to encouraging the knowledge they build to become "actionable" in the future.[10]

Maintaining awareness of WIIFM is critical to understanding your audience's needs and motivations. For example, as an author I try to use WIIFM thinking to make sure this book is worth your attention and energy. By engaging with perceived participants as though I am in a learning interaction, I am better able to imagine the self-interest of my reader base. To maintain this awareness, I try to constantly ask, *Why, and for whom, I am writing this? What do I want my readers to gain from this experience?* Reflecting on these targets keeps me focused on the all-important question: *What's in it for you as a reader/learner?* Think about your own self-interest in this learning scenario: Why are you reading this book? What do you want to gain from this experience? Thinking in this way as you plan and deliver instruction will prepare you to make a more convincing *pitch*, or the act of delivering your instructional message in a way that engages your audience and helps them understand the benefit of instruction (see chapter 11).

SHAPING YOUR AWARENESS: PERSONAL LEARNING ENVIRONMENTS

Effective teaching is about more than philosophy, soapboxes, and streamlined messages; it is also important to stay invested in your own learning process.

Maintaining current awareness of emerging instructional topics and technologies is supported by creating a robust *personal learning environment* (PLE)—the combination of applications and resources that "explicitly support one's social, professional, learning, and other activities."[11] You already have a PLE, even if you've never thought about it quite so formally—whatever resources, interfaces, or services you use to keep up with what you do or what interests you. There are many information conduits you can combine to create a viable, pedagogical PLE: books like this, journals, social networking and bookmarking sites, Twitter lists and topics, RSS feeds, search and table of contents alerts, online learning communities, brick-and-mortar or virtual conferences. It's all about managing your own approach to learning about teaching and technology.

Customizing a viable PLE is a highly personal process. Your preferences and interests come into play immediately, down to the level of whether you want to browse current journal issues in print or online. Like the research process, creating a PLE is serendipitously iterative, meaning that it informs itself as one thing unexpectedly leads to another: you bookmark a blog entry that recommends teaching students about Zotero as a citation manager, which inspires you to track down more information on the project to learn how to use it better, during which you discover another blog that has useful technology information on another topic, and so forth. Your PLE should help you stay in a rhythm of keeping track of these connections. We are all busy, and it is almost impossible to follow so many information inputs at once. That said, if you set up your learning environment in a stable and nonintrusive way, you can check in on different resources related to specific projects or areas of professional interest when you have the time and inclination. Your PLE can do wonders for combating overload by narrowing the information deluge to a manageable stream, and by no means do you have to monitor everything religiously. While I rely on the tools in my personal environment of learning, I ignore them just as regularly. Consistency is more my goal, and knowing where and how to find out about something in a time-effective way when the need arises.

A description of my own PLE: I use e-mail alerts and RSS feeds to follow journal tables of contents, and Google Reader to organize various blog feeds into a series of folders tagged with labels like "design" and "instructional tech." I save drafts of presentations and PDF articles on Google Docs and Dropbox and share items with colleagues via both. I bookmark links in

(handwritten margin notes, left side) My telling about Rok worthy knowledge · David Keeps bringing readings back to them.

Firefox and synchronize these between my home and work computers. I use Google Scholar and article databases to search for specific citations, and save them in Zotero. I network with colleagues to learn about interesting projects and new exercises. I monitor Twitter profiles and lists of educators, organizations, and librarians and use TweetDeck to search trending topics like "#OER" (open educational resources) and "shareable." I have database alerts set up for phrases like "library education" and automatically receive e-mail from organizations such as EDUCAUSE and the Pew/Internet American Life project when new articles and white papers on technology and learning are published. I browse the education and technology sections and blogs of major news outlets such as the *New York Times, Slate,* and *Wired.* I use my iPhone for accessing all of the above, as well as a tool for providing context when I run across a new topic or application on the fly. I belong to online learning communities such as LearningTimes, and attend their webcasts whenever possible. Finally, I keep my eyes and ears open in the analog world.

A few blogs I find consistently useful are *ResourceShelf, In the Library with the Lead Pipe,* the *Unquiet Librarian*, and the *Distant Librarian* for library instruction and technology; *Mashable* and *TechCrunch* for gadgets and social media; *ProfHacker* for instructional technology in higher education; and the *Centre for Learning and Performance Technologies* blog for regular teaching technology product lists such as the "Top 100 Tools for Learning." Other essential sources are the annual *Horizon Report* and *ECAR Study of Undergraduate Students and Information Technology,* both of which track game-changing technological trends within higher education, and other publications issued by research institutes such as the UK-based Joint Information Systems Committee (JISC) and professional organizations such as the EDUCAUSE Learning Initiative (ELI). URLs are provided for these and other resources in the Recommended Reading section.

Taken together, all of these sources provide a steady flow of current information on teaching, libraries, and various aspects of technology. The very act of assembling useful information sources into a PLE becomes a lesson in information literacy; by locating the tools that help you become successful at using and understanding a given technology, you begin to discover new resources and build your confidence in that area. For example, learning to set up a Yahoo Pipe Reader or NetVibes account that brings in teaching and library-related blog feeds helps you see the function and benefit of RSS and drag-and-drop interfaces.

SUMMARY

- The **"Curse of Knowledge"** afflicts experts and should be challenged by a learner-focused approach to library instruction.
- Developing an **instructional philosophy** can help focus your teacher identity.
- Your **instructional soapbox** is a method of communicating your teaching philosophy and identity.
- The **SUCCESs** model can help you find the core of an instructional message.
- The **WIIFM principle** is a way to speak to a learner's self-interest.
- You can build current and experiential awareness of instructional technologies and strategies through a robust **personal learning environment** (PLE).

REFLECTION POINTS

1. Take a stab at writing your own teaching philosophy in three sentences or less.

2. Is instruction an integral part of your professional identity, or do you consider it a secondary aspect of what you do? Do you see this role changing in the future if you transition between jobs, or as a potential result of shifts within your organization?

3. Would you say that you have an instructional soapbox? Why or why not?

NOTES

1. Chip Heath and Dan Heath, *Made to Stick: Why Some Ideas Survive and Others Die* (New York: Random House, 2007).

2. James Stronge, *Qualities of Effective Teachers,* 2nd ed. (Alexandria, VA: Association for Supervision and Curriculum Development, 2007).

3. Per Laursen, "The Authentic Teacher," in D. Beijaard et al. (eds.), *Teacher Professional Development in Changing Conditions* (New York: Springer, 2005), 206–210.

4. Carrie Donovan, "Sense of Self: Embracing Your Teacher Identity," *In the Library with the Lead Pipe*, 2009. Inthelibrarywiththeleadpipe.org.

5. Sam Wang, *Talk of The Nation,* July 22, 2009, National Public Radio. See also Sandra Aamodt and Sam Wang, *Welcome to Your Brain: Why You Lose Your Car Keys but Never Forget How to Drive and Other Puzzles of Everyday Life* (New York: Bloomsbury, 2008).

6. Claire Weinstein and Richard Mayer, "The Teaching of Learning Strategies," in M. Whitlock (ed.), *Handbook of Research on Teaching,* 3rd ed. (New York: Macmillan, 1986), 315–327.

7. Heath and Heath, *Made to Stick,* 253.

8. Ibid., 252–257.

9. Steven Bell and John Shank, *Academic Librarianship by Design: A Blended Librarian's Guide to the Tools and Techniques* (Chicago: American Library Association, 2007), 62. See also Heath and Heath, *Made to Stick.*

10. George Siemens, *Connectivism: A Learning Theory for the Digital Age,* elearnspace, December 12, 2004. www.elearnspace.org/Articles/connectivism.htm.

11. Larry Johnson, Alan Levine, and Rachel Smith. *The 2009 Horizon Report* (Austin: New Media Consortium, 2009), 4.

2

Metacognition and Reflective Practice

GOALS

- Explain the relationship between **metacognition** and **reflective practice**.
- Outline the elements of instruction: **learner**, **context**, **content**, and **educator**.
- Discuss the importance of creating a **feedback loop** to capture and respond to learner input.

Many library educators teach or design learning materials on a part-time basis, making it difficult to constantly be acquiring new skills. *Reflective practice* is the first element of instructional literacy, and is focused on pursuing instructor development as you teach or train. In this chapter I present approaches that can help you reflect in your day-to-day instruction and become more perceptive about the impact of the learning experiences you facilitate. In so doing, you can transform the natural self-scrutiny that often accompanies education into something more productive—increased confidence and flexibility.

INTENTIONALITY AND REFLECTIVE PRACTICE

According to educational psychologist Robert Slavin, "One attribute seems to be characteristic of outstanding teachers: *intentionality*."[1] Intentionality is constructive self-awareness in teaching. Intentional instructors do more than communicate well or design strong assignments; they methodically consider the impact their actions have on learners, understand the knowledge they possess, use evidence to support the strategies they select, and strive to improve their effectiveness over time. An excellent method for becoming more self-assured is to empower yourself to understand and appreciate (or at least come to terms with) teaching through a process of systematic planning and self-reflection. This requires practical, personal insight into what works in different learning situations and why.

Enter reflective practice, a mindset that transforms teaching into a learning experience and helps educators become more thoughtful about their decisions and actions.[2] This approach to instructor development encourages ongoing self-evaluation and the selection of relevant tactics to address instructional needs. Becoming more reflective has without a doubt made me a more flexible and less anxiety-ridden instructor, and has improved my ability to see myself from a learner's perspective. Not every reflective strategy I discuss will apply in every situation, but this chapter should encourage you to more intentionally consider how the materials and experiences you design affect participants and users.

METACOGNITIVE STRATEGIES

Intentionality is *metacognitive*, meaning that it involves "thinking about one's own thinking."[3] Imagine if characters in a film could hear their narrator, or if athletes listened to color commentary during a game; metacognition is like an expert voice in your head providing insight into what is happening. Everyone has this voice to varying degrees (not to mention the ability to turn it up, down, or ignore it outright).

Metacognition is an important concept in educational psychology, and a factor shown to contribute significantly to learning and instructional effectivness.[4] It encourages higher-order and critical thinking by requiring you to step back and take stock of your environment, experiences, and abilities in order to meet challenges purposefully. Information literacy is inherently metacognitive in that it encourages individuals to become aware of their search and evaluation skills and apply them to specific information needs. For students and instructors, metacognition becomes "strategic thinking about what information/strategies/skills you have, when and why to use them, and how to use them."[5]

THE ELEMENTS OF INSTRUCTION

If you haven't noticed yet, I'm a fan of breaking things down. I'm also visually oriented, so I turn to charts, models, components, and so forth to create frameworks for understanding. One such framework involves intentionally examining the four constituent elements of any instructional scenario: learner, content, context, and educator (figure 2.1).

Effective learning design involves treating each interaction as unique. Using the elements of

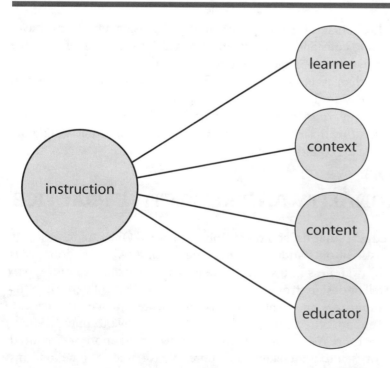

Figure 2.1

The elements of instruction

instruction as a springboard for reflection is a straight-forward method of responding more productively during instructional planning. The USER method in part II discusses related strategies in detail.

REFLECTIVE TEACHING IN ACTION

Research has shown that instructors who consciously self-reflect have greater confidence and tend to foster more positive learning environments and higher student achievement.[6] Reflective practice helps you observe and evaluate during planning in order to make pedagogical choices suitable to different learning scenarios, such as consciously considering how you might approach a web-based course with online engagement techniques rather than unconsciously attempting to replicate your face-to-face approach.[7] To exercise reflective practice, you have to maintain the desire to learn more about yourself as an educator and the intent to commit to iterative improvement. Toward this end, Slavin recommends asking six questions at the outset of any learning scenario (adapted slightly here for library instructors):[8]

1. What do I expect my learners (students, colleagues, patrons, audience, etc.) to know and be able to do as a result of my instruction (class, tutorial, presentation, or workshop)?

2. What knowledge, skills, needs, and interests do my learners have that must be taken into account?

3. What do I know about the content, development, motivation, and effective teaching strategies that I can use to accomplish my objectives?

4. What instructional materials, technology, assistance, and other resources are available?

5. How will I plan to assess learner progress toward my objectives?

6. How will I respond if my learners are not on track? What is my backup plan?

Reflective practice often involves this kind of self-questioning, which is also achievable through simple self-assessment exercises, setting personal goals as benchmarks over the course of a year or semester, or making mental notes when something either pans out particularly well or crashes and burns.

REFLECTIVE STRATEGIES FOR EDUCATORS

Heidi Jacobs argues for a broader applicability of the reflective mindset in library education: "If we are going to address the issues of librarians' roles within educational endeavors systemically, we, as a discipline, need to foster reflective, critical habits of mind regarding pedagogical praxis within ourselves, our libraries, and our campuses."[9] Reflective practice is all about motivation, honesty, and adaptability, and it can help you engage with your teaching in ways you might not expect. Every time you open a session to questions or personal insights, you give it the opportunity to become distinctive. This can also ease one of the most common frustrations of teaching librarians—not being able to interact with learners long enough to form a real connection with them. Developing an ethic of reflective adaptability is an excellent way to become more outwardly focused and refine instructional materials from the learner's vantage point. In my experience, incorporating metacognitive elements in live or synchronous online learning interactions can also prevent the boredom that can result from teaching the same concepts over and over. In the previous section, I noted that it is useful to develop a set of personal reflective strategies. This can improve your ability to find solutions to instructional "problems" as they occur.[10] The following are a few reflective approaches from my own practice:

Learn in the moment. Try not let chances to observe and evaluate pass you by, particularly during face-to-face or real-time online instruction when immediate feedback is readily available. To help me remember specifics immediately after any session, workshop, or presentation (when my residual impressions are at their strongest), I do a *three-question reflection* about the interaction: what worked, what didn't work, and whether I achieved my goals. I also quickly note anything that stood out about my own performance or that of my learners/audience, such as an interesting turn of phrase, takeaway, best moment, or problem I might have experienced with technology. I tend to use Post-its for this exercise when I deliver face-to-face sessions, because they allow me to attach my thoughts physically to whatever handout, syllabus, or notes I created as an immediate reminder of that interaction. This straightforward, low-effort exercise helps me identify and record phrases or exercises that panned out or didn't, and issues or ideas to follow up on in the future, which I then save and refer to when I know that I will be teaching similar content or want to review my performance. As with most metacognitive exercises, there are many methods for recording on-the-fly reflections. Beyond scribbling on a trusty notebook or extra handout, you can use a more centralized, cloud-based format such as Google Docs to create a document, spreadsheet, or form (survey) that is accessible from any computer or save information to a smartphone or other mobile device.

Never throw anything away. It takes five times as much work to create something from scratch as it does to work from a template, and many instructors constantly revise and reuse content from past instruction. I have even gone so far as to recycle a handout I designed for a job interview years ago (updating the content, of course). Part of being a reflective practitioner involves thinking about how what you are working on today can save you (or a colleague or student) time tomorrow. I am a natural packrat, but every so often I spend a frustrating hour searching different e-mail accounts for that one perfect attachment I know I sent myself at some point, forced to reinvent the wheel because I failed to keep a thorough record of my past learning materials. The reuse mentality can apply to any kind of output. When I write something, for example, I create the equivalent of a b-side document that I use to save the material I cut, which often comes in handy as a blog post.[11] This b-side document, the three-question reflections, and every other semi-useful scrap of content becomes part of the ongoing instructional portfolio I compile each semester and year (there is more on reuse in chapter 12).

See "shortcomings" as challenges. In chapter 1, I invited you to list your instructional strengths and weaknesses. Many find self-scrutiny unpleasant, but evaluating these points can identify what you want to focus on (instead of ignoring or avoiding what you are ashamed of). This is the difference between challenges and shortcomings—the former allows room for improvement, the latter invites you to throw up your hands (or punch yourself in the face). A personal example: When I started speaking and teaching I was a terrible "ummer," letting out countless speech disturbances (also known as filler words) such as "you know," "ah," "like," and "basically." Filler words tend to distract and take up space, but contrary to common assumption, George Mahl concluded that they are not inherent evidence of nervousness.[12] Rather, speech disturbances in public contexts are symptomatic of the mental energy it takes to verbalize under pressure.[13] According to Mahl and Stanislav Kasl, more useful indicators of nervousness in speech are hesitant, repeated, or partially uttered words.[14] I had a great deal of self-consciousness about my own use of filler words, but instead of avoiding the stage and classroom I forced myself to tackle the problem by becoming mindful of my speed and breathing, and was conscious to practice several times if possible. Over time this has made me much more deliberate in my projection, and far less likely to "um" and "like." For more about speech disturbances, I highly recommend *Um: Slips, Stumbles, and Verbal Blunders, and What They Mean*, by Michael Erard.[15]

Lighten up, toughen up. For educators, Nietzsche's "that which does not kill us makes us stronger" is an absolute. Periodically stepping outside of your comfort zone to try something new may increase the margin of error, but it can also lead to greater relaxation in the face of instructional uncertainty. Commenting on this section of the book, another friend and editor of mine equated her strategy for coping with teaching anxiety with the experience of quitting smoking, stating that in both cases she is now "expert at experiencing discomfort." I find many connections between the Buddhist concept of mindfulness and reflective teaching, particularly in this area. There is a measured vulnerability in maintaining responsive awareness, and it is therefore important to cultivate a light heart and a thick skin to roll with the punches more comfortably. Pema Chodron, Buddhist nun and de facto life coach to millions, asserts that when dealing with challenging situations, "it comes down to the question of how willing we are to lighten up and loosen our grip."[16] However painful it might be, embracing the unpleasant sensations that go along with audience scrutiny helps chip away at the discomfort bit by bit—or at least builds your tolerance. I remain mindful during instruction by staying present, fostering conversation with learners, inviting input from colleagues, and allowing the adrenaline that accompanies interacting with an audience to feed my enthusiasm. If you humanize and energize a learning interaction, it becomes much easier for all involved to use less negative scrutiny.

Shake it off, but learn from mistakes. It can be tempting to blame yourself or become discouraged by a less-than-stellar outcome, but you should try to evaluate yourself gently and productively. When something goes wrong (and notice that I pointedly did not say "*if* something goes wrong"), it is essential that you move forward at the same time that you learn from what occurred. If I slip up or experience technical issues during a live interaction, I try to acknowledge the gaffe with humor but also to file away the source of the problem in order to triage it later. It is also good practice to assess whether you can shift your strategy to mitigate in-progress issues instead of barreling through them.

Any number of methods can be used to troubleshoot in the moment, from inviting participants to suggest how you might shift gears to bringing a fresh set of eyes to a design project. In face-to-face interactions, you can monitor the effects of your instruction by paying active attention to environmental dynamics, body language, and what I think of as the "frown-print" of your learners. Facial expressions reveal a lot of useful information. The intensity of a given frown often indicates a proportionate amount of displeasure, boredom, or confusion (although not always. I myself frown constantly, particularly while learning). Observations like this allow you to respond by slowing your pace, moving around the room in live interactions, taking a break, asking a question—whatever the moment seems to require. I tend to take a mental step back and look critically at the interaction, object, or environment to identify the source of the issue—technology failure, bored learners, poor image resolution, distracting visual design, whatever—so I can triage it more effectively.

Invite feedback (and take it seriously). There are many ways to incorporate learner input into reflective practice (see chapters 6, 11, and 12). Intentional educators construct *feedback loops* to foster responsive learning experiences. If you invite participants to specify an area they would like to focus on, you should respond by incorporating the ideas you are reasonably able to address into your instructional goals—or acknowledging your inability to do so while suggesting an alternate strategy. You can also invite a colleague to observe or ask someone to review an online learning object, then take the suggestions you receive seriously and resist the temptation to feel criticized or attacked.

Be flexible. It can be tempting when pressed for time to rely on the same methods again and again, but your instructional comfort zone may not serve every audience. One benefit of reflective thinking is that it helps you adapt to the needs of an instructional scenario rather than forcing it to adapt to yours, which by no means requires radical restructuring of every learning object or class outline. Willingness to assess and revise your efforts allows your teaching practice to grow and respond organically to the learning climate in which you operate. If you stay open to changing your instructional approach in gradual and subtle ways, it can be less painful and dramatic than revolutionizing overnight. Stifle your ability to flex, and you are likely to become intimately acquainted with the meaning of terms like "burnout." This is especially valuable when working with technology in instruction, wherein not being tied to any one approach is a great asset.

REFLECTIVE STRATEGIES FOR LEARNERS

Metacognitive or reflective strategies are similarly essential in encouraging learner motivation and higher-order thinking.[17] To frame how simple facilitating reflective learner practice can be, consider an exercise I often use at the outset of real-time interactions ("Who are we and what do we want?"). This simple think-aloud activity consists of starting a session off with an interactive round of questions and answers among the entire group, customized according to the characteristics of the audience (e.g., students or librarians or faculty). In undergraduate course–related workshops with twenty-five or fewer students, I typically go around the room and ask learners to quickly (a) introduce themselves and their major, if applicable, (b) identify the topic or project they are working on, (c) name one frustration/observation about libraries, and (d) share something practical they want to get out of the session (I also tell them they can't repeat what their neighbor just said, in order to discourage twenty-five versions of "finding articles, I guess"). This sounds like a lot to cover, but it is actually quite manageable. As we go around the room, I thank each person, perhaps ask them to elaborate, or offer a few words of commentary on the inevitable teachable moments that occur—an interesting research topic, a library observation that allows me to drop a piece of practical advice, or even to compliment someone's sweater—any opportunity to lighten the not-another-library-session doldrums.

Questioning Techniques

This activity is one of many *questioning techniques* you can use to create an active and engaging metacognitive environment and encourage critical thinking among your learners. Questioning requires that you let go of some degree of control over the discursive direction taken in an interaction, which has been shown to be a consistent aspect of effective instruction (see chapters 4, 5, and 11).[18] Instead of letting learners sit passively, the entirely technology-free yet utterly active exercise described in the previous section lures them into a metacognitive mindset—to think about who they are, what they are working on, what they know about the topic at hand, and how these elements might intersect. This has the overall effect of making participants more invested in a session, because they are gently called onto the carpet in front of their peers. This exercise typically takes up at least ten minutes of a fifty- or ninety-minute one-shot or training, time well spent that achieves these goals:

- Begins the session on a personal note by establishing interpersonal connections
- Helps me understand learner disciplinary affiliation/research background
- Requires participants to reflect on their topic/interests and streamline them into a few words
- Allows participants to observe the interests/abilities/desires of their co-learners
- Creates an atmosphere of banter and interactivity in which I am responsive to their needs
- Requires students to think about what they know/have observed about libraries
- Asks them to specify a concrete goal or skill to address during the session
- Helps me gauge their levels of proficiency and engagement
- Gives me a feel for how reticent/forthcoming the classroom dynamic will be and identifies students who are likely to engage more heavily during the session, become monopolizers, or need special attention
- Allows me to adjust my goals and objectives if I realize learners are not where I expected them to be

I make it a point to begin all synchronous interactions with some form of questioning, going more or less in depth depending on how many people are involved and the degree of interactivity available. If I am speaking to a room of five hundred and all I can get is a show of hands, I still go for it as a means of giving participants immediate, guiding input into the scenario, which typically creates a sense of thoughtfulness and investment and gives the impression that I will be an interactive instructor (thus keeping people on their toes). If I am leading a webinar I invite chat questions right off the bat, or use a polling tool to give myself and the audience a chance to learn about the composition of their co-learners. I follow this back-and-forth with my own "pitch", or delivering the message of instruction directed at learner self-interest (see chapter 11). This approach allows me to engage on equal footing and frame my goals based on what learners have explicitly stated will be useful. Somewhere in my pitch, I collate and respond to these learning goals by delivering concrete objectives of what we will *do* in the session (e.g., find and evaluate five scholarly sources so that you can complete the first three entries of your annotated bibliography), which, by acting as a verbal example of the advance organizer I mention in the introduction, helps participants know what I expect them to accomplish.

The give-and-take dynamic of questioning relies not only on metacognition but also on *situated cognition,* in which environmental factors help learners contextualize the information they encounter, and *social cognition,* wherein learning is guided by the influence of the community in which it takes place.[19] Asking participants to introduce themselves and share their questions also allows me to jot down and use names, which fosters a greater feeling of personal connection even during the briefest sessions (e.g., "X mentioned she couldn't remember where to find the link for online articles; here are a few options for this." Or, "Z said he usually starts researching in Google Scholar; did you know you can access journals for free from off campus by customizing your Scholar preferences?"). This type of interplay creates an active learning *interaction* rather than a passive watching/listening episode, and by collectively establishing what is wanted from instruction on an individual level, each participant becomes more focused and aware of the goals and progress of the group.

CHALLENGING THOUGHT: CRITICAL REFLECTION

It has been my experience that learners in a library context are sometimes unwilling to consider the breadth, depth, or personal relevance of the content at hand. I have observed that, whether justified or not, learner self-perceptions of competency in information skills and methods are increasingly common, which can make library instruction appear less valuable to them. How, then, do we package our instructional approaches to bridge the gap? Because issues in information, media, technology, and access are replete with subtext, I find it consistently effective to use challenges or controversies to draw learners in and establish a collective critical dynamic. In so doing, I am able to more systematically integrate critical pedagogy into the information literacy paradigm.

According to Ira Shor, critical pedagogy is the process of encouraging "habits of thought, reading, writing, and speaking which go beneath surface meaning, first impressions, dominant myths, official pronouncements, traditional clichés, received wisdom, and mere opinions, to understand the deep meaning, root causes, social context, ideology, and personal consequences of any action, event, object, process, organization, experience, text, subject matter, policy, mass media, or discourse."[20] This involves encouraging learners to become more metacognitively aware of influence and bias. Critical thinking lends itself to investigating undercurrents in media and knowledge production cycles. According to Barry Beyer, ten skills are necessary to establish validity via critical thought:[21]

1. Distinguishing between verifiable facts and value claims

2. Distinguishing relevant from irrelevant information, claims, or reasons

3. Determining the factual accuracy of a statement

4. Determining the credibility of a source

5. Identifying ambiguous claims or arguments

6. Identifying unstated assumptions

7. Detecting bias

8. Identifying logical fallacies

9. Recognizing logical inconsistencies in a line of reasoning

10. Determining the strength of an argument or claim

Critical analysis is a useful mechanism for investigating the structures that provide access to information. Take, for example, the idea of cultural bias in subject headings. The Dewey Decimal System narrowly sandwiches information related to LGBTQ topics between prostitution and transvestism (306.76), which clearly indicates the perception of "deviant" sexuality at the time at which the headings were defined. In the Library of Congress series, though a much broader range of representative and noncritical subjects relating to "sexual life," sexuality, and gender identity are located in the HQ range, this took years of lobbying by members of the American Library Association's GLBT Round Table in the 1970s to achieve. Finally, in folksonomic tagging in social sites, a lack of controlled vocabulary allows descriptors to reflect nuanced internal subtexts, bias, and participant self-identification—meaning that whereas the acclaimed 2006 graphic memoir *Fun Home: A Family Tragicomic* is described simply as "Bechdel, Alison, 1960- -- Comic books, strips, etc." in WorldCat, in LibraryThing it carries user-created tags from "queer" to "coming of age story" to "suicide."

Critical dialogue can stimulate student thinking about the sociolinguistic and political structures guiding information access at the same time that it communicates elements of your teacher identity. In my own practice, I have found that engaging in even brief dialogue around issues like open content or the commodification of the ebook by Google and Amazon engenders unexpected learner interest in the *idea* of libraries and digital literacy, which in turn shines more meaningful light on local access and neutrality. For an excellent exploration of critical pedagogy in library education, I highly recommend Accardi, Drabinski, and Kumbier's *Critical Library Instruction: Theories and Methods.*[22]

SUMMARY

- **Metacognition** is the act of thinking about one's own thinking, which is the underlying strategy behind reflective practice.
- Effective planning involves considering the **elements of instruction**: learner, context, content, and educator.
- **Reflective strategies** focus you on your skills, abilities, needs, and decisions as you teach in the moment.
- Maintaining a **feedback loop** can help you understand the learner experience and respond to input.
- **Critical questioning** is a method for investigating information bias and access.

REFLECTION POINTS

1. Do you already use reflective or metacognitive thinking in your instruction? If so, how?
2. Think about the metacognitive aspects of the WIIFM principle outlined in the previous chapter, and how self-interest motivates different types of

learners. Compare how speaking to WIIFM motivate participants in mandatory staff trainings versus public patrons at a drop-in session. Consider how you currently (or might in the future) leverage the WIIFM principle in learning interactions based on the populations you interact with.

NOTES

1. Robert Slavin, *Educational Psychology: Theory and Practice,* 8th ed. (Boston: Pearson, 2006).

2. Donald Schon, *Educating the Reflective Practitioner: Toward a New Design for Teaching and Learning in the Professions* (San Francisco: Jossey-Bass, 1996).

3. Hope Hartman (ed.), *Metacognition in Learning and Instruction: Theory, Research, and Practice.* Neuropsychology and Cognition, vol. 19 (Dordrecht: Kluwer Academic, 2001), xi.

4. Ibid. See also John Flavell, *Cognitive Development,* 2nd ed. (Englewood Cliffs, NJ: Prentice Hall, 1985), 104.

5. Hartman, Hope, "Teaching Metacognitively," in Hartman, *Metacognition,* 150.

6. John Stronge, *Qualities of Effective Teachers,* 2nd ed. (Alexandria, VA: Association for Supervision and Curriculum Development, 2007), 30–31.

7. John Bransford, Ann Brown, and Rodney Cocking, *How People Learn: Brain, Mind, Experience, and School* (Washington, DC: National Academy Press, 1999), 17.

8. Slavin, *Educational Psychology.*

9. Heidi Jacobs, "Information Literacy and Reflective Pedagogical Praxis," *Journal of Academic Librarianship* 34, no. 3 (2008): 256.

10. Hartman, *Metacognition,* 152.

11. See Char Booth, "Falling Off the Horse, Revisited," Infomational, July 4, 2010. http://infomational.wordpress.com/2010/07/04/falling-off-the-horse-revisited/.

12. George Mahl, "Disturbances and Silences in the Patient's Speech in Psychotherapy," *Journal of Abnormal and Social Psychology* 53, no. 1 (1956): 1–15.

13. Michael Erard, "In the Beginning Was the Word, and the Word Was 'Um,'" *Morning News,* August 9, 2007. www.themorningnews.org/archives/oped/in_the_beginning_was_the_word_and_the_word_was_um.php.

14. Stanislav Kasl and George Mahl, "Relationship of Disturbances and Hesitations in Spontaneous Speech to Anxiety," *Journal of Personality and Social Psychology* 1, no. 5 (1965): 425–433.

15. Michael Erard, *Um: Slips, Stumbles, and Verbal Blunders, and What They Mean* (New York: Pantheon, 2007).

16. Pema Chodron, *When Things Fall Apart: Heart Advice for Hard Times* (Boston: Shambhala, 1997), 29.

17. Hartman, *Metacognition.*

18. Stronge, *Qualities,* 76.

19. James Greeno, "A Perspective on Thinking," *American Psychologist* 44 (1989): 134–141; Albert Bandura, *Social Learning Theory* (Englewood Cliffs, NJ: Prentice Hall, 1977).

20. Ira Shor, *Empowering Education: Critical Teaching for Social Change* (Portsmouth, NH: Heinemann, 1992), 129.

21. Barry Beyer, *Developing a Thinking Skills Program* (Boston: Allyn and Bacon, 1988), 57.

22. Maria T. Accardi, Emily Drabinski, and Alana Kumbier (eds.), *Critical Library Instruction: Theories and Methods* (Duluth, MN: Library Juice Press, 2010).

3

Learning from/with Others

GOALS

- Introduce **gleaning** as a means of gathering ideas and inspiration from your environment.
- Discuss the role of **collaboration** in instructional design and teaching effectiveness.
- List approaches, strategies, and resources for creating **communities of practice**.

Learn from others, and learn by doing. This is a good rule of thumb for improving at virtually anything: seeking inspiration and accepting criticism makes you more well rounded. Many of the ideas I present in this book I first observed among friends and teachers whose methods I admired or whose recommendations led me to a new approach or tool. Through mentorship, co-teaching, professional organizations, online forums, and other channels, I have expanded my own method base and gained a clearer perspective on my impact as a communicator and designer. Part of being a reflective educator is being aware of the observations that you make while sitting through an especially good (or bad) presentation, and not letting instances when you identify something useful pass you by. The previous chapter explored metacognition, the inward-looking aspect of reflective practice. In this chapter I examine its external foci: collaboration, observation, and learning from colleagues, students, and peers.

GLEANING

As I was writing this manuscript, one of my editors suggested that I investigate an author named Kevin Kumashiro, who has written several books on critical pedagogy including *Troubling Education: Queer Activism and Anti-Oppressive*

Pedagogy, and *Six Lenses for Anti-Oppressive Education: Partial Stories, Improbable Conversations*, which led me to a Kumashiro article on movements to curtail instructor development in the *Journal of Teacher Education*. Similarly, when my friend Emily Drabinski tweeted that she had recently finished the book mentioned in the previous chapter (*Critical Library Instruction*), I ordered a copy to inform my understanding of critical pedagogy.[1]

Research builds a composite of ideas collected through chance and diligence, which is similar to a reflective concept I call *gleaning*—incorporating the connections that naturally occur through collaboration, participation, and simply moving through the day into whatever you happen to be working on. Dictionary definitions of gleaning go something like this: "extracting information from various sources; collecting bit by bit." Traditionally, the term referred to people who gathered remnants of crops left in fields and orchards after a harvest, and modern manifestations of gleaning such as Dumpster diving were famously reexamined in a 2000 film by Agnes Varda, *Les glaneurs et la glanuese* (The Gleaners and I). Broadened to professional practice, gleaning becomes a way to rely on the external world as a source of practical inspiration. It is a mindset in which you notice potential solutions to the challenges you face and make use of the resources around you. From DIY to GTD, popular approaches to gleaning are about recognizing and celebrating the good ideas and tactics of others, and incorporating new skills into your own practice.

Gleaning grows out of a willingness to become an active and interested sponge, and involves four elements: *observation, documentation, integration,* and *acknowledgement.* As you observe teaching, presenting, and learning objects, you can consciously document how the strategies they use might support your own style. Integration should not be confused with appropriation; if you ask a coworker for an old handout or lesson plan, don't simply copy their approach to make your life easier (which is little better than opportunistic). Instead, consider their angle, recognize the work they have already put in, and supplement it with your own ideas. Acknowledging the contributions of others, whether through a citation or a word of gratitude, is essential.

A gleaning mentality encourages an attitude of constant curiosity, one of the surest ways to build instructional literacy in a continuous fashion. Becoming a diligent observer helps you perceive areas of mutual interest or resources inside and outside of your organization, such as a codeveloped workshop, site, or other type of shared effort. Being open to learning and incorporating as I go, unexpectedly, from anyone or in any situation, keeps me engaged and humble in the knowledge that I always have more to learn. In this way, gleaning gives even the most mundane forms of instructional collaboration more impact, and encourages you to build productive connections that make your organization's overall educational profile stronger and more diverse.

DOCUMENTATION

An aspect of gleaning that deserves additional consideration is documentation. When you hear about a useful e-learning application or in-class exercise, be prepared to write it down, send yourself an e-mail, create a bookmark in Delicious or Zotero—whatever it takes to keep the moment from passing. You should always give yourself the means to keep track of the useful things you run across in order to follow up on them after the fact. Effective documentation becomes increasingly possible as cloud and mobile technologies provide innovative multimodal methods for serendipitous information gathering. I used to always carry a Moleskine notebook and a pen, but I now use my "magic phone" to help me capture things I think useful via photo, voice, or notation—I snapped the cover photo for this book, for instance, while visiting the Chapel of the Chimes, a Bay Area architectural landmark.

I started consciously documenting my environment because my memory is dismal, but I quickly realized that keeping a running list of inspirations was an excellent means of bringing greater diversity into my instructional practice. I have also learned that the best insights occur when you least expect, and often come in the form of absurdly simple solutions to lingering challenges. For example, listening to NPR's *Talk of the Nation* at the gym one day, I heard Princeton neuroscientist Sam Wang discussing intensity in speech and how this affects listener memory. Knowing that this could help me make my point about infectious enthusiasm in chapter 1, but also that I would forget his name and everything he had said within ten minutes, I stopped what I was doing and typed a few bits of information on the running page of book ideas on my iPhone Notes application (figure 3.1).

Ideas come and go, but I have become much more productive at benefiting from them through reliable documentation. Microblogging services like Twitter and FriendFeed are perfect manifestations of this just-in-time principle; when you get in the rhythm of setting status updates and tweeting when things come to your attention, documentation has already become second nature. *Disclaimer:* Make sure your gleaning methods are reliable and backed up. Not long after taking the screenshot in figure 3.1, I accidentally put my phone through an entire washer-and-dryer cycle, an experience from which it never recovered. Needless to say, I was knocking wood that I had synced my information to my laptop not two days before.

GOOD ADVICE

In the introduction, I reported findings from survey research I conducted among teaching librarians. There is considerable value in exploring the knowledge of other instructors, so one of the open-ended items on this survey asked, "If you could offer one piece of advice to new instruction librarians, what would it be?" Respondents consistently underscored the importance of forming personal connections with colleagues that involved experiential learning, whether through mentorship, observation, or collaborative teaching (view responses to the survey questions in appendix A or at www.alaeditions.org/webextras/).

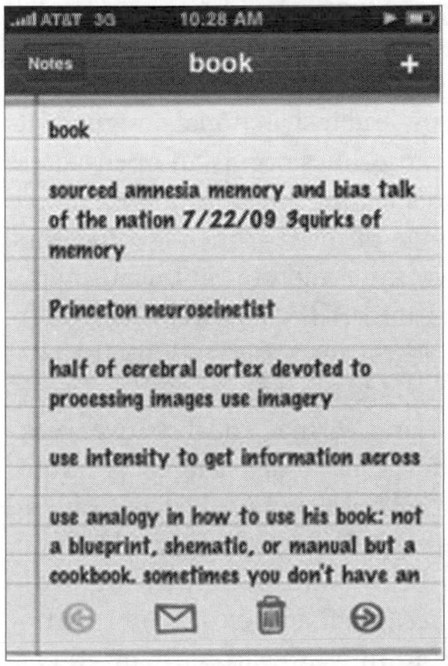

Figure 3.1
iPhone book ideas page

Out of the hundreds of thoughtful replies I received, here are a few that represent these trends:

Mentorship

Get a mentor!

The best way—without experience—you will learn is by example. Find a mentor that will let you sit in their classes.

Get mentors. Plural.

Observation

Observe. Observe. Observe. Watch as many different people teach as you can. You'll learn just as much from the people that are not great at it as from one the ones that are.

Be a sponge, observe and take in every teaching style you can, learn some styles are better for certain situations, don't be afraid to mix and match styles and experiment.

Find out who among your new colleagues has a reputation for being good at instruction, and observe several of their sessions.

Collaboration

Ask other librarians and teachers what they do. Observe others while they're teaching. Be reflective about what you do in the classroom and make notes after each class about what worked and what didn't. Communicate with instructors whose classes you're teaching and ask them what they feel their students need to know.

Find training opportunities outside of libraries. Take classes within Education Departments, collaborate with peer educators in high schools and colleges, sit in on classes to observe a veteran teacher in action.

Take the time to observe other librarians teach and participate in team-teaching, at least the first couple of times so you become more comfortable with and understanding of your role as an instructor and the goals/protocol of your institution.

BUILDING COMMUNITIES OF PRACTICE

The comments above underscore a basic principle of modern educational theory: humans are social learners.[2] In teacher education, one can build on this principle by encouraging peer-supported learning within organizations or professional groups in intentional *communities of practice* (also known as *learning communities*).[3] Programmatic or informal learning communities provide the structure and motivation for continuing education, and are a means of identifying collaborative partners with whom you can share materials, feedback, and support. For new instructors or those acquiring unfamiliar technological skills, communities of practice become a practical example of *scaffolding*—learning support in circumstances where knowledge is difficult to acquire independently.[4] In addition to providing gleaning material, insight into the teaching practices of your colleagues can catalyze shared initiatives, reduce duplication of effort, and build the collegiality necessary to maintain productive teaching and working relationships.

An important caveat: Just as we are social learners by nature, we are also various shades of socially awkward or inept. Communities of practice in instructional development can be as fraught as any other type of community; not everyone in a given learning group will be objective or interested in participating, and as I noted in the previous chapter it is easy to develop a negative self-concept from the wrong type of feedback. Part of belonging to a community of practice is considering the depth to which you want to engage with it and/or try to draw out its other members. There are many approaches to peer observation, some more intense than others. You might invite a trusted coworker to watch a face-to-face session and provide feedback limited to a specific area such as delivery pacing, or ask them to focus on learners and how they seem to react to instruction. It's nerve-racking to invite commentary, but it always serves you well in the end (either by helping you address an issue or revealing who *not* to ask next time). If you receive harsh or unhelpful feedback, console yourself with the knowledge that it likely was either offered unintentionally or as a benign manifestation of "why didn't I think of that?" syndrome.

SEEKING RESOURCES

From finding one person who gives you solid feedback to creating a programmatic instructor development

initiative in your workplace (or both), the goal of a community of practice is to find individuals with whom you can connect productively around issues of pedagogy and praxis. Most of us already belong to several learning communities through social networks, professional organizations, or local committees/task forces. It is important to determine what a positive and scalable learning community looks like for you, but sorting through the many options can become overwhelming. In the remainder of this chapter I explore different approaches to learning with/from other library educators. These lists are not comprehensive, but are meant to provide a foundation for continued exploration.

Online Learning Communities

As the capacity to support rich communication experiences online continues to expand, many digital forums have developed that provide library educators and designers with the means to interface with like-minded colleagues. Using a combination of tools such as webcasting, blogging, tagging, chat, and threaded discussion to create hybridized or all-online learning environments, these sites allow users to create personal profiles, access resources and programs, and network with professionals who share similar interests.[5]

Learning Times Library Online Conference (LTLOC, http://home.learningtimes.net/library). Steven Bell and Jon Shank's *Blended Librarians Online* learning community was the precursor to the LTLOC, a venue for academic librarians to collaborate and share instructional design challenges and strategies through online conversations and forums. In the LTLOC, Bell, Shank, and others deliver regular webcasts on topics of interest to librarians and instructional designers. Its host site, http://learningtimes.org, is an open-access collection of online learning communities oriented toward a diverse range of instructors and educators. It emphasizes networking and communication and offers a range of initiatives such as webcasts, interviews, case studies, market analysis, and discussions.

ALA Connect (http://connect.ala.org). The American Library Association's "virtual, collaborative workspace online" provides web-based learning communities and interest groups focused on instruction and all other interest areas related to library education. The Drupal-based brainchild of *Shifted Librarian* Jenny Levine, *Connect* is an aspect of the organization's ongoing effort to move toward virtualized participation. It provides ALA members from every section, committee, interest group, and task force with a framework for collaboration and communication and features a mentorship platform that encourages the exploration of working/learning relationships in particular areas. Among the many ALA areas related to library education are the ACRL Instruction Section, the Library Instruction Round Table, and the Learning Round Table.

Ning (www.ning.com). Ning is less formalized online space than the previous two examples, because it is a site that provides users with a means of defining their own social and learning communities. Several library-related Ning spaces are available. Although less explicitly active in library instruction, Ning nevertheless provides a platform for creating new online communities for library educators who want to take a more grassroots or non-organizationally affiliated approach. Within Ning, the TeacherLibrarian network and Library 2.0 have shown to be both lasting and active. Also, the Classroom 2.0 network brings together teachers interested in social media and learning from across the educational spectrum.

Conferences and Professional Organizations

Countless professional organizations, conferences, and a growing number of loosely-organized "unconferences" provide library educators and instructional designers with the means of collaborating, presenting research, and developing peer and mentorship-based relationships. Below are only a few examples of the many groups and events connected to instructor development, library education, and instructional technology.

EDUCAUSE (www.educause.edu) *and EDUCAUSE Learning Initiative* (ELI, www.educause.edu/eli). EDUCAUSE and ELI provide "vital connecting point[s] for people and information in higher education and IT. EDUCAUSE can help you . . . build a network of colleagues you can turn to for support and guidance. And through its growing offerings of Web 2.0 services, EDUCAUSE offers you several simple ways to engage with colleagues, contribute your own expertise, and increase your visibility within the community."

ALA Learning Round Table (www.alalearning.org). Recently renamed from its previous incarnation as CLENERT, the ALA Learning Round Table "promotes quality continuing education for all library personnel." A self-defined networking resource, the Learning Round Table provides many opportunities for information and strategy sharing among others engaged in instructor development. The group blog at the address listed above and the Twitter feed @ALALearning are both strong resources.

Library Orientation Exchange (LOEX, www.emich .edu/public/loex/conferences.html) *and Loex of the West* (LOTW, http://library.mtroyal.ca/lotw/). Among the conferences in highest demand for library educators, LOEX and LOTW are small-scale, annual, non-affiliated venues for research and initiatives related to library education. LOEX is also listed under *Clearinghouses of Learning Materials* below.

Continuing Education Programs

On a local level or beyond, organized programs of continuing education or instructor development are useful means of facilitating mutual learning goals. These programs tend to follow a defined curriculum and incorporate elements of mentorship, discussion, active learning, community building, and expertise and resource sharing.

University of California at Berkeley Library Instructor Development Program (IDP, http://tinyurl.com/ ucbidp). Building local learning communities is an excellent way to create support networks, identify collaborators, and inspire ongoing conversations around instructional effectiveness among others who understand your context, particularly at a time when many find their professional travel and networking curtailed due to funding cuts. For example, at UC Berkeley a fledgling initiative invites library educators from across the organization to discuss articles, attend presentations and guest lectures, and develop their skills in themed areas related to instruction. The first semester's theme was active learning, and in the second semester the group focused on instructional design. According to IDP co-coordinator Lynn Jones, "the community of practice model enables us to get to know each other outside of organizational meetings and can help develop trust necessary to work through difficult teaching problems. . . . It gives us recognition expertise among our colleagues and inspires us to improve our practice in order to share it with our peers."

ACRL Immersion (www.ala.org/ala/mgrps/divs/ acrl/issues/infolit/professactivity/iil/). Immersion is probably the best-known example of a nationally established program of library instructor development. Its curriculum includes numerous aspects of teaching effectiveness for primarily academic librarians involved in developing and delivering information literacy instruction through a series of "tracks" oriented toward different stages of instructor development (Teacher, Program, Assessment, and Intentional Teacher). Attending Immersion was an important moment in my own progression as a library instructor. More valuable than any methods or ideas I encountered, there are the ongoing relationships I have built with Immersion colleagues and mentors.

Learning 2.0 (www.plcmcl2-about.blogspot.com). The acclaimed Learning 2.0 program, created by Helene Blowers and the Public Library of Charlotte and Mecklenburg County, is originally based in the 43 Things meme (www.43things.com) and has been replicated by libraries and organizations worldwide. It is an online "self-discovery program which encourages staff to take control of their own learning and to utilize their lifelong learning skills through exploration and PLAY." Learning 2.0 can be locally implemented to engage staff in new technologies and social media and is an excellent way to foster an organizational learning community.

Clearinghouses of Learning Materials

Resource clearinghouses can be extremely helpful in keeping you from reinventing the wheel. At the local, consortial, and national levels, open-access lists of templates, instructional principles, and other pedagogical information accessed via resource repositories can steer instructors toward effective learning design and help them share standardized or institutional best practices to achieve consistency and forward programmatic learning goals.

Multimedia Educational Resource for Learning and Online Teaching (MERLOT, www.merlot.org/merlot/index.htm). According to its mission statement, "MERLOT is a leading edge, user-centered, searchable collection of peer reviewed and selected higher education, online learning materials, catalogued by registered members and a set of faculty development support services. MERLOT's vision is to be a premiere online community where faculty, staff, and students from around the world share their learning materials and pedagogy."

Library Orientation Exchange (LOEX, www.emich.edu/public/loex/). LOEX is a membership-based, nonprofit clearinghouse and historical archive of multiformat materials relating to library instruction that stopped actively seeking new submissions after 2003. Created in 1971 after the First Annual Conference on Library Orientation at Eastern Michigan University, LOEX also publishes a quarterly journal (*LOEX Currents*), sponsors conferences, and shares repository resources with its member institutions.

Animated Tutorial Sharing Project (ANTS, www.ants.wetpaint.com) *and Library Information Literacy Online Network* (LION, www.liontv.blip.tv). ANTS is a repository and working space for North American educators focused on creating and sharing open-source screencasts and other animated online tutorial

Figure 3.2

LION TV mobile interface

resources relevant to library education, organized by the Council of Prairie and Pacific University Libraries. The site features a range of open-access tutorials and identifies best practices and technical specifications of modifying and embedding digital learning objects. LION is an information literacy tutorial channel on Blip.tv with a mobile-friendly interface (figure 3.2).

Local Open Repositories

Many institutions offer web-based collections of materials and tips that can aid local instructors in instructional planning and design. Here is just one example:

UT Austin Tips and Techniques for Library Instruction (www.lib.utexas.edu/services/instruction/tips/). As a graduate student assistant working at UT Austin libraries, I regularly referred to the online repository of rules of thumb, tips, and templates compiled by the many gifted instructors at Perry-Castaneda Library. Among other resources, this repository features a clearinghouse of active learning strategies, handout templates, and more.

Social Sites and Emerging Spaces

You can find viral, impromptu, and informal shared learning experiences in many social networks and emerging applications, which not only provide the space for collaboration but are low-cost and lasting channels for identifying and sharing significant content. Responsive and community-defined interactions are a hallmark of the dynamic and user-created technology movement, meaning that community elements are inherent in many of the online spaces available to learners and instructors. These are a few examples of platforms that facilitate collaborative online learning:

Wikis. Wikis are community-contributed resource-sharing platforms, from www.mediawiki.org to www.pmwiki.org, built in many open-source and free software versions. Wikis can be an excellent means of creating collaborative local repositories of ideas, project examples, best practices, and professional connections. There are also well-known general library wikis with instruction and education-related content, such as LibSuccess (www.libsuccess.org) and LISwiki (www.liswiki.org).

Figure 3.3
#infolit in Twitter

Realtime results for #infolit

 sciencelib **Preparing for a meeting on developing content for the 1st year English classes/info lit instruction sessions #infolit**
about 10 hours ago from web

 aldtucker RT @azmichelle: **#infolit #ICT RT @tomwhitby @aldtucker @educationweek: NAEP Draft on Technological Literacy Unveiled** http://bit.ly/o3osv
1 day ago from TweetDeck

 azmichelle **#infolit #ICT RT @tomwhitby @aldtucker @educationweek: NAEP Draft on Technological Literacy Unveiled** http://bit.ly/o3osv
1 day ago from TweetDeck

 LynParker RT @rashford: **Web 2.0: Inherent tensions & evident challenges for education** http://tinyurl.com/m7pdvr **#infolit possibilities**
1 day ago from TweetDeck

Blogs. Though the biblioblogosphere may be old news to many, this does not diminish its ongoing power as a means of sharing ideas and expertise around library education. It can be particularly instructive to follow nonlibrary blogs for pedagogical and technological inspiration, such as the media-oriented *Confessions of an Aca-Fan* by NYU media studies professor Henry Jenkins (www.henryjenkins.org) or *ProfHacker* (www.chronicle.com/blogs/profhacker/) for "tips, tutorials, and commentary on pedagogy, productivity, and technology in higher education." There are countless blogs oriented toward instructional design, media, technology, and teaching effectiveness, and as always one usually leads to five others. See the Recommended Reading at the end of the book for additional blog examples.

Microblogs. Short-format, limited-character postings to sites such as Twitter (www.twitter.com) and FriendFeed (www.friendfeed.com), as well as status updating on Facebook, are now an established means of building professional community and maintaining current awareness in teaching, learning, and information technology. As librarians adopt microblogging as a conversation and resource-sharing platform, trending topics emerge that allow participants to follow individuals and activities in their areas of interest, such as the #infolit tag (figure 3.3).

Social Networks. Facebook (www.facebook.com) is another personalized online venue that allows users to create a hybrid social/professional community. Unlike Ning, Facebook primarily functions as a social space, but many library education–related professional organizations and informal interest groups exist within Facebook and use the platform to generate feedback, encourage discussion, and publicize events at conferences and the like. For example, figure 3.4 shows a Facebook event posting listed by the California Clearinghouse of Library Instruction.

Virtual Worlds. Although Second Life (www.secondlife.com) has lost some of the cachet it once held, there is nevertheless a community of library educators dedicated to exploring its viability as an interactive resource and learning platform in the Alliance Virtual Library at www.infoisland.org. The potential of Second Life and other virtual worlds is viewed by many as promising in the realm of distance education and as a means to serve users with disabilities.[6]

E-mail discussion lists. They might seem as outdated as *War Games,* but instructional lists are still an active area of professional discourse in library education.

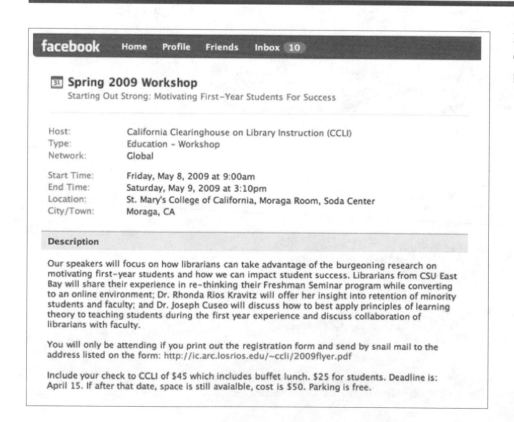

Figure 3.4
CCLI Facebook group event posting

ILI-L is a well-established and thriving instruction list (www.ftrf.org/ala/mgrps/divs/acrl/about/sections/is/ilil.cfm) that supports thousands of subscribers and is a constant source of practical ideas, research opportunities, and job postings related to instruction. This list can also provide an excellent resource for crowdsourcing solutions to immediate instructional problems.

SUMMARY

- **Gleaning** involves incorporating elements of practice that you observe in your environment into your own skill set.
- Building **communities of practice** can assist you in establishing the inspiration and structure to support ongoing instructor development.
- There are many analog and digital avenues for **mentorship**, **observation**, and **collaboration**.

REFLECTION POINTS

1. Consider your gleaning habits. Do you consciously keep track of the tips and ideas that you encounter? If so, are they centralized, or recorded in various places? If you feel that you could benefit from more intentional discovery and recording methods, brainstorm ways to shore up your approach.

2. Does your workplace have an equivalent of the Instructor Development Program or Learning 2.0?

Would (or did) this type of initiative succeed in your environment, or is a less programmatic approach to creating a learning community more desirable?

NOTES

1. By Kevin Kumashiro: *Troubling Education: Queer Activism and Anti-Oppressive Pedagogy* (New York: Routledge, 2002); *Six Lenses for Anti-Oppressive Education: Partial Stories, Improbable Conversations* (New York: Peter Lang, 2007); *Against Common Sense: Teaching and Learning toward Social Justice*, 2nd ed. (New York: Routledge, 2009); and "Seeing the Bigger Picture: Troubling Movements to End Teacher Education," *Journal of Teacher Education* 61, nos. 1–2 (2010): 1–2. Maria T. Accardi, Emily Drabinski, and Alana Kumbier (eds.), *Critical Library Instruction: Theories and Methods* (Duluth, MN: Library Juice Press, 2010).

2. Albert Bandura, *Social Learning Theory* (Englewood Cliffs, NJ: Prentice Hall, 1977).

3. Etienne Wenger, *Communities of Practice: Learning, Meaning, and Identity* (Cambridge, UK: Cambridge University Press, 1998).

4. Dale Schunk, *Learning Theories: An Educational Perspective* (Upper Saddle River, NJ: Pearson/Merrill/Prentice Hall, 2008), 299.

5. Valeda Dent-Goodman, *Keeping the User in Mind: Instructional Design and the Modern Library* (Oxford, UK: Chandos, 2009).

6. Christopher Guder, "Second Life as Innovation," *Public Services Quarterly* 5, no. 4 (2009): 282–288. For more information, see Joe Sanchez, "Implementing Second Life: Ideas, Challenges, and Innovations," *Library Technology Reports* 45, no. 2 (2009).

4

A Crash Course in Learning Theory

Learning how to think really means learning how to exercise some control over how and what you think. It means being conscious and aware enough to choose what you pay attention to and to choose how you construct meaning from experience.

—David Foster Wallace, commencement
speech at Kenyon College, 2005

GOALS

- Discuss the different types of educational theory (**learning**, **instructional**, and **curriculum**) and how they influence teaching practice.
- Describe the major theoretical schools of **behaviorism**, **cognitivism**, and **constructivism**.
- Discuss the Learning Pyramid and the concept of **active learning**.
- Explore the four factors of learning: **memory**, **motivation**, **environment**, and **prior knowledge**.
- Examine the relationship between educational theory and **instructional design**.

According to Robert Slavin, "Effective teaching is neither a bag of tricks nor a set of abstract principles; rather, it is intelligent application of well-understood principles to address practical needs."[1] In this chapter and the next, I explore the "well-understood principles" of teaching and learning. You don't need exhaustive theoretical knowledge to become a stronger educator, but a grasp of the fundamentals can be instrumental in gaining insight into learners and selecting intelligent instructional strategies. The David Foster Wallace quote that opens this chapter captures something essential: learning is translating information and experience into meaningful knowledge, a process over which individuals exert a great deal of metacognitive control. In educational contexts, knowledge formation is heavily influenced by teachers, who directly (through pedagogical strategies) and indirectly (through instructional objects) impact how much energy learners devote to the translation process. The more clearly you understand the factors guiding learning, the better prepared you become to select methods and define outcomes that motivate participants to construct meaning from the experiences you facilitate. By extension, the easier it becomes to triage the inevitable questions that arise from working in a library instructional environment: *Why do people start to fade about thirty minutes into my class? Would it be useful to try inviting students to provide running backchannel commentary during a workshop via Twitter? Why does no one volunteer when I ask a question? Do I need to create a print handout? Is this an appropriate image placement on this slide? How can I approach this topic so that people will not only "get" it, but care?*

WHY THEORY?

The most compelling rationale for understanding learning theory is to make things easier on yourself. No matter how much you teach, you can use the tested, investigated work of others to avoid making redundant mistakes or structuring your approach in a way you know will negatively affect learner retention. Read the next two chapters with this in mind: drawing on existing ideas means less trial by fire for you. There is research behind every teaching and design strategy that works, research that suggests evidence-based responses to instructional challenges. Theoretical grounding facilitates reflective practice by suggesting targeted questions to ask about your own teaching effectiveness.[2] *Am I making any sense?* becomes *Do I create opportunities for learners to apply information skills in real-world settings? When responses are given, do I elaborate with useful feedback? Do I present concepts in ways that stimulate higher-order thinking?*

FROM RESEARCH TO PRAXIS

Applying theory can be as simple as using an analogy rather than a straightforward description or selecting a question type that will have more impact at the beginning of a learning object than at its conclusion. I refer to learning and instructional research when I'm confronted with unfamiliar teaching scenarios, when I need to understand the pedagogical impact of emerging technologies, or to sharpen my insight into the learning dynamics of different populations. For example, in my last job transition I knew I would be leading more staff and faculty trainings, so I spent time researching *andragogy,* the teaching of adults according to their specific characteristics. I also find that awareness of principles and findings translates to a larger idea reserve when I am compelled to switch gears if something isn't working.

EDUCATIONAL THEORY EXPLAINED

In this context, a theory is a "scientifically acceptable set of principles . . . that provide frameworks for interpreting observations and serve as bridges between research and education."[3] Educational theory can be divided into three branches:[4]

> *Learning theories* examine why and how knowledge is formed (the focus of this chapter).
>
> *Instructional theories* address the methodology (pedagogy) and applications (praxis) of teaching (the focus of chapter 5).
>
> *Curriculum theories* focus on the content of instruction in a particular subject area. (This area is somewhat outside the scope of this book, but represented in my discussions of information fluency and critical pedagogy).

Until recently, research into learning and research into teaching were relatively separate. On the surface this may seem odd, but to those who investigate them, teaching and learning are not synonymous or even necessarily connected. Learning has traditionally been the domain of psychologists interested in development and cognition in human as well as animal subjects, whereas educators have been more concerned with learning that results from instruction. Therefore, learning theories are more often conceptual and descriptive, whereas instructional and curriculum theories tend to communicate actionable strategies.[5]

Learning theory provides the background for instructional techniques. The first major modern school of educational thought—*behaviorism*—investigated animal responses to different kinds of stimuli (meat = salivating dog; meat plus bell = salivating dog; bell without meat *still* = salivating dog), which inspired the common practice of providing positive reinforcement for correct answers. A second school of thought—*cognitivism*—explores the capacities of human memory, which inspires teaching and design techniques that reflect the brain's information processing abilities. The most recent school—*constructivism*—explores the effects of individual perception and the social environment, which have led to more collaborative and self-directed learning strategies. Here and in chapter 5, I focus on these well-established theoretical areas. In chapter 6, I consider emerging schools of thought, such as *connectivism*, that deal with shifting literacies and the impact of technology on learning.

THEORY IN LIBRARY EDUCATION

It is common for disciplines or professions to share a body of theory, and some educational perspectives are common among library educators. *Information literacy* is a curriculum theory that has since the late 1980s forwarded the "conceptual frameworks, mental models, and critical thinking" skills necessary to locate and evaluate information.[6] *Active learning*, an instructional theory first conceived by philosopher John Dewey (1859–1952), describes techniques that engage audiences and invite them to interact meaningfully rather than passively. Active learning emphasizes "the link between learning and doing" and is itself an extension of constructivist learning theory, which posits that individuals create meaning through direct experiences that shape their views.[7] In the remaining chapters of part I, my goal is to situate and broaden this theoretical base by exploring supporting and alternative ideas in teaching and learning. It is useful to have a model for applying theory in library practice; the USER method is a framework for research-supported instructional planning.

According to David Carr, libraries are "public places intended for learners, and for lives of self-invention and pursuit. At their best, they are forums for communication, independent learning, and self-preservation."[8] In addition to supporting instructional design, educational theory is applicable outside of classroom and e-learning settings, and can provide insight into creating library systems and spaces that are more intuitive and user focused by reducing the "noise"—the distracting extraneous information—in your sites, communications, facilities, and information products. Learning theory provides the foundation for interpreting how users interact with the objects that explain, organize, guide, and facilitate their search for and application of information, and it can aid the process of discovering instructional opportunities outside the traditional teacher-learner paradigm.

DEFINING LEARNING

What does it mean to say that someone has "learned" something? Is learning a correct answer, a cognitive process, or a state of being? Does it occur during instruction, or at the point when knowledge is applied in the future? There are many definitions of the term, none universally accepted. Common to many definitions is the notion that learning is "a change in an individual caused by experience."[9] George Siemens challenges change as the primary evidence of learning, defining it instead as "actionable knowledge" that can be called upon at some future time.[10] What is inarguable is that learning is natural to lived experience; throughout our lifetimes, the sensory stimuli that surround us offer nearly constant opportunities to create associations (red means stop), discover lessons (the meaning of the term *hangover*), perceive rules (stealing is wrong), and perfect skills (tying your shoes). We gain knowledge at different rates for different reasons based on a vast array of motivations, and the process is inherently guided by our unique characteristics, developmental states, and aptitudes, as well as our social and cultural context. It is the educator's challenge to perceive the individual and environmental factors that help people learn naturally in the day-to-day and leverage them effectively in more "formal" instructional contexts. According to Dale Schunk, the evidence of meaningful learning is that the knowledge it produces is enduring as opposed to temporary; a second challenge therefore becomes building learning experiences and objects that last.[11]

PERSPECTIVES ON LEARNING

Learning has been investigated from many angles. What began as a philosophical and religious inquiry broadened over time, as more scientifically oriented disciplines such as psychology and sociology developed. Transformations in literacy have shaped this inquiry; oral traditions were common among early recorded and classical societies, making memory and rhetoric central to the earliest investigations.[12] In more recent years, the impact of new media and information technology has again shifted the focus.[13]

Classical Learning Theories

The study of learning began with fundamental questions about the origin of knowledge: How do humans first come to "understand" anything? Do we inherit our ideas and insights, or do we arrive in the world as "blank slates"? Plato (c. 424–347 BCE) developed a school of thought known as *rationalism* (all knowledge derives from reason). Aristotle (384–322 BCE), a student and contemporary of Plato's, inspired a contrary approach known as *empiricism* (all knowledge derives from experience).[14] Platonic rationalism posited that humans are born equipped with an innate capacity to put mind over matter and think through experiences, whereas Aristotelian empiricism took the opposite position, arguing that the source of human knowledge is the direct experience that individuals use to guide their actions. Fast-forward many centuries to Enlightenment philosopher John Locke (1632–1704), a later empiricist who took Aristotle's blank slate, or tabula rasa, concept further. Locke contended that there is no human knowledge that does not derive from immediate sensory experience. A later rationalist, Immanuel Kant (1724–1804), believed that rather than perceiving the world as it categorically exists through our senses, we use reason to impose our own order on the environment.

Fact vs. Mind vs. Self/Society

The questions tackled by Plato, Aristotle, Locke, and Kant remain central to the modern study of learning and instruction. Is knowledge based in instinct, experience, or both? Do we learn by doing, or by seeing and interpreting? Empiricism and rationalism dominated the response to these questions until the Enlightenment-age development of the scientific method. In the mid-nineteenth century the formation of the new academic disciplines radically changed the emphasis of the investigation of learning. Whereas philosophers sought to intuit how people make sense of the world around them, psychologists began to actively investigate the question using experimentation and observation.

As the behavioral sciences shifted their inquiries away from the philosophical, three dominant approaches emerged: *behaviorism*, *cognitivism*, and *constructivism*. In the early years of the modern study of learning, psychologists focused almost entirely on the formation of fact, or how to encourage appropriate responses to questions and other stimuli (behaviorism). Attention transitioned to an emphasis on mind, or the mechanisms through which people perceive, process, and recall information (cognitivism). Interest has more recently focused on the self and the social—that is, the individual and cultural factors that affect production of knowledge (constructivism). These paradigms developed in response to one another, each building on the foundation laid by its predecessors but

motivated by issues researchers perceived had been left unexplored or underemphasized. Each has its own definition of learning and, by extension, differing perspectives on the role of the educator. Cognitivism and constructivism exert more influence on current learning and instructional theory; behaviorism has lost some of its foundational authority. In the following section, I profile each theoretical approach and present their instructional strategies in the next chapter.

BEHAVIORISM

The study of psychology grew from the systematic observation of subjects, so it is not surprising that modern educational theory is rooted in the idea that the evidence of learning is outward behavioral change. For the behaviorist, learning is demonstrated when a correct response (answer) is given to a particular stimulus (question): when 2 + 2 is the stimulus, 4 is the desired response. In this train of thought, instruction has less to do with influencing internal factors such as cognition or emotion and much more to do with facilitating a productive balance between stimulus and response.

Behaviorists often relied on animal experimentation to explore their ideas. In the late 1920s, Ivan Pavlov developed his theory of *classical conditioning* by demonstrating that, whereas dogs naturally salivate when given food (unconditioned response), by ringing a bell (neutral stimuli) each time food is dispensed over time you can train dogs to salivate each time a bell rings, even when no food is present (conditioned stimulus).[15] A contemporary of Pavlov, Edward Thorndike, developed the concept of *trial and error* by observing cats in boxes learning to make lasting associations between stimuli (pressing a bar) and a desired response (escape!) over time, also known as the Law of Effect.[16] In the 1950s, B. F. Skinner explored the role of consequences in behavioral learning by observing rats and pigeons in an apparatus known as the Skinner box. His concept of *operant conditioning* (distinguished from Pavlovian classical conditioning by its focus on consequence and choice rather than unconscious reaction) presented the idea that pleasant consequences (rat presses bar, rat receives treat) can be used to encourage a desired behavior or correct response, just as unpleasant consequences can discourage an undesirable behavior or an incorrect response (rat presses bar, rat receives shock).[17]

Behaviorism gave rise to the kind of well-controlled, instructor-focused classrooms depicted in old reel-to-reel educational films: rows of rapt children at desks, parroting answers in unison to clearly answerable questions. Learners are seen as black boxes; information goes in, answers come out. For the behaviorist, the important consideration is how to ensure correct and consistent responses by shaping actions with consequences. Practice and repetition are key, followed by testing to provide evidence of learning. Positive feedback for correct answers (reinforcement) is pivotal, as is the organized presentation of material. Absent from the behaviorist school of thought is emphasis on the process by which knowledge is formed or the factors affecting its interpretation. Creativity, agency, community, and discovery do not factor significantly into the behaviorist equation.

COGNITIVISM

As the study of psychology became more sophisticated, those investigating the learning process began to observe the mental changes occurring inside individuals as they encountered information, and the factors affecting information interpretation, retention, and transferal. By the mid-twentieth century, an alternate approach known as cognitivism began to address what many theorists viewed as the more problematic aspects of behaviorism: that learning is passive rather than active, that knowledge is externally imposed, and that the evidence of learning is as simple as a correct answer. Cognitivists known as Gestalt theorists challenged the idea that learning is the result of behavioral conditioning, proposing instead that in the real world it is a series of internal processes that result in moments of insight that cannot be satisfactorily explained by trial and error or repetition. Cognitivism in effect internalized the study of learning, shifting its focus from outward behavior to the psychology and science of information processing and to some degree to the motivational and emotional factors that contribute to knowledge formation.

Cognitivism and its many subfields remain central to the study of educational psychology and by extension exert great influence on contemporary teaching and learning. Cognitivists believe that we "experience the world in meaningful patterns or organized wholes" and that by organizing information and processing prior knowledge we make the intellectual connections that underpin higher-order thinking.[18] A central aspect of cognitivism is its focus on the intellectual transitions that occur as a learner passes through various stages of maturity. In the early 1950s, influential theorist Jean Piaget studied successive steps of child development, forwarding the idea that our ability to think moves from concrete to abstract and that in order to be absorbed effectively, content must be presented at the correct developmental stage.

Piaget also argued that an individual is constantly building and revising "mental models" (schemata) to categorize information and make sense of experiences.[19] When individuals draw connections between new pieces of information, they gradually revise old ideas to account for new input. Applying this, theorist David Ausubel argued that, by presenting an "anchoring idea" that links new content with familiar concepts or experiences, an instructor lays the foundation for a learner to be able to contextualize new information and make it personally relevant and usable.[20] The concept of metacognition also springs from the cognitivist approach; by reflecting on their own goals and abilities in a given instructional scenario, individuals perceive personal benefit and develop strategies according to their own learning strengths.

CONSTRUCTIVISM

The contemporary approach known as constructivism (sometimes *constructionism*) developed in response to perceived shortcomings in cognitivism and behaviorism and has in the past several decades resulted in significant learner-centered changes in teaching methodology. Early constructivists John Dewey (1859–1952) and Lev Vygotsky (1896–1934) took issue with the right/wrong focus of behaviorists, who in their view neglected to explore learning as a social process informed by prior experience, beliefs, and individual ability. The central idea of constructivism is that both the individual and the social context exert a profound influence on the learning process, and that learners create meaning from their environments by interpreting them through personal attributes, values, and perceptions. Literally, individuals construct knowledge by building their own context for the information they encounter, which incorporates elements of individual agency and social learning less dominant in other theories. In constructivism the evidence of learning is not necessarily in behavioral change, and much of how we learn occurs through observation, translation, and imitation (mimesis, socialization, and modeling).[21]

The concept of learner-centered instruction is one of the most lasting contributions of constructivism. Constructivists sought to shift the focus of instruction from passive to active, from educator to learner, and from cognition to learning community. John Dewey was instrumental in forwarding the notion that learning is an active rather than a passive state and a practical, evolutionary function expressed in real-world problem solving.[22] For Dewey, learning is the natural consequence of working through the challenges of daily life. Therefore, meaningful instruction should build upon engaging learners with realistic, relevant problems in an authentic, community-based atmosphere.

Lev Vygotsky focused on the sociocultural aspects of learning in his theory of the *zone of proximal development* (ZPD). He argued that each individual has a certain degree of potential to learn in a given situation, which is then facilitated or prevented by the instructional environment. In essence, the ZPD is "the amount of learning possible by a given student given the proper instructional conditions."[23] *Situated learning*, another central tenet of constructivist thought, asserts that learning is influenced by many cognitive and contextual factors and that meaningful retention and transfer are encouraged by "situating" content in a way that allows learners to interact with its the real-world application. Constructivists also perceive that learning is individualistic and subject to ability

and preference; I consider designing for individual learning characteristics in chapter 9.

DECONSTRUCTING THE LEARNING PYRAMID

If you are at all familiar with the concept of active learning, chances are good that you have also seen the Learning Pyramid (figure 4.1). The Learning Pyramid is one of the most lasting, viral images in teacher education and is regularly used to forward the constructivist premise that instruction is more meaningful when it is realistic, engaged, and reflective. It diagrams the effectiveness of learning methods involving different levels of auditory, visual, kinesthetic, and interpersonal activity, suggesting that the more involved and communicative the instructional task, the more individuals remember as a result. In a classroom setting, this ideally translates into participation, dynamic lesson pacing, learner involvement, and problem-based exercises.[24] In an online setting,

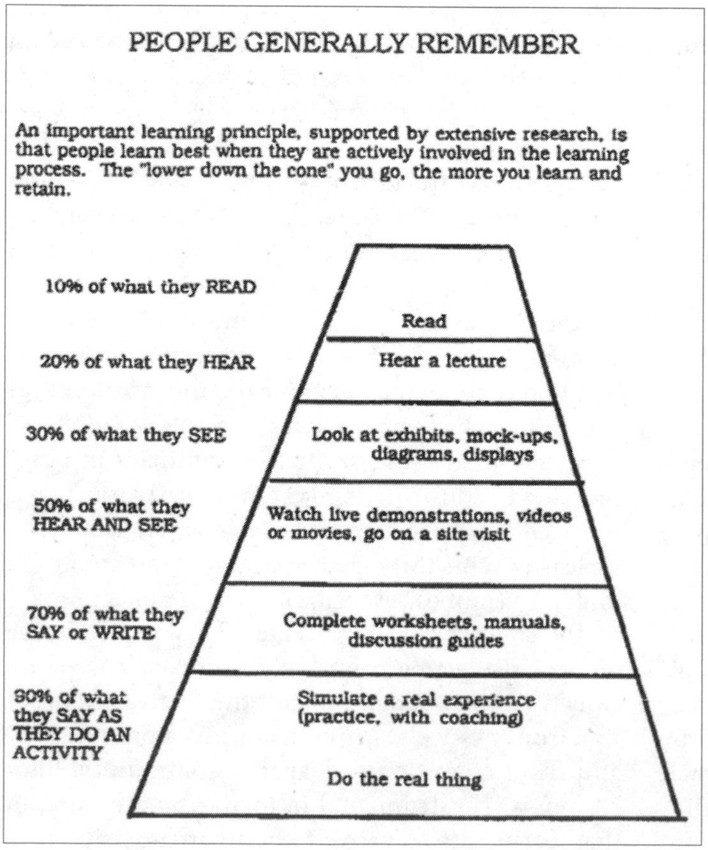

PEOPLE GENERALLY REMEMBER

An important learning principle, supported by extensive research, is that people learn best when they are actively involved in the learning process. The "lower down the cone" you go, the more you learn and retain.

10% of what they READ — Read

20% of what they HEAR — Hear a lecture

30% of what they SEE — Look at exhibits, mock-ups, diagrams, displays

50% of what they HEAR AND SEE — Watch live demonstrations, videos or movies, go on a site visit

70% of what they SAY or WRITE — Complete worksheets, manuals, discussion guides

90% of what they SAY AS THEY DO AN ACTIVITY — Simulate a real experience (practice, with coaching)

Do the real thing

Figure 4.1
Learning Pyramid

(reproduced with permission by NTL Institute for Applied Behavioral Science, 300 N. Lee Street, Suite 300, Alexandria, VA 22314. 1-800-777-5227) active learning incorporates elements of interactivity, discovery, and collaboration. This is all well and good based on the theoretical approaches I have discussed thus far. So, what about the Learning Pyramid needs to be deconstructed?

Despite its popularity, the Learning Pyramid is the theoretical equivalent of an urban legend: Somewhat based in reality, but way overblown. Try searching Google Images for "learning pyramid." You will find hundreds of variations in an array of shapes and sizes; details differ from image to image, and equivocal red-flag words like *generally, seem to,* and *may* abound. Many have tried to substantiate its claims, but the figures that associate memory with activity cannot be verified.[25] Although its origins are murky, the Pyramid seems to have been created in the 1960s by a for-profit company known as the National Training Laboratories, which adapted the idea from a graphic known as the "Cone of Experience" originally created by media educator Edgar Dale in the mid-1940s.[26] To this day, if you ask the National Training Laboratories to support its claim that the Learning Pyramid is based in "extensive research," you will receive this reply:

> Thanks for your inquiry of NTL Institute. We are happy to respond to your inquiry about The Learning Pyramid. Yes, it was developed and used by NTL Institute at our Bethel, Maine campus in the early sixties. . . . Yes, we believe it to be accurate—but no, we no longer have—nor can we find—the original research that supports the numbers. We get many inquiries every month about this—and many, many people have searched for the original research and have come up empty handed. . . . Yet the Learning Pyramid as such seems to have been modified and always has been attributed to NTL Institute.[27]

Why is the Learning Pyramid so compelling, and what if anything can it actually teach us? For one thing, it is a perfect example of an idea that has stuck. It is simple, concrete, seemingly credible, and validates the shared experience of teachers, trainers, and presenters the world over—that learners seem to benefit more from engagement than passivity. The Learning Pyramid provides an easy map to instructional effectiveness (If I want them to remember something, all I need to do is have them teach each other) and gets to the heart of what educators want (an engaged audience) and what we fear (a bored audience) in a visually digestible way (imagine if you needed only to look at

the Pyramid for a few minutes instead of reading this and the next chapter).

The chaos of pedagogy and praxis are enough to make anyone search for a digestible guideline, and this is why the Learning Pyramid masterfully misleads so many educators. I remember the first time I saw it in an instructional training program; it seemed like a revelation. *Finally, an explanation of how people actually learn,* I thought. No longer would I drone on at the head of the class; instead, I would use interactive technology and peer education at every opportunity. The ideas behind the Pyramid inspired me to experiment with new media, develop varied and more interactive classes, and interact differently with learners, all of which worked wonders for my instructional confidence and effectiveness. That said, I was also basing instructional decisions on unsubstantiated claims and forcing technology and interactivity into contexts where they sometimes didn't seem to work that well: too much of a good thing.

Think critically for a moment about the Pyramid's claims and you will see the problem. Rather than one method being inherently better than another, James Lalley and Robert Miller cite research that finds each of the learning approaches in the Learning Pyramid are potentially effective in the right context.[28] Learning is influenced by a range of variables, meaning that individuals learn differently according to preference, aptitude, media, and environment. Additionally, some content lends itself more readily to one method over another: a podcast of a traditional lecture may be the most efficient way to present one subject, whereas immersive hands-on activity in a face-to-face classroom may lend itself to another. They argue instead that learning happens on more of an engagement continuum than a learning pyramid, wherein prior experience, individual and group motivation, and instructional context is critical to determining the effectiveness of specific learning and instructional methods.

INTERNAL AND EXTERNAL CONDITIONS OF LEARNING

Exploring the conditions that influence learning is a method for determining context and continuum. Robert Gagné, one of the founders of instructional design, believed that there are both *internal* and *external conditions* that affect individual learning. Internal conditions include cognition, emotion, and desire, whereas external conditions are the environment, instructor, and cultural influences at work in a learning interaction.[29] It is the interplay between external and internal conditions that determines what a learner takes away from an instructional scenario, which helps an educator anticipate the strategies that will work more effectively in one context over another. An example that may resonate with many readers: If you are leading a course-integrated workshop for students who have a poor opinion of their primary instructor (external condition), their level of motivation to pay attention to any aspect of your session is likely to be much lower (internal condition). In this situation, you might maneuver to have the instructor actually *not* attend the session, which is contrary to typical practice. Without the instructor present, you might find that the students who actually show up are more likely to be receptive.

This scenario points to an important insight: many factors affecting the ability or motivation to learn have little to do with the instructor. For example, learners' physical and mental states are hugely important to how they able to interpret, recall, and apply information—distress frustrates our ability to pay attention. Affective (i.e., emotional) as well as cognitive factors guide how we incorporate new data and use experiences to build on prior knowledge, and cultural contexts determine not only how information is interpreted but whether the subject matter is within a learner's frame of reference to begin with.[30] Equipped with this understanding, you can more clearly recognize the external conditions that are within your range of influence (e.g., physical environments, digital interfaces, course content, instructional delivery) while tailoring your message to nurture conditions internal to your audience (e.g., learning styles, personal goals, motivation).

CONTEXTUAL VARIABLES AND INSTRUCTIONAL REALISM

Thinking about the conditions of learning also helps you understand that, if there is a problem in a learning interaction, it may not only be you causing it. I think of this as *instructional realism*. When you approach a class, tutorial, or training, you can do your best to be aware of the conditions of learning, but awareness does not necessarily equal control. It is important to identify the factors that you actually have the ability to influence in order to focus your energies on them. The more environmentally oriented of these factors

are known as *contextual variables*, which are similar to learning conditions but specific to teaching spaces, organizational cultures, and so forth. These can exert a great deal of influence on a live interaction.

Think about a few negative contextual variables that may have shaped on-the-ground learning scenarios in your past, such as low workplace morale, poor climate control or noise in a classroom, or sessions that begin at 8 a.m. or right after lunch. In virtual instruction, any number of technical issues are hugely important contextual variables, and mitigating the potentially negative among them is an important part of e-learning design.[31] Reflecting on analog or digital contextual variables before an interaction is a method of determining what it would take to address them, such as speaking with the physical plant or building manager about temperature adjustments, prompting a viewer to use a specific browser for performance, leveraging humor to alleviate frustration, rescheduling an after-lunch session, or employing more active instructional techniques if you anticipate an unmotivated group.

THE FOUR FACTORS OF LEARNING

If you've ever gotten a flat tire, the importance of the internal and external conditions of learning becomes clear. To illustrate what I mean, consider the experience of three individuals who learned to fix a flat via different methods. The first is me: As a teenager in driver's ed, I half-ignored a crusty reel-to-reel film from the 1950s on how to fix a flat—pull off, turn on hazards, locate jack, etc. . . . . *zzz.* Compare this to a friend of mine, regularly taken to the side of a Texas interstate during rush hour by her father, who timed her changing simulated blowouts with a stopwatch. (Amazingly, she remembers this fondly.) Now consider a third example: A former colleague of mine confronted a longtime fear of car trouble at an auto repair class geared toward empowering women to handle mechanical tasks they were socialized to find intimidating. There, she watched an instructor explain and simulate the tire changing process, which she was then able to practice several times with a partner.

Fast-forward to what happens to each of us when our tires actually blow: I discover that the car I have owned for years is missing its jack, my friend's internal clock starts ticking and she switches into pit crew mode, and my old colleague locates her manual and thinks deliberately through each step before heading for the trunk. Three ways of learning the same task, all of which produce completely different results. What occurred in each learning scenario to affect our real-life performance so drastically? From an educator's perspective, why were my friend and my former colleague better prepared to handle the situation? Though on the surface the answers seem straightforward, considered in greater depth they offer significant insight into the ways learners engage meaningfully with instruction (as opposed to superficially, or not at all).

To examine key differences in the tire-changing scenarios, I first explore what I consider to be the four core factors that influence individual learning—*motivation, environment, prior knowledge,* and *memory* (figure 4.2). Each is instrumental in shaping how individuals interpret instructional content and context, and by extension how readily they are able to recall the information and skills they encounter and transfer them to real-life, or authentic, situations.[32] Arguably the end goal of all instruction, *transfer* and *recall* are central concepts in educational theory that come up several times in chapter 5.

Memory

It may seem obvious, but there is much more to remembering than memorization. The lasting application of knowledge to facilitate future tasks, insight, and skills is the point of instruction; teaching is therefore an exercise in conditioning memory. According to *information processing theory,* individuals use their sensory registers (sight, touch, hearing, etc.) to encounter and sort environmental information, some of which is transferred to short-term memory (also known as working memory), and some of which is discarded. Short-term or working memory stores "bits" of content for only a few seconds before either discarding or incorporating them into long-term memory.[33] The term *cognitive load* describes the work, weight, or stress that the brain experiences as it processes information, which is directly affected by how content is organized and presented.[34] If you have ever tried to multitask and concentrate on something closely at the same time or follow a presentation accompanied by slides stuffed too full of text, you have experienced cognitive overload, or when your mind literally strains to process more information than it can manage.

In these situations, you transfer less information to long-term memory because your internal processes are overcapacitated and forced to filter too many bits at a time. To some extent learners control how much of their mental energy they direct toward an instructional scenario, but cognitive load management is not equivalent to paying attention (although some people's defensive reaction to overload is refusing to receive any further information). There is a physiological limit to how much information the human

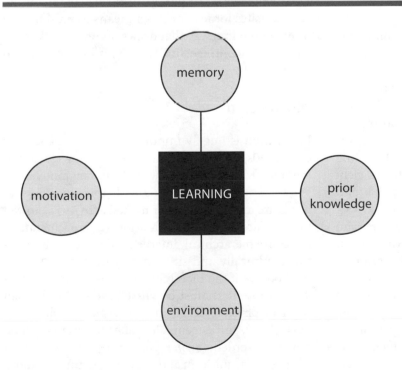

Figure 4.2
Factors of learning

brain can process, known as *working memory capacity.* You might be familiar with the phrase "seven plus or minus two"? Breakthrough research by psychologist George Miller in the 1950s determined that people are able to store about seven pieces or units of information in their working or short-term memory, give or take a few, at any moment.[35] If too much capacity is directed toward filtration, the ability to determine relevance and significance diminishes.

The authors of *Made to Stick* offer an exercise that provides insight into information transfer from short to long-term memory.[36]

Below are two short series of letters. Concentrate on committing the first series to memory for ten seconds or so, but don't read ahead—block the second letter series with you hand or a sheet of paper if necessary. After about ten seconds, look away and write down as many letters as you can remember.

J FKFB INAT OUP SNA SAI RS

Now, repeat the exercise with the second series of letters:

JFK FBI NATO UPS NASA IRS

In the first part, the rule of seven plus or minus two predicts that you were likely able to remember five to nine letters total, which you also probably jumbled or wrote out of sequence. In the second part, you might have nailed the entire series. By a slight shift in spacing, seemingly random groups of letters morph into familiar abbreviations, thus becoming far easier for your working memory capacity to handle. By acting as *mnemonics*—memory aids that make more efficient use of cognitive processing capacity—familiar and roughly associated terms such as NATO and NASA help you reference existing knowledge structures and "hang on" to more bits of information than when the letters appeared disjointed. You unconsciously improved your own recall by associating new information with something already known, a process called *elaboration.* While an overly simplistic example, the principle of "chunking" content into cognitively manageable and retrievable units makes more efficient use of information processing capacity.[37]

Prior Knowledge

In the tire-changing scenarios, my teenage self would have been quite out of my depth if I had not known what a car was in the first place, and a tacit understanding of North American politics and culture in the 20th century is required for the abbreviation exercise to have any impact. Every piece of information a learner receives to be incorporated into memory must call upon an existing framework of facts, concepts, and processes that make said piece of information interpretable, no matter how basic. Each of us builds mental patterns to classify the information we encounter and translate it into working knowledge; it is essential to connect instructional content to what is already known or significant as a means of helping learners make meaningful associations. *Schemata,* the cognitive models we leverage to "organize large amounts of information into a meaningful system," build a structure for translating data into meaningful knoweldge.[38]

Prior knowledge thus has profound effects on how learners incorporate information into memory, because what individuals bring to a scenario affects everything from the amount of attention they direct toward instruction to their comprehension of the material itself. Learners also pass through developmental stages informed by aptitude and experience; Piaget's *readiness* concept dictates that instruction be carefully matched to the student's level.[39] In the next chapter and in part II, I discuss determining prerequisites for learning as a means to present new information in a way that draws on previous knowledge and encourages its meaningful synthesis into lasting skills.

Motivation

Motivation is hugely important to learning. In the early 1940s, psychologist Abraham Maslow described the "hierarchy of needs" that guide human motivation. When certain mental, emotional, and physiological needs are met, higher-order mental activity is allowed to take place. According to Maslow's approach, human needs are hierarchical, interdependent, and "biologically, culturally and situationally determined."[40] At the bottom of the hierarchy of needs are *deprivation needs,* those that must be satisfied to ensure human survival: physiological soundness, safety, "belongingness" (love), and esteem. Only after these are satisfied can higher-order *growth needs* can be pursued, such as knowledge acquisition and the desire to understand, a motivation-driven process Maslow described as *self-actualization*.[41]

Theorists also distinguish between *intrinsic* and *extrinsic* motivation.[42] Intrinsic motivation is how inherently interesting or valued a subject is to a learner; extrinsic motivation results from incentives designed to encourage engagement with subjects of low intrinsic value. Although library educators are less likely than, say, a breakdance instructor to encounter students with high levels of intrinsic motivation, we definitely interact with learners from across the motivational spectrum. Elective learning scenarios such as drop-in classes or web-based professional development courses are more likely to have intrinsically motivated participants, as are those involving graduate-level university students and continuing learners. Attendees at required instructional events such as staff trainings or introductory information literacy sessions are more likely to need extrinsic strategies to engage their attention. Motivational strategies for in-person and virtual instruction are presented in chapter 5.

Environment

Environment is perhaps the most broadly interpretable factor of learning. I mentioned earlier in the chapter that affective (or emotional) factors contribute heavily to learning, and the environment becomes the psychological infrastructure for interaction, attention, and participation.[43] The atmosphere and dynamic facilitated by an instructor are therefore instrumental in determining learner engagement. In face-to-face instruction, the learning environment spans practical factors such as room dimensions, furniture, and seating capacity; climate and ambient elements like lighting and temperature; technical factors such as computing technology and presentation media; cultural elements such as language accessibility and inclusiveness; and instructional elements such as tone, pacing, classroom dynamics, discussion management, and opportunities for interaction. In web-based and mobile instruction, the learning environment is determined by delivery medium, technological accessibility, connection speed, degrees of interactivity, and the underlying stability of the e-learning platform itself, whereas in relatively static instructional objects such as web pages, videos, course guides, or even print handouts, it is determined by layout and design.

Technology is now often central to the environment of learning in both of face-to-face and virtual instruction. When used ineffectively, technology can thwart engagement as readily as it can facilitate it, a distinction easily perceived by participants. The annual *ECAR Study of Undergraduate Students and Information Technology* has consistently shown that learners are open to technology-enriched instruction when it supports their course experience, but that they still overwhelmingly value personal contact in learning. As one 2009 respondent noted, "There needs to be a balance between human interaction and IT-based learning."[44] Determining the technological familiarity, needs, and characteristics of your audience is a means to avoid using tools in ways that obscure your message or present too steep a learning curve. As the platforms and presentation media available to instructors continue to develop, this involves considering each application for its context-specific appropriateness and capacity to facilitate outcomes (see chapter 6).

THE FOUR FACTORS IN ACTION

Based on the above elaboration, consider how motivation, environment, prior knowledge, and memory influenced each individual in the tire-changing examples outlined earlier in the chapter (see table 4.1).

In my case, I was bored and distracted (motivation) and lacked the insight to perceive that I was missing out on a necessary skill (prior knowledge). The content was far removed from its practical application, and the presentation technology was dismally outdated (environment). Therefore, I retained little from the experience (memory).

In my friend's case, her father found a way to address some of the more common aspects of teenage antipathy, such as making the need for knowing the skill real by simulating the experience of a roadside flat (environment), and her retention increased accordingly (memory). The authentic learning experience, emotional connection with her instructor, and sensation of benchmarking her performance over time made the content highly relevant (motivation), and her father's description of the process and its value prepared her to want to learn (prior knowledge).

In my colleague's case, she was able to master the steps of a previously intimidating process (prior knowledge) in a controlled, nonhectic setting (environment) that used humor and structured peer engagement as support mechanisms (memory), which increased her confidence and ability to overcome fears about a process that had long remained daunting (motivation).

Table 4.1 **The Four Factors of Learning in Action**				
	MEMORY	**MOTIVATION**	**PRIOR KNOWLEDGE**	**ENVIRONMENT**
1) Driver's Ed	• discouraged by distraction and ineffective delivery medium	• negligible	• little experience either with driving or being stranded	• passive • detached
2) Side of the Road	• encouraged by engagement and repetition	• emotional • competitive	• supplemented by instructor knowledge	• immevrsive • authentic
3) Ladies' Auto Repair	• encouraged by structure and support	• self-directed • goal-oriented	• self-perceived low prior knowledge a source of motivation	• active • social

SUMMARY

- Teaching and design strategies are founded in educational research, an understanding of which can help you select instructional approaches that match your strengths and support the needs of your learners.
- **Learning theories** explain how and why learning occurs, **instructional theories** address the methodology of teaching and pedagogy, and **curriculum theories** focus on the content or subjects of instruction.
- Learning is a **persistent change** or **actionable knowledge** in an individual caused by experience, observation, practice, or synthesis in either formal or informal settings.
- Classical learning theories include **rationalism** (knowledge is based in reason) and **empiricism** (knowledge is based in experience).
- Three major schools of learning theory are **behaviorism** (learning is observable and conditioned), **cognitivism** (learning is cognitive, structural, and internal), and **constructivism** (learning is social, active, and contextual).
- **Active learning** occurs on an **engagement continuum** rather than a learning pyramid, varying based on learner needs, characteristics, and preferences.
- There are **internal** and **external** conditions that influence individual learning. Internal conditions are cognitive, emotional, and desire related; external conditions are environmental, cultural, and instructor related.

- Four factors affecting learning are **memory**, **motivation**, **environment**, and **prior knowledge**.

REFLECTION POINTS

1. Is your teaching approach more representative of behaviorism, cognitivism, or constructivism? Do any of these schools of thought appeal to you instinctively?

2. Think about the idea of an engagement continuum versus a learning pyramid, wherein the contextual specifics and experience level of participants affect their level of interest and learning style. How might this continuum affect your approach to engaging different types of audiences?

3. Think about your own learning process in a recent instructional scenario, such as staff training or an online workshop. What contextual factors affected your performance or attention?

NOTES

1. Robert Slavin, *Educational Psychology: Theory and Practice*, 8th ed. (Boston: Pearson, 2006), xvii.
2. James Stronge, *Qualities of Effective Teachers*, 2nd ed. (Alexandria, VA: Association for Supervision and Curriculum Development, 2007), 30–31.
3. Dale Schunk, *Learning Theories: An Educational Perspective*, 5th ed. (Upper Saddle River, NJ: Pearson, 2008), 3.
4. Charles Reigeluth (ed.), *Instructional Design Theories and Models: A New Paradigm of Instructional Theory*, vol. 2 (Mahwah, NJ: Lawrence Erlbaum, 1999), 12.
5. Ibid., 23.

6. Esther Grassian and Joan Kaplowitz, *Information Literacy Instruction: Theory and Practice* (New York: Neal-Schulman, 2000), 22.

7. Dennis Phillips and Jonas Soltis, *Perspectives on Learning*, 4th ed. (New York: Teacher's College Press, 2004), 17.

8. David Carr, *A Place Not a Place: Reflections and Possibility in Museums and Libraries* (Lanham, MD: AltaMira Press, 2006), 6–7.

9. Marcy Driscoll, *Psychology of Learning for Instruction*, 2nd ed. (Boston: Allyn and Bacon, 2000).

10. George Siemens, *Connectivism: A Learning Theory for the Digital Age*, elearnspace, December 12, 2004. www.elearnspace.org/Articles/connectivism.htm.

11. Schunk, *Learning Theories*, 2.

12. Walter Ong, *Orality and Literacy* (London: Routledge, 2002).

13. Nicholas G. Carr, *The Shallows: What the Internet Is Doing to Our Brains* (New York: W.W. Norton, 2010).

14. Schunk, *Learning Theories*, 10–11.

15. Ivan Pavlov, *Conditioned Reflexes*, trans. G. V. Anrep (New York: International, 1927).

16. Edward Thorndike, "The Law of Effect," *American Journal of Psychology* 39 (1927): 212–222.

17. Burrhus Skinner, *Science and Human Behavior* (New York: MacMillan, 1953).

18. Phillips and Soltis, *Perspectives*, 34–35.

19. Jean Piaget, *The Origins of Intelligence in Children* (New York: W. W. Norton, 1963). See also Grassian and Kaplowitz, *Information Literacy*, 42.

20. David Ausubel, *The Psychology of Meaningful Verbal Learning* (New York: Grune and Stratton, 1963). See also Phillips and Soltis, *Perspectives*, 69.

21. Albert Bandura, *Social Learning Theory* (Englewood Cliffs, NJ: Prentice Hall, 1977).

22. Phillips and Soltis, *Perspectives*, 38–39.

23. Schunk, *Learning Theories*, 245.

24. Mark Windschitl, "The Challenges of Sustaining a Constructivist Classroom Culture," *Phi Delta Kappan* 80, no. 10 (1999): 751–755.

25. James Lalley and Robert Miller, "The Learning Pyramid: Does It Point Teachers in the Right Direction?" *Education* 128, no. 1 (2007): 64–79. See also A. Kovalchick and K. Dawson (eds.), *Educational Technology: An Encyclopedia* (Santa Barbara, CA: ABC-Clio, 2003), www.learningandteaching.info/learning/myths.htm.

26. Edgar Dale, *Audio-Visual Methods in Teaching* (New York: Dryden Press, 1946).

27. "About the Learning Pyramid," homepages.gold.ac.uk/polovina/learnpyramid/about.htm.

28. Lalley and Miller, "Learning Pyramid."

29. Robert Gagné, Walter Wager, Katherine Golas, and John Keller, *Principles of Instructional Design*, 5th ed. (Belmont, CA: Thomson/Wadsworth, 2005), 5–7.

30. Schunk, *Learning Theories*, 226.

31. Ibid., 23.

32. John Bransford, Ann Brown, and Rodney Cocking, *How People Learn: Brain, Mind, Experience, and School* (Washington, DC: National Academy Press, 1999), 17.

33. Richard Atkinson and Richard Shiffrin, "Human Memory: A Proposed System and Its Control Processes," in K. W. Spence and J. T. Spence (eds.), *The Psychology of Learning and Motivation*, Advances in Research and Theory 2 (New York: Academic Press, 1968), 89–95.

34. Schunk, *Learning Theories*, 298–299.

35. George Miller, "The Magical Number Seven, Plus or Minus Two: Some Limits on Our Capacity for Processing Information," *Psychological Review* 63 (1956): 81–97.

36. Chip Heath and Dan Heath, *Made to Stick: Why Some Ideas Survive and Others Die* (New York: Random House, 2007), 51–52.

37. Linda Lohr, *Creating Graphics for Learning and Performance* (Upper Saddle River, NJ: Pearson, 2008), 51. See also Ruth Clark and Chopeta Lyons, *Graphics for Learning: Proven Guidelines for Planning, Designing, and Evaluating Visuals in Training Materials* (San Francisco: Pfeiffer, 2004), 118.

38. Schunk, *Learning Theories*, 155.

39. Jean Piaget and Barbel Inhelder, *The Psychology of the Child* (London: Routledge and Kegan Paul, 1969).

40. Abraham Maslow, "A Theory of Human Motivation," *Psychological Review* 50 (1943): 370–396.

41. Abraham Maslow, *Motivation and Personality*, 2nd ed. (New York: Harper and Row, 1970).

42. Martin Covington, "Self-Worth Theory Goes to College: Do Our Motivation Theories Motivate?" in D. M. McInerney and S. Van Etten (eds.), *Big Theories Revisited*, Research on Sociocultural Influences on Motivation and Learning 4 (Greenwich, CT: Information Age, 2004). See also Slavin, *Educational Psychology*, 334–338.

43. Claire Weinstein and Richard Mayer, "The Teaching of Learning Strategies," in M. C. Wittrock (ed.), *Handbook of Research on Teaching*, 3rd ed. (New York: Macmillan, 1986), 315–327.

44. Shannon Smith, Gail Salaway, and Judith Caruso, *The ECAR Study of Undergraduate Students and Information Technology: Key Findings*. www.educause.edu/ecar/, 12, 2009.

5

A Correction Course in Instructional Theory

We must look for those elements of learning theory that pertain to the events about which an instructor can do something.

—Robert Gagné et al., *Principles of Instructional Design*

GOALS

- Explore the instructional approaches of **behaviorism**, **cognitivism**, and **constructivism**.
- Introduce the concepts of **direct** and **discovery instruction**.
- Describe the instructional implications of **memory**, **motivation**, **prior knowledge**, and **environment**.
- Provide examples of **extrinsic** and **intrinsic** motivation.

Now that you have endured a crash course in learning theory, how do you begin to translate this information into practice? By this point you have probably determined that instructional approaches are numerous and the justifications for selecting them complex. Instead of memorizing every idea that exists, you can understand broad principles that encourage learning and, on the basis of the characteristics and needs of your audience, use these ideas to design effective messages and learning experiences. The trick is knowing enough about the elements of instruction—learner, content, context, and educator, categories I first discussed in chapter 2—to match theoretical approaches to your targets, technologies, and learning activities.

Many library educators feel pressured to blend new technologies and activities into every session, believing that this is the only way to create dynamic instruction. Like learning styles, teaching styles are an expression of your aptitudes and preferences. Although it is important to challenge yourself to expand your knowledge and skill set as an educator, it is equally critical to reflect on your own interests and the resources that are available to you. Designing new learning objects and activities is a time-intensive process, and introducing different elements into your repertoire risks backfire or can entail more work than you expected. David Cook and Ryan Sittler rightly argue that there is no right or wrong instructional approach, only approaches that are "*useful* or *not so useful* in particular learning situations." Developing a stronger sense of "practical pedagogy" can help you avoid the creating off-the-mark experiences or taking on more than you can handle.[1]

PRINCIPLES OF INSTRUCTIONAL THEORY

It is impossible to reach every student all of the time. Part of what is so daunting about designing instruction is that at any given moment there are participants who already know it all (or at least think they do), those who know a fair amount (and could probably stand to know more), those who know next to nothing (or at least fear they do), and those who know nothing at all (and are bored or frustrated out of their minds). This requires you to ask, *How do I balance my instructional message between the know-it-alls and the know-next-to-nothings while engaging the know-somethings and resuscitating the don't-cares?* There are countless theoretical responses to this question, but Dale Schunk identifies five common principles among them:[2]

- Learners progress through stages/phases.
- Material should be organized and presented in small steps.
- Learners require practice, feedback, and review.
- Social models facilitate learning and motivation.
- Motivational and contextual factors influence learning.

In other words, people learn best when instruction is incremental, organized, responsive, social, and engaging.

INSTRUCTIONAL STRATEGIES FROM THE MAJOR SCHOOLS OF LEARNING

In chapter 4, I described how the principal schools of educational theory—behaviorism, cognitivism, and constructivism—understand learning: Behaviorist learning results from stimulus and response and is encouraged by repetition and reinforcement. Cognitivist learning is the interpretation of sensory information into mental structures that facilitate transfer and recall. Constructivist learning translates experience into knowledge via social processes and

cultural contexts. Understanding this conceptual shift from repetition to organization to socialization helps demonstrate why some educators might favor one approach, depending on the scenario, objective, or learners in question.

All provide potentially useful instructional principles, but each school of thought tends to mesh more naturally with some applications than others. For example, behaviorist methods are successful in fact- and competency-based learning (e.g., job training), cognitivist instruction tends to translate well to concepts and procedures (e.g., search strategies), and constructivist approaches lend themselves more readily to higher-order thinking (e.g., problem solving and critical analysis). To bring their practical implications into relief, Peggy Ertmer and Timothy Newby recommend asking a series of questions about each theoretical approach:[3]

1. How does learning occur?
2. What factors influence learning?
3. What is the role of memory?
4. How does transfer occur?
5. What types of learning are best suited to this theory?
6. What aspects of this theory are important to instructional design?
7. What teaching strategies facilitate learning?

Table 5.1 summarizes behaviorism, cognitivism, and constructivism in response to these questions.

It is not necessarily desirable to choose one theoretical model over another. As a library educator, you are likely to work with diverse media and interact with audiences of differing skill levels and backgrounds. It will therefore be useful to incorporate best practices from each perspective in order to accommodate a range of learning needs and styles, a process known as *differentiating instruction* (see more on differentiation in chapters 10 and 11). To assist you in the differentiation process, I summarize the core instructional strategies of each school of thought in the next few sections.

Behaviorist Instruction

For the behaviorist practitioner, environments and objects are designed to create conditions under which learning is predictable, interactive, structured, and reinforced. Instruction includes a clearly outlined set of goals that are communicated to the learner, assessment strategies that demonstrate whether the targets were reached, an incremental approach that involves repetition of key content, and consistent opportunities for learner participation and instructor feedback. Schunk elaborates on these characteristics:[4]

- Reinforcement should happen often and at the appropriate time.
- Material should be presented in increments or small steps.
- Learners should be actors rather than passive receivers.

Table 5.1 Comparing Instructional Theories

	BEHAVIORIST	COGNITIVIST	CONSTRUCTIVIST
How does learning occur?	• through guided behavioral change made evident by accurate answers/consistent performance	• through mental processes that result in the formation of concepts and schema	• through experience, sociocultural influence, and metacognition
What factors influence learning?	• *external* (environment, instructor)	• *internal* (cognitive processes, readiness, aptitude)	• *internal* (emotional) • *external* (social, environmental)
What is the role of memory?	• repetition and reinforcement facilitates memorization	• short- and long-term memory interact to facilitate schema building	• activated and influenced by meaningful learner experiences
How does transfer occur?	• encouraged by positive reinforcement, learners make associations in the form of "correct" answers	• learners form mental models in order to apply concepts and ideas to new scenarios	• through perception of personally relevant context and application of knowledge
What types of learning are best suited to this theory?	• fact-based • practical	• concept-based • procedural	• problem-based • collaborative
What aspects are important to instructional design?	• provide feedback to reinforce learning • provide opportunities for practice and exchange	• present information with targeted efficiency in order to stimulate memory and the formation of structured knowledge	• provide learners with opportunities to investigate content in authentic settings
What teaching strategies facilitate learning?	• instructor-centered • learner/instructor interaction • information organization and repetition	• instructor-centered • strategic information presentation • targeted media use • cognitive load management • learner scaffolding	• learner-centered • authentic simulation • collaborative activity • hands-on practice • questioning techniques • critical inquiry

- Feedback should occur immediately after a learner responds.
- Students should be allowed to pace themselves or move through content at different rates.

Takeaway: The most applicable tenets of behaviorist instruction are (a) clearly communicating learning targets, (b) assessing learning and performance outcomes on the basis of these targets, (c) providing opportunities for participation and self-guided practice, (d) taking an organized approach to content communication, and (e) offering consistent, productive input that guides knowledge-building.

Cognitivist Instruction

For the cognitivist practitioner, educators are the conduit through which information is organized and presented. Individuals build knowledge structures at the pace that their cognitive processes allow, meaning that instructional content should flow in manageable chunks via different media to sustain attention, explained to learners in terms of their prior knowledge,[5] and structured to encourage the efficient transfer of information from working to long-term memory. Furthermore, learners benefit from developing metacognitive self-awareness of how they process and retrieve information.

Takeaway: Useful cognitivist instructional strategies include (a) capturing and maintaining learner attention, (b) connecting learning material to existing knowledge and needs, (c) separating content into units and modules, (d) pacing instruction to account for information-processing capacity, and (e) promoting metacognitive strategies.

Constructivist Instruction

For the constructivist practitioner, learning is contextual and social. The interactions that occur during instruction are guided by the interplay of participants and the beliefs and experiences they bring to the table—the "social-cultural environment" of learning.[6] Constructivist methods should align with learner outcomes, meaning that interactions are much less focused on the transmission and receipt of information than on the creation of an environment that is authentic and situated.[7] The constructivist educator should "provide the conditions that stimulate thinking" and participate in the learning experience alongside the student.[8] Instruction commonly involves creative and exploratory assignments,

reciprocal teaching, critical dialogue, and collaborative learning. Scaffolding provides learner support, which can gradually be removed as knowledge is gained.[9]

Takeaway: The most relevant tenets of constructivist instruction involve (a) creating authentic interactions in which learning is clearly situated within its real-world application, (b) providing opportunities for active and peer-based communication, (c) a less prominent and more supportive role for the instructor, and (d) fostering critical awareness of the social and cultural factors affecting learning.

DIRECT VS. DISCOVERY INSTRUCTION

Strategies from each school of thought can be broadly divided into *direct,* wherein the educator or instructional object is the central force guiding the learning environment, and *discovery,* wherein the environment of learning is actively shaped by participants (also referred to as *student-centered learning*). The underlying purpose of direct instructional techniques such as lecture, demonstration, and narrated screencast is to present information efficiently and systematically, whereas the underlying purpose of discovery techniques such as simulation and peer education is to invite learners to think for themselves.[10] In direct instruction the educator takes center stage, whereas in discovery instruction the educator acts as a guide or resource. Both approaches are integral to library education, where it is often critical to present material succinctly as well as provide opportunities for hands-on practice during the same learning interaction.

Characteristics of Direct Instruction

Most closely aligned with behaviorism and constructivism, direct instruction presents information in an organized yet ideally interactive method that helps the learner relate it to previous knowledge and perceive future applications. Direct instruction methods have also been referred to as *meaningful reception learning* and *expository teaching.*[11] Slavin lists a series of steps characteristic of direct instruction lessons that are applicable to both virtual and face-to-face contexts:[12]

1. *State learning objectives and orient students to the lesson:* Tell students what they will be learning and what performance will be expected of them.

2. *Review prerequisites:* Go over skills and concepts needed to understand the content.

3. *Present new material:* Give new information using examples and demonstrating concepts.

4. *Conduct learning probes:* Pose questions to assess learner understanding.

5. *Provide independent practice:* Give learners opportunities to practice content and skills.

6. *Assess performance or provide feedback:* Review independent practice and provide input.

7. *Provide distributed practice and review:* Illustrate future contexts for application and review objectives.

Direct instruction is well suited to demonstrations of functional, procedural, or factual knowledge (e.g., showing how something works, describing characteristics), and is highly useful when there is a need to present a great deal of content quickly and efficiently (sound familiar?)[13] The following examples from Reigeluth highlight everyday applications of the direct instructional format, which I have updated and supplemented with library-specific examples:[14]

Demonstration: Highlight the useful features of a website or database in a session or tutorial.

Discussion: Gather a panel of experts at a staff development event to discuss digitization and e-book readers.

Lecture: Discuss the information architecture of search engines versus licensed library resources.

Socratic method: Present a scripted series of questions to lead learners to a specific point.

Drill and practice: Demonstrate a series of search steps and ask learners to replicate them.

Tutorial (noninteractive): Develop a web video that demonstrates how to install and configure Zotero.

Guided discussion: Moderate a classroom discussion on bias and authority.

Podcast/vodcast: Translate a typical research session into a series of recorded episodes.

Pecha Kucha or Lightning Talks: Organize a series of rapid six-minute presentations on emerging technologies.

Direct instruction should not be misinterpreted as a necessarily passive experience. Rather, it should involve questioning techniques and challenging conversation to encourage critical thinking and assess student mastery. The "Who are we and what do we want?" exercise described in chapter 2 is an example of direct instruction in which learners are highly engaged and actively involved in metacognitive thinking. As the list suggests, the direct approach is also not necessarily limited to "traditional" presentation styles. Noninteractive podcasts, vodcasts, and videos all fall under the heading of direct instruction. The Pecha Kucha or Lightning Talk format, in which each presenter is limited to twenty slides or images for twenty seconds apiece, is another fast-paced and unconventional direct application that can feature several topics quickly and efficiently, particularly useful demoing emerging technologies.

To identify local technology "experts" and foster a community of learning at the UC Berkeley Library, colleagues and I organized an Emerging Technology Lightning Talks forum that allowed staff to showcase diverse technologies from professional development perspectives. After the forum, attendees rated which topics they were interested in learning more about, which helped us determine the technology training schedule the following semester. The forum was such a success that it has become a regular event to showcase local knowledge and generate participation in longer-format trainings. Audience feedback indicated direct instruction at its best; in the words of one attendee, "I really liked the short and sweet presentation format. Lots of information in easily comprehensible ways."

Characteristics of Discovery Learning

According to Schunk, instruction "becomes more meaningful when students explore their learning environments rather than listen passively to teachers," and it is this constructivist perspective that informs the discovery approach to learning.[15] Discovery learning, also referred to as *problem-based* or *inquiry-based* learning, takes place when students form knowledge by way of inquiry and direct experience.[16] Because "aha moments" naturally occur during the problem-solving process, discovery instruction often involves presenting learners with scenarios and questions and encouraging intuition and creativity. Discovery methods do not focus on right or wrong answers, but encourage deductive thinking and collaboration. Phillips and Soltis list core characteristics of this approach:[17]

- Students will be actively engaged with interesting and relevant problems.
- They will be able to discuss with each other and with the teacher.
- They will be active inquirers rather than passive.
- They will have adequate time to reflect.
- They will have opportunities to test or evaluate the knowledge that they have constructed.
- They will reflect seriously about the constructions produced by other students and by the teacher.

Discovery methods to some extent require participants to self-regulate, that is, to cultivate metacognitive awareness of their personal learning strategies, and lends itself to evaluation and critical assessment of instructional topics.[18] Reigeluth lists the following common discovery instruction methods, which I have revised and supplemented with library-specific examples:[19]

- *Interactive tutorial:* Present learner-defined navigational options in a screencast on information evaluation.
- *Open discussion:* Allow attendees to brainstorm their own agenda in a webinar.
- *Unconference/barcamp:* Organize a nonhierarchical forum or discussion on attendee-defined topics.
- *Seminar:* Invite learners to develop a portfolio around a specific problem over a semester.
- *Group project:* Invite groups in a podcasting workshop to produce and share a short piece in class.
- *Role play:* Ask staff in a public services training to act out a potential interaction.
- *Apprenticeship:* Mentor a new teaching librarian through direct instructional training.
- *Games:* Create an online jeopardy game with concepts in information fluency.
- *Case study:* Create a real-life example of an information-based challenge for learners to solve.

The object of discovery instruction is to help learners interact authentically with concepts and content in order to form an independent judgment on its application. Using discovery methods, a traditional lecture-based university course might be replaced by an online, project-based format in which students collaborate with peers at international institutions or build portfolios while interning with nonprofit or nongovernmental aid organizations. A librarian might "embed" in this experience and facilitate discovery by helping students set up search alerts and identify relevant Twitter and RSS feeds on topics of interest, or by shadowing classroom chats and discussion forums and suggesting interesting resources as a form of real-time research assistance. Similarly, in a staff training on a new website design or application interface, attendees could break up into groups tasked with becoming "expert" at the positives and negatives of a particular area of the site or tool, then designate a representative to critically share their discoveries.

INSTRUCTING FOR ENGAGEMENT

As we gain insight into the social and cultural forces that shape learning and incorporate technological advances into educational practice, the definition of instructional effectiveness is changing. Whereas the role of the instructor was once to dominate the classroom and communicate fixed content to a largely passive audience, there is now a growing emphasis on facilitating communities of learning and emphasizing the role of collaborative knowledge building and stimulating analog as well as digital conversations. Within this context it is tempting to view discovery learning as the superior method of instruction, but it is important to remember that there is nothing inherently wrong with direct instructional methods such as lecture, demonstration, and guided discussion, provided that they are participatory, active, and used in balance with discovery methods.

Think back to the discussion of the Learning Pyramid and engagement continuum in the last chapter. By overgeneralizing about how people learn, it wrongly dismisses many "nonactive," or direct, teaching methods that are essential to library instruction. According to learning theorist K. Patricia Cross, "Passive learning is an oxymoron; there is no such thing."[20] Your selection of direct or discovery strategies can be aided by considering what makes something *active* in a specific learning context, which begins with recognizing that activity means different things to different people. A postdoctoral chemistry fellow listening to a lecture by a Nobel Prize winner is likely to be highly engaged by this "passive" delivery method, whereas effective visual design on a slide-based presentation can draw a nonspecialist audience into a largely nonparticipatory forum, such as the direct instruction TED talks referenced in chapter 1. Active learning is about involving and supporting participants in a learning experience by stimulating them to think critically, participate in a dialogue, or share their knowledge with their peers, which can occur as readily in a guided demonstration as it can in an unconference. Engaged learning is active learning, no matter the delivery mechanism or level of direct peer-to-peer participation. The vital characteristic to maintain is authenticity, the clear context of real-world application that connects learning targets to practical needs. Whether you are in a face-to-face, online, or hybrid instructional role, your goal should be to blend direct and discovery methods into an engaging learning environment that allows learners to *experience* the "What's in it for me?" principle.

Conflating activity with participation can result in the adoption of games or activities created solely for their own sake, without a primary focus on how a specific group of learners might learn best. Paul Kirschner and colleagues challenge the notion that independent discovery learning is inherently effective, arguing instead that direct methods and scaffolding provide necessary learner support.[21] As I stated at the beginning of the chapter, effective instruction is incremental, organized, responsive, social, and engaging. Instructor guidance is also important, even in the most constructivist or learner-centered interaction. You can and should experiment with ways to involve learners more directly in instruction, such as incorporating response and quiz elements, facilitating discussion, allowing participants to suggest topics and agendas, or creating group learning activities. The best way engage participants is to use a contextually relevant instructional design, provide supportive guidance, encourage discussion or interaction, vary the instructional methods you use at intervals, and encourage critical and reflective thinking.

Discovery-based approaches can be easily incorporated into direct instruction lessons and vice versa in a way that facilitates both of these goals; a face-to-face class could be given an exploratory group assignment that allows them to experience discovery techniques within a primarily demonstration-oriented direct instruction lesson. Mixing direct and discovery techniques has the added effect of engaging different learning styles and better addressing the needs of all participants.

LEARNING FACTORS AND INSTRUCTIONAL METHODS

The core aspects of learning I outlined in the previous chapter—memory, motivation, environment, and prior knowledge—have distinct implications for instruction.

Memory

Memory is a factor of learning over which an instructor has a great deal of influence, because the pace and design of content and activities are guided heavily by your input. There are many strategies for maximizing transfer from short-term to long-term memory and designing activities that help learners gain realistic experience with instructional content to increase recall.

COGNITIVE LOAD MANAGEMENT

The principle of cognitive load management can help you streamline learning objects and create interactions that allow learners to identify salient details for themselves. Managing cognitive load is like pouring liquid into a funnel: information must be introduced gradually and with an eye to capacity, or you run the risk that a learner will not be able to incorporate it. To take this metaphor a few steps further, the thicker the liquid (the more complex the material), the slower you will want to pour, depending, of course, on the size of the funnel and the receptacle in question (the engagement, ability, and prior knowledge of the learner). Think back to the SUCCESs acronym in chapter 1: Simple, Unexpected, Concrete, Credible, Emotional, Story-based messages. Many elements of the SUCCESs approach are rooted in memory research, simplicity first and foremost. Information processing theory states that the human brain has a finite capacity to "handle" information, meaning that even the most complex subject should be explored in a manner that recognizes limitations.

Effective message design is crucial in managing cognitive load, because engagement and attention increase the likelihood that a learner will direct the necessary amount of cognitive capacity toward comprehension. Defining what you want your audience to understand helps you guide the presentation of materials and avoid overload. The common adage "Teach concepts, not tools" applies here; make sure learners gain practical, transferable insight and skills rather than, for example, exhaustive knowledge of searching protocol in only one resource. In practice, this might mean focusing less on the details of a database interface ("click here, then click here" . . . ad nauseam) than on broadening discussion to include what advantages an article database has in the first place, how learners might evaluate the items they find in whatever database they happen to use, and where they can go for additional help. Trust that if learners build a relevant authentic framework, they will discover the finer points for themselves when the need arises.

MENTAL MODELS

Gestalt theory stresses that "organized material improves memory because items are linked to each other systematically."[22] Presenting information in manageable, organized, and related pieces facilitates the construction of mental models (schemata), structures that associate new content with prior knowledge and values. When learners "makes sense" of something unfamiliar, they situate it within existing knowledge structures. The acronym exercise from the previous chapter provides an example. Most of us already have a personal context for JFK or FBI (e.g., Dallas, Marilyn Monroe, J. Edgar Hoover), which we use to manufacture imagery or cues to help us recall each acronym. The more contextual and relevant that the information is made, the better learners are able to fold it into existing schemata.

Mental models are applicable in learning situations that involve higher-order thinking, decision making, and problem solving.[23] Consider how presenting Twitter within a hierarchy or schema of user-generated content might help different groups of learners build mental models around information exchange in social media. A concept map portraying social media in political communication might be used to stimulate undergraduates to discuss how, in grassroots protest, Twitter's short, efficient, community-focused messages and topical threads can be used with relative anonymity via mobile devices (figure 5.1). In the context of staff training, a similar map could help participants understand Twitter as an instructor development tool that can be used to share content, glean strategies, and connect with potential collaborators somewhat more widely than Facebook, which tends to enable ongoing personal connections within more tightly defined professional groups.

CHUNKING AND AVOIDING THE CURSE

The Curse of Knowledge (also discussed in chapter 1) often tempts library educators to cram excessive detail into our brief learning interactions and objects. One of the more challenging aspects of effective instructional design is realizing that *less is more,* almost without exception. By focusing on minutiae or providing so much direct instruction that there is little time for

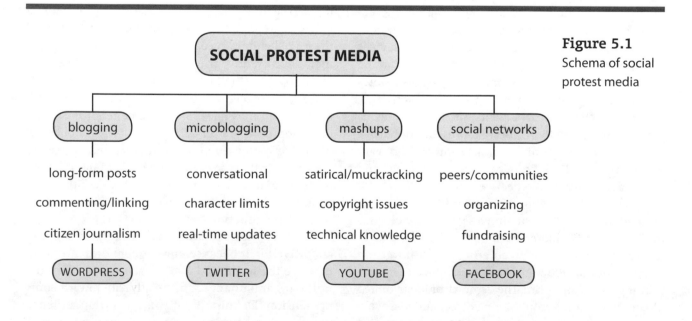

Figure 5.1
Schema of social protest media

discovery, we actively interfere with a learner's ability to construct meaningful skills and knowledge. Chunking, the breaking down of content into units, is a strategy that encourages effective information transfer.[24] In the acronym exercise, twenty random characters were chunked into six familiar abbreviations, which reduced the bits of information competing for the cognitive space required to travel from working to long-term memory. The idea is to organize content into manageable pieces, which helps regulate the structure of instruction and manage cognitive load. A chunk can be a lesson component, tutorial module, graphic section in a handout, and so forth (see chapters 10 and 11). One simple way to achieve this in more time-constrained situations is using the *rule of threes*—a relatively arbitrary but surprisingly effective strategy of setting a maximum of three objectives, three outcomes, three lessons, three units, three exercises, three examples, etc. in order to keep your planning and message in check. I find the that rule of threes forces me to remember that the streamlined ideas are the most memorable, while also imposing a go-to structure for breaking a tutorial or workshop into more concise components.

Prior Knowledge

In any learning scenario, the prior knowledge of your audience should be a key element of your planning. Teaching and training librarians often assume that our audiences understand our terminology and processes, overloading participants with too much content in hopes of covering as many bases as possible. It is much more effective to go lighter on content and heavier on context—to help learners see how the subject, technique, or resource fits into the knowledge structure they already have so that it becomes more meaningful.[25] It is crucial to reflect on what you assume your audience knows and does not know and find a productive and challenging balance between the two. This often involves using the familiar to introduce the unfamiliar, such as demonstrating research techniques to undergraduates by beginning on their turf with Google, then moving to Wikipedia, and then on to library-licensed content via proxy linking in Google Scholar or using the "find this in a library" link in Google Book Search to navigate to a local catalog.

A learner who has been personally frustrated with libraries or research in the context of their day-to-day experience might pay more attention to someone explaining how to prevent this type of frustration. On the flip side of this coin, prior experience or frustration with instructional content can also cause learners to dismiss the skill or resource in question as not worth the trouble, much like what I did at around the time I hit high school math. We have likely all had the experience of learning that a student in one of our sessions has taken the same class four times already; it is a relative certainty that this student will not pay rapt attention, even though the content I present may be totally different from that in the previous classes. I think of this as the "been there, done that" syndrome, which can crop up in any teaching situation. Whenever possible, library education should identify concrete and immediate instances of information need or frustration and help an audience perceive the personal, practical ability of the material being presented to prevent such frustration from occurring.

PREREQUISITES FOR LEARNING

A student cannot engage with instruction without at least cursory knowledge of its content, so it is particularly important to consider the prerequisites you require of participants in an instructional interaction.[26] At the outset of a teaching or learning design opportunity, ask two questions to determine what knowledge a learner should bring to the scenario: *What knowledge do I assume learners have? What knowledge do I require of learners in order for the material to be useful?* Miss the mark on either of these, and chances are that participants will notice. Prerequisites for learning allow you to avoid presenting content that is either too rudimentary or too advanced. By anticipating what an instructional situation requires to be comprehensible, you are better equipped to strike a balance between challenge and accessibility. Determining prerequisites for learning is informed by analyzing the needs and characteristics of your learners (chapter 9) and supports the process of defining goals, objectives, and outcomes (chapter 10). You can use a variety of assessment measures during and after instruction to judge whether your prerequisites for learning were accurate (chapter 12).

THE WIIFM PRINCIPLE

In libraries, instruction is typically intended to give foundational discovery, information technology, and critical thinking skills applicable in independent search or research situations. The concepts we teach should therefore connect directly to authentic information-needs and technology-use scenarios. Keep the WIIFM ("What's in it for me") principle in mind to give your audience specific insight into how, when, and why the information you present will be meaningful and useful to them.[27] If you are trying to hammer the idea of the permanence of information sharing on social networking sites to a group of younger learners, show how easy finding digital TMI (too much information: table dancing, keg stands, etc.) actually is by asking the group to dig up an image of themselves online they didn't know existed, or by displaying tame-ish examples to the group. To illustrate the risks of plagiarism, demonstrate the tools instructors use to root it out by tracking down content from free-term-paper sites such as www.cheathouse.com or scholarly papers using free plagiarism detectors such as those at www.plagiarismdetect.com, www.plagium.com, or www.copytracker.org.

EXPERIENCE

The experience level of your audience can help you consider the potential effectiveness of direct versus discovery learning on the objectives and needs of a given situation and determine how to strike a differentiated balance.[28] For example, when you are teaching subject-specific resources, graduate students are more likely to be engaged by a lecture or demonstration of the full range of available databases in a subject than undergraduates, who may be in the early stages of the research process and would benefit more from exploring one interdisciplinary database hands-on. Independent or collaborative immersion is often an effective instructional technique for learners with low prior experience, but in some technology-focused instances these attendees may have an actual or self-perceived barrier to understanding. In this dynamic that frequently arises in staff trainings and other scenarios that involve adult learners, it is important to make the subject accessible by introducing and demonstrating it thoroughly as well as by gauging prior experience. Consider methods for establishing prior knowledge in advance of a staff training on microblogging or other form of social media:

- Publicize the session as tailored to either novice or advanced users, depending on your target.
- Require registration and reply to RSVPs with a few pre-assessment questions or criteria for attendance.
- Send a survey to participants prior to leading the training.
- Informally poll attendees at the beginning of the session.

- Require participants to watch the Common Craft tutorial on Twitter (www.commoncraft .com/twitter) or other orientation module prior to attending to ensure that all share a level of understanding.

In this scenario, if your attendees have low prior knowledge, immediate immersion and hands-on practice may not be the best strategies to lead with. A demonstration of microblogging followed by a discussion of its potential applications in libraries (direct instruction) might be a more comfortable route than immediately jumping into the application (discovery instruction). Using guided demonstration as a scaffolding technique eases participants into independent practice and can build both confidence and interest. In this case, less experienced learners benefit from first encountering direct instruction that provides background and then engaging in the discovery strategies of creating accounts, following and messaging their classmates, and learning Tweet semantics.

Motivation

Among the many factors affecting motivation are individuals' goals for the learning interaction, their perceptions of its personal value, and expectations of their own performance. In chapter 4, I outlined two types of motivation—intrinsic (internal to the learner) and extrinsic (based on instructor-created incentives)—and noted that the nature of the content we tend to work with means our learners are less likely to be highly intrinsically motivated. The better that learners understand what a learning object or experience will do for them in terms of attaining goals or completing tasks, the more they will perceive its intrinsic value. This may have more to do with conditions internal to a learner than the instructor, but there are still strategies you can use to encourage it in a learning scenario:

Intrinsic Motivational Strategies

- Schedule the learning interaction to coincide with an immediate need.
- Consistently address audience self-interest using the WIIFM principle.
- Communicate using the language of participants. Don't distance yourself with library-speak.
- Make the practical, beneficial outcomes of instruction accessible/perceptible.
- Make a personal connection that helps audiences engage with you.

Timing is always an essential component of intrinsic motivation, and you should try to position instruction at the point closest to practical need. Schedule course-related instruction so that it coincides with an assignment; place digital learning objects prominently and widely on a website so that they are easy to access when a need arises. In asynchronous contexts such as screencast tutorials, web-based courses, or FAQ/help pages, placing learning objects as near potential sources of frustration as possible enables them to offer "just-in-time" help where intrinsic learner motivation is naturally high. For example, a series of online tutorials on search strategies could be clearly linked from the catalog's help or "no results found" pages. Martin Covington also recommends taking a transparent attitude toward "sharing with students the motivational rationale around which their course was created"—in other words, invoking the WIIFM principle from the instructor perspective.[29]

Library-related instruction does not necessarily inspire intrinsic motivation in all learners, meaning that library educators are regularly called to address extrinsic motivation through incentivization. Common extrinsic motivational strategies include requiring attendance for a course grade, developing an engaging or humorous delivery style to heighten personal investment in a workshop, speaking to the WIIFM principle, providing positive reinforcement for correct answers, using instructional games, or distributing prizes for participation.

Extrinsic Motivational Strategies, Face-to-Face

- Demonstrate interest in learner progress.
- Provide positive feedback and reinforcement.
- Offer incentives such as extra or service credit for attendance.
- Integrate learning games or opportunities for playful competition.
- Structure collaborative/paired work and reporting aloud into class activities.

In synchronous online and mobile learning situations like a live webinar, many of these strategies can be readily incorporated, whereas in asynchronous virtual instruction, the question of extrinsic motivation is more complex. Classroom strategies such as providing immediate rewards for participation may not work so easily in this context, but some can be successfully translated to the online environment (e.g., feedback elements or a graded quiz in an online tutorial). Depending on the character of the interaction, consider how you might work motivational incentives into a real-time or asynchronous learning object or interaction

Extrinsic Motivational Strategies, Virtual

- Provide proof of completion for credit at the end of an interaction.
- Add interactive elements such as polls and quizzes.
- Indicate learner progress (50 percent complete, etc.) throughout.
- Stimulate community-building and collaboration using social media.
- Use elements of good visual design to increase learner attention (see chapter 11).

Environment

Affective factors shape the environment of learning, and developing your ability to create a positive dynamic in all types of interactions is key. An instructor's role in shaping the learning environment is influenced by her or his personal relationship to teaching, expectations of student learning, and own motivation to create a positive learning experience. A confident and enthusiastic instructional persona increases learner engagement (see chapter 11).[30] Instructional tone is largely dependent on the intrinsic motivation of the facilitator, and those who are perceived as interested in the interaction are more effective at capturing and sustaining attention. In the brief interactions typical to library instruction, a personal tone can help you establish rapport with students more quickly. In classroom or synchronous online scenarios as well as asynchronous digital forums and social media interactions, it is also essential that students feel safe in expressing opinions and asking questions. *Humanism* is a constructivist approach that stresses the holistic support of students, that is, the emotional and mental as well as behavioral.[31] Schunk lists four guidelines that can assist you in fostering a humanist learning environment:[32]

- Show positive regard for students.
- Separate students from their actions.
- Encourage personal growth by providing students with choices and opportunities.
- Facilitate learning by providing resources and encouragement.

The use of neutral and inclusive language and balanced subjects in sample searches prevents you from alienating specific groups or appearing insensitive or biased. In participatory online learning situations or classroom discussions, you can establish ground rules that encourage respectful dialogue. It is also important to remember that teaching spaces have unique environmental characteristics. If you have several options for live instruction, you can develop a sense of which scenario or audience fits which type of space. Whenever possible in a face-to-face context, familiarize yourself with the room and its characteristics, from teaching technology to lighting to background noise, so that you are more comfortable and able to anticipate problems. Post the contact information of offices or individuals who can help you troubleshoot technical issues in the moment, and always consider ways you might salvage the situation should total meltdown occur.

SUMMARY

- Effective instruction tends to be **incremental**, **organized**, **responsive**, **social**, and **engaging**.
- **Behaviorist** instruction involves learning targets, assessment, learner participation, organized content communication, and consistent, productive reinforcement.
- **Cognitivist** instruction involves capturing learner attention, using advance organizers, separating content into units and modules, pacing instruction, and promoting metacognition.
- **Constructivist** instruction involves authentic interactions, learning situated within its real-world application, active and peer-based communication, a supportive role for the instructor, and critical awareness of the social and cultural factors affecting learning.
- In **direct instruction** the educator is responsible for guiding the learning interaction, whereas in **discovery** or **student-centered instruction** learning is shaped by participants.
- It is important to define **prerequisites for learning** at the outset of an interaction.
- Learners can be engaged via **intrinsic** and **extrinsic** motivational strategies.

REFLECTION POINTS

1. Imagine that you have been given the task of introducing a completely redesigned online catalog in an academic library to library staff, graduate students, faculty, and undergraduates, all of whom have different levels of experience with the old catalog and discovery interfaces in general. Will there also be differences in how you make a face-to-face session "active" for each of these four groups?

2. How might you be able to affect the intrinsic motivation of the different participant groups in the above reflection point?

NOTES

1. David Cook and Ryan Sittler (eds.), *Practical Pedagogy for Library Instructors: 17 Innovative Strategies to Improve Student Learning* (Chicago: Association of College and Research Libraries, 2008), 3.
2. Dale Schunk, *Learning Theories: An Educational Perspective* (Upper Saddle River, NJ: Pearson/Merrill/Prentice Hall, 2008), 22.
3. Peggy Ertmer and Timothy Newby, "Behaviorism, Cognitivism, Constructivism: Comparing Critical Features from an Instructional Design Perspective," *Performance Improvement Quarterly* 6, no. 4 (1993): 50–70.
4. Schunk, *Learning Theories*, 64.
5. David Ausubel, *The Psychology of Meaningful Verbal Learning* (New York: Grune and Stratton, 1963).
6. Dennis Phillips and Jonas Soltis, *Perspectives on Learning*, 4th ed. (New York: Teacher's College Press, 2004), 53.
7. Schunk, *Learning Theories*, 240.
8. John Dewey, *Democracy in Education* (New York, MacMillan, 1958), 168.
9. Roger Bruning, *Cognitive Psychology and Instruction* (Upper Saddle River, NJ: Pearson/Merrill/Prentice Hall, 2004). See also Sadhana Puntambekar and Roland Hubscher, "Tools for Scaffolding Students in a Complex Learning Environment: What Have We Gained and What Have We Missed?" *Educational Psychologist* 40 (2005): 1–12.
10. Cook and Sittler, *Practical Pedagogy*, 2008; Robert Slavin, *Educational Psychology: Theory and Practice*, 8th ed. (Boston: Pearson, 2006), 245–248.
11. David Ausubel, *Educational Psychology: A Cognitive View* (New York: Holt, Rinehart and Winston, 1968).
12. Slavin, *Educational Psychology*, 210.
13. Cook and Sittler, *Practical Pedagogy*, 7.
14. Charles Reigeluth, *Instructional-Design Theories and Models* (Hillsdale, NJ: Lawrence Erlbaum, 1983), 22.
15. Schunk, *Learning Theories*, 282.
16. Jerome Bruner, "The Act of Discovery," *Harvard Educational Review* 31 (1961): 21–32.
17. Phillips and Soltis, *Perspectives on Learning*, 52.
18. Slavin, *Educational Psychology*, 248.
19. Reigeluth, *Instructional-Design*, 22.
20. Patricia Cross, "Opening Windows on Learning," *League for Innovation in the Community College*, June 1998, 21.
21. Paul Kirschner, John Sweller, and Richard Clark, "Why Minimal Guidance during Instruction Does Not Work: An Analysis of the Failure of Constructivist, Discovery, Problem-Based, Experiential, and Inquiry-Based Teaching," *Educational Psychologist* 41 (2006): 75–86.
22. Schunk, *Learning Theories*, 155.

23. Ruth Clark and Chopeta Lyons, *Graphics for Learning: Proven Guidelines for Planning, Designing, and Evaluating Visuals in Training Materials* (San Francisco: Pfeiffer, 2004), 125.

24. Linda Lohr, *Creating Graphics for Learning and Performance* (Upper Saddle River, NJ: Pearson, 2008), 51. See also Clark and Lyons, *Graphics*, 118.

25. David Ausubel, "The Facilitation of Meaningful Verbal Learning in the Classroom," *Educational Psychologist* 12 (1977): 162–178.

26. Benjamin Bloom, *Human Characteristics in School Learning* (New York: McGraw-Hill, 1976).

27. Carl Rogers and H. Jerome Freiberg, *Freedom to Learn* (New York: Merrill, 1994); Steven Bell and John Shank, *Academic Librarianship by Design: A Blended Librarian's Guide to the Tools and Techniques* (Chicago: American Library Association, 2007).

28. Schunk, *Learning Theories*, 207.

29. Martin Covington, "Self-Worth Theory Goes to College: Do Our Motivation Theories Motivate?" in D. M. McInerney and S. Van Etten, *Big Theories Revisited*, Research on Sociocultural Influences on Motivation and Learning 4 (Greenwich, CT: Information Age, 2004), 93.

30. James Stronge, *Qualities of Effective Teachers*, 2nd ed. (Alexandria, VA: Association for Supervision and Curriculum Development, 2007), 28–29.

31. Bernard Weiner, *Human Motivation: Metaphors, Theories, and Research* (Newbury Park, CA: SAGE, 1992).

32. Schunk, *Learning Theories*, 465.

6

Teaching Technologies

GOALS

- Discuss instructional technology literacy in terms of **experience, evaluation**, and **customization**.
- Outline the **toolkit** approach to evaluating the practical **affordances** of teaching technology.
- Investigate **connectivist learning theory**.
- Describe strategies for supporting and guiding the **learner PLE**.

In earlier chapters I explored the first two components of instructional literacy: *reflective* practice and *educational theory*. The third component, *teaching technologies*, may present the most daunting pedagogical challenge for many readers. According to David Jonassen and colleagues, instructional technology can be used as a tool to support the construction of knowledge, an information vehicle to encourage exploration, a method of providing context to help students learn in action, a medium to facilitate communication, or an intellectual partner to promote reflection.[1] My goal in this chapter is to outline strategies for understanding and applying a diverse range of technologies as a practical, outcomes-focused component of your instructor development.

SMOKE AND MIRRORS

I have to admit that I dreaded writing this chapter. It's not hard to understand why: When you discuss teaching, learning, and technology, there is a vast expanse of (constantly shifting) ground to cover. Much of the material on technology in teaching waxes rhapsodic about the potential of emerging applications, then stops short at explaining how to put them to work. The same issue is reflected in technology competencies in library education. Standard 6.7 of the ACRL Proficiencies for Instruction Librarians and Coordinators states that a skilled library instructor "integrates appropriate technology into instruction to support experiential and collaborative learning as well as to improve student receptiveness, comprehension, and retention of information," which leaves working instructors to wonder how they can determine what tools are "appropriate," and when best to apply them.[2]

This is what I think of as the "smoke and mirrors" effect: the promise of teaching technologies can be clear as day, but understanding how to use them effectively remains murky. The technology insight educators want is highly practical: reliable learning activities, delivery strategies, and assessment measures to gauge our impact. However, context specificity makes my job in this chapter (defining best practices in these areas) difficult.

A serendipitous e-mail from my father helped me wrap my mind around this challenge. A political science professor in Texas, he is what you might call an "old school" lecturer. For years, I have listened to him dismiss students who asked him to create PowerPoint slides to accompany his talks. "The day I use Power-Point is the day I retire" were his exact words, I believe. Solemn vow notwithstanding, he recently snuck this into one of his messages: "The semester is off to a decent start so far. I am converting to power points for my lecture outlines, against my longstanding preference, and finding that I actually like it . . . much to my surprise. Oh well, out of the stone age." This grudgingly positive comment highlights a simple fact about instructional technology: When you overcome hurdles or prejudices and interact hands-on with a particular device or platform, you often uncover its unexpected potential to help you respond to learners, address problems, and diversify your practice.

AWARENESS AND CHANGE

As I see it, the two biggest challenges in instructional technology are maintaining current awareness and adapting to constant change. Both have very real implications for on-the-ground library educators trying to integrate emerging *social*, *information*, and *communication technologies* (SICTs) into teaching and public services. Maybe you and your colleagues spent countless hours building MySpace pages and colonizing a Second Life island only to realize at roll-out time

that your users had moved on to greener Facebook pastures. Or, you might recently have discovered that the locked-down classroom computer needs a software update at about the same time you tried to play a streaming video in class, or that your painstakingly created local course guide software doesn't appear to play very nice with the newest version of Internet Explorer.

Teaching with technology means that you are to some degree always on the edge of the unknown. The key to managing this fraught reality is by focusing on the following instructional literacy strategies as you work with SICTs:

1) *Experience:* Gain hands-on, authentic insight into emerging social, information, and communication tools.
2) *Evaluate:* Critically evaluate their potential to achieve specific learning outcomes.
3) *Customize:* Integrate tools into instruction based on the needs and objectives of a learning scenario.

This three-tiered approach helps you first demystify an emerging platform like cloud computing (e.g., remotely accessible web-based information storage through services like DropBox and Google Docs), then discern the practical value of its learning applications (e.g., remote collaboration and distance access), and finally assess if these can respond to concrete instructional needs (e.g., storing backup copies of instructional materials or co-authoring content). Investigating the technology landscape in this manner allows you to use existing SICTs while staying attuned to future developments. As you build the teaching technology aspect of your instructional literacy, it is important to be persistent, adaptable, and (particularly for the early adopters) conscious of maintaining reasonable expectations. Whether you are technophilic (like myself) or technophobic (like my father), this practical approach may help you find that integrating technology into instruction is less painful than you imagined.

EVALUATING AFFORDANCES

When I refer to "instructional technology," "SICTs," "teaching tools," I am describing a constantly expanding array of dynamic products and applications. I am also describing the crusty old projector in your computer classroom. I have observed that educators often tend to think about technology tools in stark categories of familiar (things we have used successfully) and unfamiliar (things we are afraid to try). Familiar technologies are the decidedly unmysterious workhorses we use constantly, such as course management systems, word processing and presentation software, and even e-mail. We develop close relationships with these tools and come to understand their quirks, and it is usually easy to perceive if we need to sharpen our skills or advocate for a better setup where they are concerned. Unfamiliar technologies, on the other hand, are the black box side of the equation. These are the SICTs we might have heard about but haven't yet put to use in an instructional setting, or the bleeding-edge trends we barely understand. Either way, the unfamiliar tools can create the sensation of needing to "catch up," or simply lead to overt mystification.

Every SICT in existence is unfamiliar to everyone at one time in its life cycle, so ongoing familiarization should be an expected part of teaching with technology, rather than a source of trepidation. Transforming confusing or unknown applications into tools that achieve practical ends begins by building the three-stage experiential instructional technology literacy process I outlined above into your professional practice. I am the first to admit that this can be time consuming, but, similar to educational theory, it is not necessary to become expert with every gadget under the sun. Rather, establishing the practical *affordances* of SICTs is a far more reasonable strategy. In web and application design, affordances are those qualities of an object that lend themselves to being used.[3] In education, affordances become the teachable properties of specific technologies, eminently useful as you plan outcomes, design learning activities and objects, and deliver instructional messages. I identify ten instructional affordances of social, information, and communication technologies:

assessment: template/customizable evaluation and analysis

collaboration: shared effort, cooperation, and/or crowdsourcing

communication: contact and exchange among participants

customization: personalizable features or appearance

documentation: information recording for future access and use

play: diversion and/or creative expression

portability: mobile communication, creation, and access

productivity: task-oriented learning and time management

sharing: dissemination of ideas or information for public consumption

visualization: graphical information display

Examining these affordances requires integrating current and emerging SICT-focused resources into your personal learning environment, and a willingness to experiment with the devices and approaches you encounter. To assist you in discovering reliable outlets for building current technology awareness, I list essential information and instructional technology blogs, sites, and organizations in the recommended readings at the end of the text.

EXPLORING OPTIONS

There are innumerable hosted, freeware, and open source SICTs that provide creative opportunities to break out of the one-shot paradigm to extend a learning interaction, and just as many that can make the environment in a one-shot session more dynamic. In *Information Literacy Meets Library 2.0,* a chapter contributed by Brian Kelly describes the now-familiar first wave of 2.0 technologies (e.g., blogs, wikis, and virtual worlds) that started to emerge in the mid-2000s.[4] In table 6.1, I supplement Kelly's descriptions with each item's pedagogical affordances and specific product examples. In table 6.2, I expand his original list with additional emerging technology options of potential instructional value to library educators.

REMEMBER TO FLOSS

In "Free: Why $0.00 Is the Future of Business," Chris Anderson explores the pervasive cultural expectation for no-cost communication and productivity tools.[5] There are plenty of costs associated with developing and customizing emerging technologies in an organizational or educational setting, and Free (Libre) Open Source Software (FLOSS) alternatives to fee-based services regularly present themselves as useful alternatives. For many hosted or fee-based applications a free option is likely already to exist or be in development; many of the tools in tables 6.1 and 6.2 are FLOSS examples. Additionally, countless social, mobile, and

Table 6.1 "Web 2.0" Technologies and Applications

TECHNOLOGY	DESCRIPTION	PROPERTIES	TOOLS
Blogs	applications that are commonly used to provide diaries, with entries provided in chronological order	• assessment • communication • documentation • sharing	• WordPress • Blogger
Wikis	collaborative web-based authoring tools	• collaboration • documentation • productivity • sharing	• Wikipedia • LISwiki
Syndicated Content (RSS)	technologies that allow content to be automatically embedded elsewhere	• communication • customization • portability	• blog and news feeds • Twitter
Podcasts & Videocasts	syndicated audio and video content, which is often transferred automatically to portable MP3 players such as iPods	• communication • play • portability	• iTunes • Audacity
Mashups	services that contain data and services from multiple sources	• customization • play • visualization	• WikiScanner • VisualTwitter
Social Sharing Services	applications that provide sharing of various types of resources such as bookmarks, photographs, etc.	• collaboration • customization • sharing	• SlideShare • Flickr
Communication Tools	various tools including chat applications and Internet telephony tools that can provide various forms of communication ranging from simple text messaging systems to audio and video communications	• collaboration • communication • documentation • productivity • portability	• Skype • Google Voice
Social Networks	communal spaces that can be used for group discussions and sharing of resources	• communication • customization • play • sharing	• Facebook • LinkedIn
Folksonomies & Tagging	a bottom-up approach to providing descriptive labels for resources, to allow them to be retrieved	• collaboration • customization • sharing	• Delicious • Technorati
Virtual Worlds	3D simulations in which an avatar (which represents the user) can interact with other avatars	• collaboration • communication • play • visualization	• Second Life

Table 6.2 Emerging Technologies

TECHNOLOGY	DESCRIPTION	PROPERTIES	TOOLS
Augmented Reality	interactive visual search and recognition tools that interpret environmental factors and translate them into information	• communication • play • sharing • visualization	• Layar • Wikitude
Classroom Response Systems	handheld in-class devices that allow students to indicate answers in real time and visualize response data	• assessment • communication • play • visualization	• iClicker
Cloud Computing	virtual, web-based data storage and access	• collaboration • portability • productivity	• DropBox • Google Docs
Content Management Systems	programs that enable dynamic and usable web editing, authoring, and management	• communication • collaboration • customization • documentation	• WordPress • Drupal
Course Management Systems	integrated file sharing and communication platforms for use in educational settings	• assessment • collaboration • communication • customization • productivity	• Moodle • Sakai • Blackboard
Geotagging/ Geolocation	applications that assign location-based information to images and other information formats	• communication • portability • visualization	• Flickr • Google Earth
Gesture-Based Computing	devices and interfaces that perceive and respond to independent user motion	• communication • play • productivity • sharing • visualization	• Natal • Wii
Location-Based Services	mobile applications that customize information and experience based on geographic location and proximity	• communication • play • portability • sharing • visualization	• GoWalla • FourSquare
Microblogging	short-form blogging sites limited to a certain number of characters	• sharing • collaboration • communication	• Twitter • FriendFeed
Mobile Devices/ Apps	devices and applications that enable mobile connectivity and portability in addition to other functionality	• communication • play • portability • productivity	• Twitter • Facebook • Google Apps

(cont.)

Table 6.2 cont.

TECHNOLOGY	DESCRIPTION	PROPERTIES	TOOLS
Personalized Interfaces	customizable individual interfaces, typically web-based, in which content and communication streams are combined and aggregated	• communication • customization • portability • productivity	• iGoogle • NetVibes
Semantic Applications	web applications that share and translate metadata with other applications	• communication • collaboration • portability • sharing	• Freebase • FOAF (Friend of a Friend)
Tangible User Interfaces	touchscreen computing devices that allow users to input commands and manipulate information by touch	• documentation • play • visualization	• Microsoft Surface • iPad • SmartBoard
Universal Communicators	mobile and fixed applications that consolidate and interoperate with multiple communication streams	• communication • collaboration • productivity • sharing	• VoxOx
Visualization Tools	web and computer applications that translate display information into visuals, images, and graphics	• assessment • communication • play • visualization	• Wordle • Twittervision • Mindomo
Widgets/ Add-ons/ Extensions	functional mini-applications used on a computer desktop, dashboard, mobile device, or web browser that enhance its core functionality	• assessment • collaboration • customization • productivity • sharing	• Zotero • Delicious

collaboration platforms exist exclusively in cost-free form, and flexible open application programming interfaces (APIs) from Twitter, Google Code (www.code.google.com) and other sources can be remixed for free locally to create instructional mashups. Table 6.3 is a (by no means comprehensive) conversion chart that illustrates FLOSS counterparts to common proprietary teaching technologies.

Finding FLOSS products is usually as straightforward as searching "open source captivate" or "free alternative photoshop." They are now so pervasive that it takes only a try or two to stumble on something economically scalable (see figure 6.1). An extensive Wikipedia entry provides a breakdown of free and open source products from the sciences to assistive technology to education. You can also consult the Wikipedia FLOSS Project Directories list, which points to online communities like www.SourceForge.net that catalogue available options.[6]

UNDERSTANDING TECHNOLOGY AND LEARNING

Teaching technology literacy involves more than evaluating affordances; it also means understanding how SICTs are changing the way people learn, use libraries, and interact with information. Most of us perceive that changes are occurring, but are hard-pressed to find reliable data that can be translated into instructional strategies or tailored to our own users. It helps to maintain a local perspective as you learn about overarching SICT use and consumption trends, because your own learner community will

Table 6.3 FLOSS Conversion Chart

TECHNOLOGY TYPE	PROPRIETARY	FLOSS
Audio Capture/Editing	• GarageBand • Soundbooth	• Audacity, audacity.org • Ardour, ardour.org
Citation Management	• EndNote • Refworks	• Zotero, zotero.org
Classroom Control Systems	• NetControl2	• iTALC, italc.sourceforge.net
Concept Mapping	• Inspiration	• MyMind, sebastian-krauss.de/software • Mindomo, mindomo.com
Course Management Systems	• Blackboard	• Moodle, moodle.org • Sakai, sakaiproject.org
Digital Archives	• Dspace	• Omeka, omeka.org
Font Downloads	• myfonts.com	• FontStruct, fontstruct.com
Screen/Video Capturing	• Snagit	• Jing, jingproject.com
Image Editing	• Photoshop	• GIMP, gimp.org • Picasa, picasa.google.com
Knowledgebase	• Interspire	• KBPublisher 2.0, sourceforge.net/projects/kbpublisher
PDF Viewing/ Annotating	• Acrobat Pro	• Skim, skim-app.sourceforge.net • Adobe Reader, get.adobe.com/reader • Blio, blio.com
Presentations	• PowerPoint	• Google Docs, docs.google.com • Prezi, prezi.com
Productivity	• Office	• Open Office, openoffice.org • Google Docs, docs.google.com
Project Management	• Microsoft Project	• OpenProj, openproj.org
Screencasting	• Captivate • Camtasia	• CamStudio, camstudio.org • Jing, techsmith.com/jing/
Subject/Course Guides	• LibGuides	• Library a la Carte, http://alacarte.library.oregonstate.edu • Drupal, drupal.org
Surveys/ Assessments	• SurveyMonkey • Zoomerang	• freeonlinesurveys, freeonlinesurveys.com • Google Forms, docs.google.com
Video Production	• FinalCut Pro • iMovie	• Avidemux, http://fixounet.free.fr/avidemux • Kino, kinodv.org • Cinelerra, cinelerra.org
Web Calling	• AT&T • Vonage	• Google Voice, google.com/voice • Skype, skype.com
Web Editing/ Authoring	• Dreamweaver	• Aptana, aptana.com • KompoZer, kompozer.net
Webcasting/ Screensharing	• Connect • WebEx	• DimDim, dimdim.com • Ustream, ustream.tv

invariably differ in substantive ways from national or international data. When you recognize how your users' communication, learning, play, and search habits are changing, you can more realistically evaluate the best methods to support them. In this section, I scan current research on generational technology trends, learning theories, and educational movements affecting teaching and learning practice in libraries.

Closing the "Future" Gap

Cyberpunk author William Gibson famously said, "The future is already here. It's just not very evenly distributed."[7] This is definitely the case with tech adoption, where use and expertise differ based on access, privilege, and preference. In virtual and mobile instruction, technological access barriers are real impediments to learning—there are many communication media that require high-speed connectivity, still rare in many rural and lower-income urban regions. On the other hand, while the 2009 *ECAR Study of Undergraduate Students and Information Technology* shows that age-based gaps in SICT use are still apparent, these appear to be narrowing as time wears on. For example, texting and social networking services are most heavily used by 18–24-year-olds, but older populations consistently adopt the same systems at slower rates.

In any generation or population you will find a scale of technology access and awareness, and it is important to think critically about your use of instructional technologies in order to hit a common denominator. This is where prior for learning, discussed in chapter 5, become immediately useful. If you use a specific application in a learning interaction or object, first consider prior knowledge or access rather than assuming either exists. You can also employ questioning techniques in an in-progress scenario to gauge how much scaffolding is necessary. Simply asking learners about their familiarity with a tool or concept and prompting them for specific use examples provides insight into how deeply you may need to explore features and functionality. In addition to adjusting your expectations of student understanding, hearing the experiences of their co-learners allows participants to contextualize the SICT in question.

Learning Theory 2.0: Connectivism

Despite their pre-Internet origins, principles from behaviorism, cognitivism, and constructivism adapt well to technology-supported instruction. For example, cognitive load management is instrumental in arranging the components of digital learning objects. Constructivism values participatory learning, the foundation of user-generated content. The behaviorist

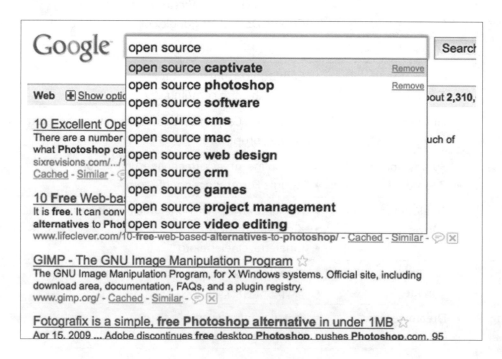

Figure 6.1
Finding FLOSS options

strategy of offering constructive feedback is essential in facilitating successful online interactions. Revisionist perspectives on technology and learning have also emerged, notably George Siemens's connectivist theory, which posits that pervasive networking and mobility has fundamentally changed how people interact with information, and, by extension, their learning processes. Connectivism is compared to constructivism for its focus on participation and nonlinear exploration rather than on learning as a cumulative endpoint, but its major departure is an emphasis on the effects of information architecture on learning itself. Siemens identifies several trends to justify this new approach to educational theory:[8]

- Many learners will move into a variety of different, possibly unrelated fields over the course of their lifetime.
- Informal learning is a significant aspect of our learning experience. Formal education no longer comprises the majority of our learning. Learning now occurs in a variety of ways—through communities of practice, personal networks, and through completion of work-related tasks.
- Learning is a continual process, lasting for a lifetime. Learning and work-related activities are no longer separate. In many situations, they are the same.
- Technology is altering (rewiring) our brains. The tools we use define and shape our thinking.
- The organization and the individual are both learning organisms. Increased attention to knowledge management highlights the need for a theory that attempts to explain the link between individual and organizational learning.
- Many of the processes previously handled by learning theories (especially in cognitive information processing) can now be off-loaded to, or supported by, technology.
- Know-how and know-what is being supplemented with know-where (the understanding of where to find knowledge needed).

Explicit in connectivism is the need to facilitate insight into information organization, which enables clearer understanding of the resources available within a local context. This suggests a powerful role for library educators and clear alignment with information literacy theory, which "enables learners to . . . assume greater control over their own learning" by developing familiarity with the cycle of information production

and use;[9] both approaches emphasize moving between media and method depending on context.[10] Library educators are uniquely positioned to connect disparate information communities; the notion of librarians as "disciplinary discourse mediators" reflects a connectivist orientation toward scholarly communication.[11] With generalist insight into information resources and the discourse of disciplines and communities, teaching librarians can foster connections within an increasingly complex world.

Shifting Literacies: Media, Information, and Technology

In recent years theorists have explored the influence of emerging technologies, social media, and gaming on literacy, proposing that new SICTs are radically transforming core elements of how people create and communicate.[12] In an influential white paper on "participatory culture," Henry Jenkins and colleagues outlined essential skills for working and learning in the twenty-first century, including play, performance, simulation, appropriation, multitasking, distributed cognition, collective intelligence, judgment, transmedia navigation, networking, and negotiation.[13] The 2009 MacArthur Foundation *Living and Learning with New Media* report charted youth technology interaction as moving fluidly from "hanging out" (social engagement) to "messing around" (light information engagement) to "geeking out" (intense subject-matter engagement), and that significant knowledge-building occurred at all levels without participants necessarily thinking of the process as learning.[14] The influence of this shift in libraries is felt from public services to collection development, while emerging literacies increasingly intersect with the instructional purview of library educators.[15] Social and mobile technologies are an implicit part of this process, as interpersonal, professional, and academic communication increasingly occurs in nontraditional realms far more "open" than print-based media or closed person-to-person exchanges.

Creating Openness

David Wiley states that "the challenge is not to bring technology into the classroom. . . . The challenge is to capture the potential of technology to lower costs and improve learning for all."[16] As libraries struggle with budget deficits and shrinking staff, open educational resources can broaden instructional development and create fertile ground for new ideas in online learning and distance instruction. By providing more people with more opportunities to learn in more ways, SICTs are creating a vastly more accessible learning experience than has traditionally been available. Curtis Bonk, author of *The World Is Open*, identifies ten transformational trends in educational technology:[17]

1. Web searching in the world of e-books

2. E-learning and blended learning

3. Availability of open-source and free software

4. Leveraged resources and open courseware

5. Learning object repositories and portals

6. Learner participation in open information communities

7. Electronic collaboration

8. Alternate-reality learning

9. Real-time mobility and portability

10. Networks of personalized learning

In addition to the instructional materials repositories and participatory learning communities described in chapter 3, the open education and "edupunk" movements illustrate Bonk's trends through initiatives like Howard Rheingold's Drupal-based downloadable Social Media Classroom (www.socialmediaclassroom .com) and institutions such as MIT Open CourseWare (www.ocw.mit.edu), the Open University (www.open .ac.uk), and Peer2Peer University (www.p2pu.org).

TEACHING WITH/ABOUT/ AROUND TECHNOLOGY

Thus far I have outlined a strategy for identifying technology affordances, profiled specific tools, and surveyed emerging ideas in tech-assisted pedagogy. In the remainder of this chapter, I confront any smoke and mirrors I may have inadvertently created with an in-depth examination of on-the-ground technology implementation in library education. In the day-to-day, instructional technology in libraries usually functions as one (or more) of the following: a pedagogical tool, an instructional topic, or a source of frustration. I therefore examine our collective practical reality from three angles: 1) teaching/learning *with* technology during instruction, 2) teaching/learning *about*

technology as an aspect of curriculum, and 3) teaching/learning *around* technological challenges that arise.

Teaching *with* Technology

Teaching *with* technology is about seeing SICTs as means to ends, insight that is most effectively built on personal and experiential knowledge and best translated into thoughtful targets during instructional design. Understanding the competencies of your audience, the resources available in your environment, and your own comfort zone as an instructor allows you to more seamlessly integrate pedagogy and technology. Developing actionable knowledge of instructional affordances enables you to recognize the potential of a specific tool or approach to "fit" a teaching moment.

THE TOOLKIT APPROACH

Every social, information, and communication technology has pedagogical potential. Using experiential evaluation and PLE-supported investigation, you can build a personal technology "toolkit" that connects specific SICTs to instructional and learning outcomes. The *experience*, *evaluation*, and *customization* strategy outlined in the beginning of the chapter encourages you to examine concrete affordances (assessment, collaboration, communication, customization, documentation, play, portability, productivity, sharing, and visualization) and provide yourself with authentic insight into the platforms listed in tables 6.1–6.3. The toolkit approach follows the principle of situated learning: relying on secondary sources is always helpful, but getting a feel for a tool (when it is possible) provides a clearer indication of how you can use it in your own context.

When you encounter a new (or even familiar) application or piece of equipment in your personal learning or teaching environment, you can systematically reflect on its characteristics, outcomes, potential caveats, and instructional affordances. Table 6.4 provides a sample evaluation of an interactive touch-screen whiteboard, a relatively common (and often underutilized) on-site library instructional technology tool. By compiling this list, you consider the active, creative, and practical uses to which the whiteboard could be put, a reflective process that can lead to more confident applications of the tool in class. This is a thought and action exercise, one in which you should schedule time to interact with the board hands-on.

The toolkit evaluation works equally well with web-based and mobile SICTs, and experiential familiarity is always the core objective. Hands-on experience may not be possible, however, with expensive programs or hardware such as e-readers and gaming consoles. That said, you can seek input from colleagues or other information sources, set up application trials, inquire whether commercial services provide on-site demonstrations or loaners, investigate if another part of your institution owns the equipment, or take test/play field trips to retailers—all workaround strategies for demystifying devices. The toolkit evaluation can easily be a mental exercise, but you can also use the template grid in appendix A and at this book's web-extra site (www.alaeditions.org/webextras/).

TOOLKIT CASE STUDY: GOOGLE WAVE

The toolkit approach is an excellent way to confront unfamiliar technologies. An emerging tool worthy of affordance evaluation at the time I was writing this book was Google Wave, a real-time collaboration environment that merged the functionality of Google Docs, Talk, and other applications. Perceiving it as a promising platform for teaching and learning, early in its beta cycle many librarians (myself included) explored Wave's pedagogical implications. Ironically, shortly after I submitted my completed manuscript in the summer of 2010 using Wave as a toolkit evaluation example, Google made the unexpected announcement that they would discontinue it due to lackluster interest and ongoing development of more popular products with similar functionality. This news left

me (and likely many other authors) with an interesting dilemma—*should I write Wave out of the text in favor of another tool, or use it as an opportunity to address an important lesson about the transitory nature of instructional technology?* I chose the latter option, and retain the original case study with a few modifications to reinforce a basic message of technological impermanence. Because little in the live or virtual classroom can be relied upon as absolutely certain, as you develop the ability to evaluate products on the fly you should also cultivate adaptability and avoid putting all of your faith into a single approach.

The following series of steps describes the experiential evaluation process I undertook to familiarize myself with Wave, which can roughly translate to any emerging tool:

1. I first heard about Wave from gadget blogs I regularly monitor.

2. After noticing it for a few weeks in the social media buzz, I checked with EDUCAUSE and other educational technology sites to see if they had produced Wave profiles or feature reviews.

3. Next, I wrangled myself a tester invitation from a friend who tweeted that she had a few left.

4. I then set up my Wave account, logged in, and started poking around.

Table 6.4 Sample Interactive Whiteboard Toolkit Evaluation

CHARACTERISTICS	OUTCOMES	CAVEATS	Instructional Affordances	Customization	Communication	Collaboration	Visualization	Sharing	Productivity	Portability	Documentation	Assessment	Play
• touchscreen display • screen recording/ capture • interactive markers/keyboard	• multimodal stimulation • engagement/ participation	• smaller screen may make text invisible	Learner		√	√	√						√
	• capture/share notes • highlight features visually	• could be difficult to switch settings quickly • expensive	Instructor					√	√		√		√

5. After exploring the interface for a bit, I watched the built-in tutorials created by the Google development team, which provided insight into the tool's intended purpose.

6. After getting an initial feel for the application, I scanned a few more blog reviews and watched several YouTube how-to videos.

7. Finally, I experimented in more depth by configuring options and systematically trying Wave apps, using Help when necessary.

After about an hour of what might accurately be described as "purposeful playing," I completed a toolkit evaluation to reflect more concretely on the applications, affordances, and caveats I noticed (table 6.5). What initially struck me as valuable about Wave was its real-time visual collaboration potential, an interesting way to facilitate backchannel commentary in face to face or online instruction. I perceived that its threaded, multimodal conversations could create a viable environment for rich online consultations with students engaged in long-term research, thanks to its ability to embed different types of learning objects and overlap with other Google products. At the time

I encountered the application it didn't provide the depth of cross-functionality with Docs and other Google tools that I wanted, so I did not venture far into using it as an instructional tool. That said, performing the evaluation made me familiar enough with Wave to be able to cogently describe it to colleagues and students, keep an ear open for enhancements that interested me, and use it in informal collaboration. Upon hearing of its imminent disappearance, I proceeded to move several ongoing Wave collaborations to Docs, and directed my focus toward Twitter and other microblogging apps for facilitating backchannel discussion.

USING TECHNOLOGY TO MEET CHALLENGES

Another way to approach teaching with technology is on problem-solving terms; the toolkit mindset involves imagining technological solutions to instructional challenges. An example: With online access and enrollment on the rise, one mounting concern among teaching librarians is reaching distance learners and patrons. In this case, instructional technology offers many solutions. Webcasting and live streaming are increasingly desirable e- and m-learning approaches that have recently seen tremendous strides in affordability and quality; what once required thousands of dollars in equipment and fees now takes a computer,

Table 6.5 Sample Google Wave Toolkit Evaluation

CHARACTERISTICS	OUTCOMES	CAVEATS	Instructional Affordances	Customization	Communication	Collaboration	Visualization	Sharing	Productivity	Portability	Documentation	Assessment	Play
• live collaboration • multimedia • mashups increase functionality	• collaborative effort • PLE tool acquisition	• presents steep learning curve • not a lot of functionality	Learner		√	√	√				√		√
	• learner engagement • distance interaction	• still buggy • options already available in other platforms	Instructor		√	√	√	√			√		√

a webcam, and a compatible web service such as DimDim or WebEx. Ustream is another of many free services that allow you to broadcast live streaming video, offering additional features such as an iPhone viewing application and live audience polling. Web communication startups usually provide user-friendly instructions that cut the learning curve down to as few steps as possible, as in figure 6.2. Designing learning materials for the online environment presents plenty of challenges, and Susan Sharpless Smith's *Web-Based Instruction in Libraries,* now in its third edition, provides a wealth of information on formats, approaches, and strategies.[18]

Teaching *about* Technology

In addition to using technology in pedagogical capacities, librarians constantly cover SICTs as the focus of their instructional content. Teaching *about* technology involves creating learning experiences that effectively address the "What's in it for me?" potential of search, communication, and academic productivity tools. Jeremy Boggs lists three technological "roles" for educators: role model, tech support, and cheerleader.[19] I suggest a fourth that reflects librarians' dedication to informed inquiry: *critic*. Library educators can leverage each of these roles in order to become, in effect, application technology and end-user productivity

experts in our learning communities. By integrating "digital wisdom" into the information fluency curriculum and modeling knowledgeable and creative technology use, we can help our constituents and colleagues shape stronger personalized environments for working, leisure, and learning.[20]

GUIDING THE LEARNER PLE

Learning is becoming far more customizable; whereas the instructional environment was once rigidly structured, connected individuals are now more able than ever to use social and collaborative media to pick and choose the services they use to stay informed (or procrastinate by staring at lolcats). This shifting learning paradigm provides teaching librarians the opportunity to use our generalist knowledge to impart strategic knowledge about productivity and research skills that can be integrated into participant personal learning environments. I have thus far described the PLE as a method of building instructor awareness, but it is also an excellent springboard for speaking to the ever-important WIIFM principle among learners.

The PLE encompasses the physical as well as the digital learning environment. The library-as-place movement of recent years has enhanced interest in creating flexible and inviting physical locations using modular furniture, layered buildings, and collaborative space allocation. The library triple-play of spaces,

Figure 6.2
Ustream how-to page

resources, and services holistically supports the environment of learning, and becomes a means of grounding instruction in authentic contexts and encouraging users to reflect on how information tools and concepts can help them get things done. Nancy Foster and Susan Gibbons's *Studying Students* initiative produced a fascinating ethnographic perspective on the personal research and study habits of University of Rochester undergraduates, insight that allowed librarians at that institution to embed more productively in the social and learning context of their community.[21]

In my own practice, I have found that using the role model/tech support/cheerleader/critic typology mentioned above provides a helpful learner engagement strategy during live instruction. For example, in library staff trainings for the campus learning management system, I encourage participants to imagine how it might support on-campus PLEs by demonstrating how I use it in my own practice (role model). In addition to troubleshooting problems with the system during active portions of the workshop, I provide learning support and extend the interaction by suggesting links to further information, making my slides available online, and offering to provide one-on-one consultations if they have questions or difficulty in the future (tech support). Throughout the session, I present with enthusiasm and encouragement, billing the LMS as a convenient way to provide outreach to students and faculty, collaborate with colleagues on web-based initiatives, and collocate project resources overload (cheerleader). At the same time, I add an evaluative element to my pitch, suggesting potential frustrations and workarounds at important junctures (critic).

TECHNOLOGY FOR ACTIVE LEARNING

John Bransford and colleagues list five ways to use technology in active instruction: to provide real-world contexts for learning, connections with outside experts, visualization and analysis tools, scaffolds for

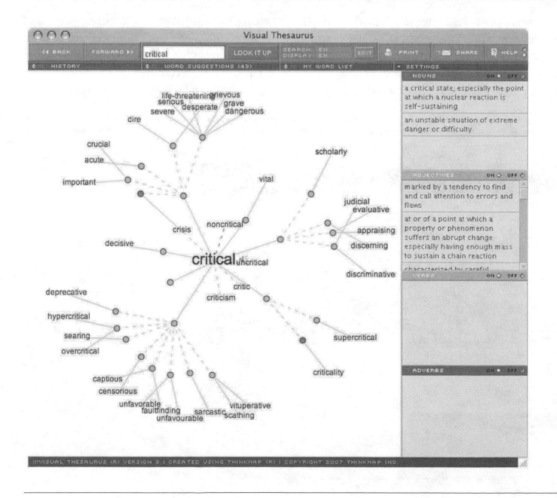

Figure 6.3
Visual Thesaurus for keyword brainstorming exercise

problem solving, and opportunities for feedback and revision.[22] As simplified versions of the ten instructional affordances I presented earlier in the chapter, these categories provide inspiration for creating active technology exercises once you begin to step through the USER method. Rather than simply demonstrating a platform or application, engaging students actively with a tool allows them to construct an experience of how it might operate in their own context. An example of an immersive activity in the "visualization" category: When I want to engage a group of undergraduates in thinking of alternative search keywords and topical narrowing, I introduce the dynamic Visual Thesaurus site (www.visualthesaurus.com). Although it is subscription based, you can try three "visual searches" for free before being prompted to buy, plenty of chances for students to break into concepts in an entertaining graphical manner (figure 6.3). Time and again, learners appreciate the chance to "play" with terms associated with their topic, which in turn motivates them to think of alternative angles.

Teaching about technology also involves becoming aware of the importance of suggesting alternative applications for different types of learners. In the same exercise I also invite participants to try another favorite site of mine, Wordnik (www.wordnik.com), an online dictionary project "aiming to collect all the words

in the English language." Created by Erin McKean, lexicographer and former principal editor of *The New Oxford American Dictionary* (don't miss her awesome TED talk on redefining the dictionary),[23] Wordnik integrates social media, personalized accounts, a drag-and-drop interface, and visualization tools to make the traditional dictionary experience much more engaging. Additional features include a display of the changing historical popularity of a word, feeds of real-time mentions in Twitter and Flickr, and a computation of the word's point value in Scrabble (figure 6.4). In class assessments, students frequently cite Visual Thesaurus and Wordnik specifically as valuable, dropping comments like "I loved the visual thesaurus website."

As an additional alternative visualization exercise, I sometimes use My Mind, Prezi, or MindOmo, all FLOSS concept-mapping software, to create simple diagrams that demonstrate relationships between concepts (figure 6.5). I also mention that visually inclined students can sign up for or download the software for free to take notes, brainstorm, or diagram ideas around a topic or argument. *Caveat:* In this and all technology-enhanced learning activities, you will want to make sure workstations or webcasting tools are updated and compatible with the sites you will be displaying; otherwise be prepared to deal with real-time headaches.

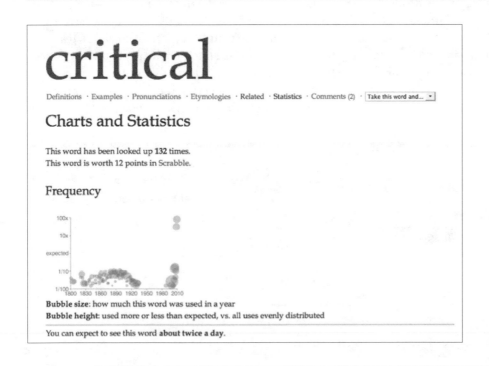

Figure 6.4
Wordnik as a visualization tool

Teaching *around* Technology

This last caveat raises an important point: Teaching *around* technology is a recognition of the fact that SICTs can create as many problems as they solve, but a critical mindset during instructional design helps you avoid hype and focus on solutions. The phrase "the medium is the message" implies that the method you use to communicate an idea is its most important characteristic.[24] In instructional planning, technology should play a converse role: A tool or application should help you convey and engage rather than obscure and confuse. By allowing the message of instruction to take the lead, technology becomes a method to support and extend the learning interaction.

CHALLENGE YOUR ASSUMPTIONS

Teaching around technology also implies thinking of SICTs as neither a substitute for meaningful interaction with an age-specific group, nor a panacea for teaching challenges.[25] For years, experts have debated whether technological learning characteristics vary across different age groups. Marc Prensky's famous digital native/immigrant typology is an example of early thinking on the subject; individuals born after roughly 1980 ("digital natives") were argued to be culturally and cognitively changed as a result of immersion in new technologies, more capable of multitasking and adapting to new applications than those born before them ("digital immigrants"). I have long been skeptical of statements that characterize Millennials as technology fluent and older learners as hopelessly out of date, a suspicion research is beginning to confirm.[26] Younger learners may have a greater propensity for early adoption, but evidence

dictates that this does not necessarily indicate differences in aptitude or learning style or a concurrent interest in learning technologies that use the same platforms.[27] A passage in the 2009 *ECAR Undergraduate Students and Information Technology* report expresses this well:

> No matter how extensively the mobile revolution—or any other technology-based disruption for that matter—impacts higher education, respondents to our survey consistently tell us that they want to see the use of IT balanced with the human touch in their academic environment. In their responses to the final open-ended question of our survey, students wrote explicitly about a preference for "real books and real people" and said "shiny new tech is still no substitute for well-trained, passionate instructors."[28]

CONFRONTING MYTHS

Becoming an effective instructional technologist involves striking a balance between technolust and technophobia. Moving past hype, information overload, format confusion, peer pressure, and simple intimidation to view SICTs with practical realism encourages their balanced and productive incorporation into your teaching and learning practice. One method for retaining balance and the human touch is to critically examine technology myths. A few of the most common among library educators:

Myth #1: If it's not brand new and fancy, it's not technology. Learning tools by no means have to be bleeding edge to "count." A piece of chalk is a teaching technology if it is used to help learners make connections with the content. The toolkit mindset encourages you to judge all instructional media, from a notecard to an iPad, using the same criteria you used to evaluate

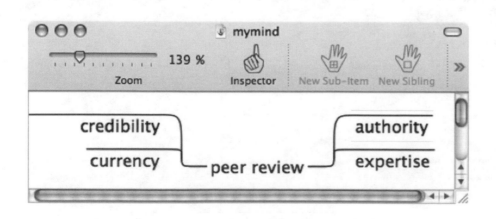

Figure 6.5
MyMind concept map

educational theories introduced in chapter 5—as either useful or not useful.

Myth #2: If I don't use gadgets to enhance live instruction, no one will pay attention. Southern Methodist University music school dean Jose Bowen coined the phrase "teaching naked"—using social media and games to prepare students for learning before class, which allows for a technology-free, face-to-face interaction. According to Bowen,

> Flashy powerpoints with video and synchronous e-conferences are impressive, but the best reason to adopt technology in your courses is to increase and improve your naked, untechnological face-to-face interaction with students. . . . simple, new technologies can greatly increase your students' engagement outside of the classroom and thus prepare them for real discussions (even in the very largest classes) by providing content and assessment before class time. The goal, in other words, is to use technology to free yourself from the need to "cover" (i.e., describe ad nauseam) foundational content in the classroom, instead using face-to-face time to demonstrate the continued value of direct interaction and discussion.[29]

For library educators, teaching naked becomes a way to imagine how you can extend instructional opportunity before and after an interaction, and a method for remembering that message should come before medium.

Myth #3: Everyone's doing it that way, so I should too. Actually, this is the opposite of what you should do. Every teaching librarian engages differently with technology, and we all find ourselves in environments that call for distinct tools and approaches. Instead of mimicking the strategies of others, glean the basics, gather inspiration and advice, then tailor your application of the technology in question to a specific scenario.

Myth #4: I need a Facebook page, a Twitter feed, and my own vlog on Blip.tv. Maybe you do, maybe you don't—bells and whistles are great, but only if you have the time and inclination to use them to benefit learners or forward your own professional development. My advice is this: try to start small and use technology to fix small frustrations with your most common practices; for example, replacing paper evaluations with Google Forms surveys saved me time and drawer space and has become a tip I regularly share with colleagues (I discuss this online assessment strategy in more detail in chapter 12).

TECH FAILS AND FIXES

Earlier in the chapter I mentioned the difficulty of finding a foolproof approach to instructional technology. The full truth of the matter is that not only is there no such thing as foolproof, there is vast potential for fool*ish*: you should always try to anticipate what can go wrong before the fact. I have experimented with many tools in a variety of instructional scenarios, and the only certainty is this: the more tricks you pull out of your bag, the greater the chance that one of them will backfire. I have had the pleasure of screeching feedback, dropped Skype calls, busted speakers, fritzing monitors, unintentionally dirty search results, corrupted files, broken USB drives, dead DVRs, Second Life sexual harassment, my own phone ringing, dead links, hard drive crashes, accidental file trashes, blanking on passwords, and PowerPoint slides that developed animate intelligence—I could go on.

To reduce the likelihood of any of the above, I have learned to simplify and select straightforward and reliable technological strategies that I can depend on. In the case that something does fail, contingency thinking and learning from mistakes will serve you well. Consider lessons from two of my own fail/fix experiences:

1) PDFed

In workshops with activities that require participants to record a substantial amount of information (e.g., an undergrad session that deals with defining keywords, identifying disciplinary language, and locating research sources), I often create a customized handout that features fill-in-the-blank sections. Provided that my teaching environment includes a screen and projector, by converting a Word document into PDF and then adding empty text fields in the places I want to type (figure 6.6), I also make a "fillable" digital copy to model exercises in real time. Having this e-version also makes it easier to add the handout to the course management system for later or in-class use or send it to the primary instructor if they want to distribute it to students via e-mail.

Fail: I was hurrying one of the first times I tried this approach, so instead of drawing a separate fillable field for each blank, I copied and pasted the same field throughout and didn't test the outcome. Imagine my surprise when I discovered that the first word I typed appeared simultaneously in every copied field – the class watched "racism" emerge real-time in about fifteen different places at once.

Fix: Needless to say, this was a ghost-in-the-machine moment that flustered me to the point of derailing my in-class composure. To recover what remained of my footing, I scrapped the PDF and grabbed a marker to replicate the tech-failed exercise on the dry-erase board.

Lesson: Test, test, and retest before you go live.

2) Dis(as)t(er)ance Learning

I had the opportunity while working at Ohio University to liaise with an affiliated master's-level research methods class at a university in Ghana. Students had remote access to OU's licensed education databases, but few utilized these resources; I identified this as the main instructional problem I wanted to solve. I decided to give participants an overview of off-campus research access using synchronous online webcasting and screensharing tools.

Fail: I worked out a complicated method using DimDim and Skype to stream presentation slides and the library website while speaking, but despite a decent test run the live connection on their end was too erratic to support such a bandwidth strain. Furthermore, weak classroom speakers made the audio almost impossible to hear.

Fix: I attempted to present as slowly as possible and cover only the most important points, and assured the class that I would create a supplementary tutorial and send around a linked guide that would be more stable over an intermittent connection. In retrospect, students would have been much better served had I simply created a guide or video in the first place. In this case, the reality of their access constraints should have factored more heavily into my selection of technologies.[30]

Lesson: Keep it simple.

TECHNOLOGY ADVOCACY

Another aspect of teaching around technology will likely be familiar to all readers: advocacy. Imagine that you have decided to assign an in-class group learning activity consisting of compiling a research bank of sources on different topics. You know one affordance of wiki software is that it facilitates group editing, so you test a few options to see what works best. The one you select requires you to upgrade a plugin on your classroom workstations, but you soon learn that local IT policies prevent this due to security concerns. This leaves you with three choices: forego the wiki idea, learn how to use a less robust option, or advocate for a change or exception in policy. This dilemma is common when working with instructional technology in an institutional setting. Many organizations prohibit installing some FLOSS tools on staff machines or restrict social media use during work hours, which can create a tension with the increasingly free and collaborative nature of SICTs. If institutional openness is hard to come by, the privilege to engage in experimentation or use new approaches is something you may need to advocate for within your organization.

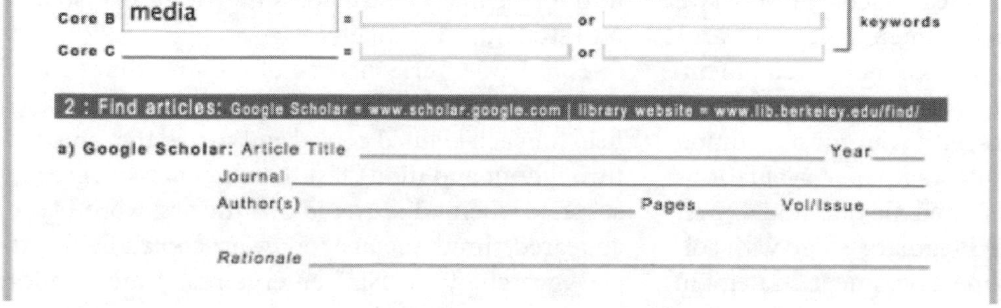
A crash course in academic research. CW R1B

1 : Break it down.

> A **researchable topic** consists of **core concepts** that can be broken down into **keywords**. Identify three core elements in your topic and list two synonyms, antonyms, related terms, or themes for each.

Tip: Use **wordnik.com** or **visualthesaurus.com** to help you brainstorm terms.

Core A racism = prejudice or xenophobia
Core B media = or
Core C = or
keywords

2 : Find articles: Google Scholar = www.scholar.google.com | library website = www.lib.berkeley.edu/find/

a) Google Scholar: Article Title ______ Year ______
Journal ______
Author(s) ______ Pages ______ Vol/Issue ______

Rationale ______

Figure 6.6
Fillable PDF handout (detail)

INSIGHT INTO USABILITY

A second aspect of advocacy involves technology usability. We work with the catalogs, websites, information services, interfaces, and products provided by our institutions, even if they are difficult to teach. We become used to explaining local platforms to learners, which puts us in the interesting position of being, in essence, usability experts able to address problems ourselves or communicate (constructively) to other stakeholders about the interface and functionality issues highlighted during instruction. Think about how many steps it takes to find an article database or to seek further help in your own website; there is often room for improvement. Over time, if some of these concerns are addressed (e.g., putting a metasearch box on a library home page, or changing a misleading label in the catalog), our sites and services become better attuned to the user perspective, and in our instruction we are more able to help users come away with valuable knowledge.

SUMMARY

- Approaching technology in terms of **experience, personalization,** and **practicality** opens the door to useful and productive pedagogical strategies.
- **Connectivism** is a theoretical approach that emphasizes the impact of information technology on learning.
- Cultivating a **toolkit mindset** toward instructional technology is a way to evaluate the teachable properties of specific SICTs and create active learning exercises based on these properties.
- Teaching **with**, **about**, and **around technology** are perspectives that help you think through common SICT teaching challenges.
- To reduce the risk of failure, (1) **test, test, and retest**, and (2) **keep it simple**.
- Become an **advocate** for better local technology and usability practice.

REFLECTION POINT

1. Imagine that you are a school media specialist in a rural school district who has just been hit with a big assignment. To qualify for additional federal funding, your administration is submitting a grant proposal to create a cultural education exchange program with an urban South American grammar school. Administrators want to establish virtual classrooms in which local and distance students can learn, share lessons, and communicate with one another in real time. As the resident "expert" you have been asked to investigate free and inexpensive web-based options and suggest several different technological methods of facilitating the goals of the project. Think about your teaching technology strategy in this scenario:

1. Where would you begin? What resources are necessary for you to pursue and track your findings?

2. How would you identify and evaluate the tools and technologies available?

3. How could you leverage the training, knowledge, and skills of your community of practice to help you?

NOTES

1. David Jonassen, Kyle Peck, and Brent Wilson, *Learning with Technology: A Constructivist Perspective* (Upper Saddle River, NJ: Merrill, 1999).

2. Association of College and Research Libraries, Standards for Proficiencies for Instruction Librarians and Coordinators, www.ala.org/ala/mgrps/divs/acrl/standards/profstandards.cfm, 2007. External resources can provide insight into how other educators are trained to teach with technology, such as the International Society for Technology in Education's National Educational Technology Standards, which outline competencies for K–12 instructors and students (www.istc.org). Reviewing these standards can indicate salient skill areas for library educators.

3. Joanna McGrenere and Wayne Ho, "Affordances: Clarifying and Evolving a Concept," Graphics Interface 2000 conference paper, 179-186.

4. Brian Kelly, "Library 2.0 and Information Literacy: The Tools," in P. Godwin and J. Parker (eds.), *Information Literacy Meets Library 2.0* (London: Facet, 2007), 19–36.

5. Chris Anderson, "Free: Why $0.00 Is the Future of Business," *Wired* 16, no. 3 (2008), accessed from www.wired.com.

6. List of Free and Open Source Software Packages: www.en.wikipedia.org/wiki/List_of_open_source_software_packages; List of Free Software Project Directories: www.en.wikipedia.org/wiki/List_of_free_software_project_directories.

7. William Gibson, NPR interview, *Talk of the Nation*, November 30, 1999.

8. George Siemens, *Connectivism: A Learning Theory for the Digital Age,* elearnspace, December 12, 2004. www.elearnspace.org/Articles/connectivism.htm, 3.

9. Association of College and Research Libraries, *Information Literacy Competency Standards for Higher Education* (Chicago: American Library Association, 2000).

10. Daniel Callison, "Key Words in Instruction: Information Fluency," *School Media Activities Monthly* 20, no. 4 (2003).

11. Michelle Simmons, "Librarians as Disciplinary Discourse Mediators: Using Genre Theory to Move toward Critical Information Literacy," *Libraries and the Academy* 5, no. 3 (2005): 297–311.

12. Joan Lippincott, "Student Content Creators: Convergence of Literacies," *EDUCAUSE Review* 42, no. 6 (2007): 16–17.

13. Henry Jenkins, Katie Clinton, Ravi Purushotma, Alice Robison, and Margaret Weigel, *Confronting the Challenges of Participatory Culture: Media Education for the 21st Century* (Cambridge, MA: MIT Press, 2006), 3–4.

14. Mizuko Ito et al., *Living and Learning with New Media: Summary of Findings from the Digital Youth Project*, MacArthur Foundation Report on Digital Media and Learning. http://digitalyouth.ischool.berkeley.edu/report, 2008.

15. Vibiana Cvetkovic and Robert Lackie, *Teaching Generation M: A Handbook for Librarians and Educators* (New York: Neal-Schuman, 2009).

16. Wiley quoted in Anya Kamenetz, "How Web-Savvy Edupunks Are Transforming American Higher Education," *Fast Company*, September 1, 2009.

17. Curtis Bonk, *The World Is Open: How Web Technology Is Revolutionizing Education* (San Francisco: Jossey-Bass, 2009), 8.

18. Susan Sharpless Smith, *Web-Based Instruction: A Guide for Libraries* (Chicago: American Library Association, 2010).

19. Jeremy Boggs, "Three Roles for Teachers Using Technology," *Clioweb*, February 7, 2009, www.clioweb.org/2009/02/07/three-roles-for-teachers-using-technology/.

20. Mark Prensky, "H. Sapiens Digital: From Digital Immigrants to Digital Natives to Digital Wisdom," *Innovate: Journal of Online Education* 5, no. 3 (2009), accessed from www.innovateonline.info/.

21. Nancy Foster and Susan Gibbons, *Studying Students: The Undergraduate Research Project at the University of Rochester* (Chicago: Association of Research Libraries, 2007).

22. John Bransford, Ann Brown, and Rodney Cocking, *How People Learn: Brain, Mind, Experience, and School* (Washington, DC: National Academy Press, 1999), 17.

23. Find McKean on *TED* at www.ted.com/talks/erin_mckean_redefines_the_dictionary.html.

24. Marshall McLuhan, *Understanding Media: The Extensions of Man* (New York: McGraw-Hill, 1964).

25. Siemens, *Connectivism;* Prensky, "H. Sapiens Digital."

26. Joint Information Systems Committee and Centre for Information Behaviour and the Evaluation of Research, *Information Behaviour of the Researcher of the Future*, www.jisc.ac.uk/whatwedo/programmes/resourcediscovery/googlegen.aspx, 2008.

27. Ibid.; Sue Bennet, Karl Maton, and Lisa Kervin, "The 'Digital Natives' Debate: A Critical Review of the Evidence," *British Journal of Educational Technology* 39, no. 5 (2008): 775–786; Gregor Kennedy et al., "First Year Students' Experiences with Technology: Are They Really Digital Natives?" *Australasian Journal of Educational Technology* 24, no. 1 (2008): 108–122; Ito et al., *Living and Learning;* Siva Vaidhyanathan, "Generational Myth: Not All Young People Are Tech-Savvy," *Chronicle Review,* 2008. www.sivacracy.net/2008/09/my_essay_on_the_myth_of_the_di.html.

28. Shannon Smith, Gail Salaway, and Judith Caruso, *The ECAR Study of Undergraduate Students and Information Technology: Key Findings.* www.educause.edu/ecar/, 12, 2009.

29. Jose Bowen, "Teaching Naked: Why Removing Technology from Your Classroom Will Improve Student Learning," *National Teaching and Learning Forum* 16, no. 1 (2006), accessed from www.ntlf.com.

30. Michael Henniger, *The Teaching Experience: An Introduction to Reflective Practice* (Upper Saddle River, NJ: Pearson/Merrill/Prentice Hall, 2004), 214.

7

Instructional Design

The goal of instructional design is to make learning more efficient and effective and to make learning less difficult.

—Gary Morrison et al., *Designing Effective Instruction*

GOALS

- Examine the characteristics of **design** and **design thinking**.
- Describe the foundational **ADDIE design cycle** (Analyze, Design, Develop, Implement, Evaluate).
- Explore the origins of **instructional** and **experience design** and their applications in a library setting.
- Describe the practice of **balancing your teaching brain**.

In earlier chapters I have focused on *reflective practice*, *educational theory*, and *teaching technologies*— components of instructional literacy that support the development of your teacher identity, provide insight to the learner perspective, and foster current awareness of tools and methods. In this chapter I examine the fourth component, *instructional design* (ID). ID is a systematic instructional planning approach that channels this insight and awareness into efficient, learner-focused pedagogy.

WHY DESIGN?

I have been fascinated by the idea of design for as long as I can remember. I notice the appearance and usability of everyday things and am curious about their origins, which manifests in a preoccupation with signs, graffiti, product labels, architecture, old appliances, and the like. Design draws on a shared aesthetic and kinesthetic language to impact the way we experience the world around us, which has great power to influence perception and action. For example, during the Great Depression, North American auto manufacturers shifted focus from mechanical improvements and developed "planned obsolescence" and the modern make/model system. By making slight design changes to car bodies year after year, car

Activity 7.1 Frustration/Flaw/Fix

	Frustration	Flaw	Fix
Example: Blender	While trying to unscrew blades, I realize I am inadvertently tightening them.	Blade attachment screws on counter-clockwise.	Attachment should tighten clockwise.
1)			
2)			
3)			

companies discovered that they could sell the image of a well-designed automobile and foster an active culture of consumption. Executives at General Motors plotted the height of tailfins decades in advance, and function followed form in the worst crisis of modern capitalism.[1]

In this scenario, design shaped desire by creating a reliable system of anticipation that captured and sustained consumer attention. To understand design's capabilities in educational settings, it is useful to consider the subject in a broader context. The word itself has diverse applications. John Heskett notes that "design has so many levels of meaning that it is itself a source of confusion. It is rather like the word 'love,' the meaning of which shifts radically depending on who is using it, to whom it is applied, and in what context."[2] The motivations for a design approach span from practical to commercial to artistic to altruistic (or any combination thereof): Product designers make everyday objects more usable; architects and interior designers create attractive functional spaces; fashion designers bring style to everyday necessity; graphic designers shape visuals to inform (and influence); experience designers consider how to create usable objects and interfaces; and instructional designers make the process and products of learning more effective.

Design requires the same sort of intentionality used in reflective practice: No matter its purpose, a design is the conscious effort to guide use or perception. A more involved definition might then be that design is the process of translating goals or ideas into outcomes that shape experiences. Cultivating a design mentality in instruction encourages awareness of how your learning interactions and objects are actually used and experienced, and "universal" principles can facilitate the creation of instructional designs with wider and more lasting application.

THE FLAW/FRUSTRATION/ FIX PROCESS

The flip side of design's universal language is our common ability to notice when things don't work or look quite right (generally far more apparent than when they *do*). Poor design obviates itself in any number of small daily frustrations. I often notice ordinary usability experiences that expose design flaws, like online forms that erase *all* of my personal information when I forget to add my zip code before clicking "submit," or the blade attachment on my blender that inexplicably screws on lefty-tighty/righty-loosey. The natural reaction to this is engaging in what I think of as the "frustration/flaw/fix" thinking: You find yourself frustrated by an experience or object, unconsciously locate its design flaw, and, whether it is a productive exercise or not, mentally troubleshoot the problem (as in willing the online form to remember at least some of my information, so I don't have to fill it all out again). This is the point at which, if you can't fix the issue yourself, you move on to something else, submit critical feedback, or return a product for a refund. In activity 7.1, jot down three frustration/flaw/fix moments you have experienced.

DESIGN THINKING

When you go through the flaw/frustration/fix exercise, you are actually engaging in *design thinking*. Design thinking is a creative and systematic approach to problem solving common to many professions.[3] It is found in many of the concepts I have presented thus far, including streamlined message design using SUCCESs.[4] An example of this approach in action: Around the time I arrived at UC Berkeley, the Library had begun the long process of transitioning to a new integrated library system (ILS). At a staff forum on the switchover, the head of UC Berkeley's ILS implementation team explained the timeline and record transition process by dumping strips of paper between two cardboard boxes, one labeled "Pathfinder (old Catalog)" and the other "Millennium (new ILS)." The moment she pulled out the first box the energy in the room shifted—people craned their heads forward and started to laugh. Instead of exacerbating collective anxiety about new workflows or falling back on the Curse of Knowledge, her unexpected delivery method broke presentation protocol and translated a potentially arcane subject into a concrete and simple visualization. She presented herself with credibility and used the box metaphor to create a story that would help staff understand what lay ahead.

We rarely have much more time than a short workshop or screencast to communicate our messages. In the perpetual outreach challenge that is library instruction, finding accessible and humorous ways to incorporate design thinking seriously counts. By asking, *How can I make this experience better/easier/ more efficient/more understandable?* in a library context, you can use a frustration/flaw/fix mentality to improve the experience of your learners and users. Design thinking is not about attaining perfection, but by investigating different angles of a problem or performance scenario, you become better prepared to develop a workable solution. There is no way to make an experience or product truly universal, and any left-hander (myself included) will tell you that design tends to follow the needs of the majority. That said, you can learn to recognize the diversity in any audience as a way to accommodate a wide range of people. This does not occur in a vacuum but through the process of *prototyping*, an iterative cycle of testing, evaluating, and revision based on user feedback. Prototyping assumes that before a product is "finished" it benefits from outside perspectives that lead to gradual adjustment.

ADDIE: THE CORE OF DESIGN THINKING

One thing instructional designers and librarians share is a mutual obsession with acronyms and abbreviations. Who could forget such American Library Association greats as FAFLRT, LSSDDPMAG, and RTSDCCSSAC?[5] The answer is, anyone could. Unlike these examples, some abbreviations are actually mnemonic devices that help encapsulate ideas too complex to remember easily (e.g., ROY G. BIV for Red Orange

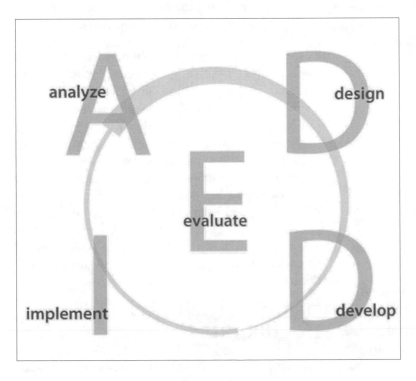

Figure 7.1
ADDIE design cycle

Analyze
Understand the core needs and characteristics of the product's users.

Design
Create a strategy that addresses the needs and characteristics of these users.

Develop
Construct and revise the product.

Implement
Deliver the product to its intended audience.

Evaluate
Assess the impact and effectiveness of the product.

Yellow Green Blue Indigo Violet). Though it might seem glib, concepts in design and education are often described with acronyms to give them a foothold in your memory. Mnemonically speaking, ADDIE is to design what ROY G. BIV is to the color wheel. ADDIE stands for Analyze, Design, Develop, Implement, and Evaluate— the five steps at the core of design thinking (figure 7.1). Each step of ADDIE is part of a cycle, but whereas analysis, design, development, and implementation are sequential, evaluation is continuous throughout.

From start to finish, ADDIE is the process of reflection used to create, refine, and deliver a product to its intended audience. What makes ADDIE so useful is that it describes the sequence by which any object, interaction, or experience—from an online tutorial to a hydrogen-powered car—is developed and assessed. Among instructional designers, ADDIE is so commonplace that its origins cannot be attributed to a specific creator.[6] Even though other design fields may not be explicitly aware of ADDIE, they tend to follow a similar design process. For example, employees at IDEO, a well-known product design firm that created the original Apple mouse, use the following five-step approach:[7]

Understand the market, the client, the technology, and their perceived constraints on the problem.

Observe real people in real-life situations to find out what makes them tick.

Visualize new-to-the-world concepts and the customers who will use them.

Evaluate and refine the prototypes in a series of quick iterations.

Implement the new concept for commercialization.

According to Steven Bell and John Shank, the IDEO method is a prototyping framework similar to ADDIE but tailored to the commercial marketplace.[8]

DESIGN PRINCIPLES AND MODELS

Instructional design consists of *principles* that explain how learning occurs in different situations and *models* that explain how to put theory into practice.[9] Robert Gagné lists a series of principles that link all design models:[10]

Design is more about improving learning than improving teaching. Preparing for any educational scenario should be an exercise in putting the needs, characteristics, and aptitudes of the learner first. If you do this, you will naturally improve your instructional delivery.

Learning is a process influenced by many factors. Learning is complex. It is the result of a combination of conditions and influences that can be understood, addressed, and supported in order to create more effective instruction.

The design approach can be tailored to fit different learning scenarios. There is no one way to teach, and design is flexible depending on the needs and requirements of both instructors and learners.

Design is iterative—it informs itself in an ongoing cycle. A cycle of reflection and adaptability is built into the instructional design approach, while evaluation and feedback revise the facilitation of learning.

Design is a process consisting of steps and substeps. Each part of the design process can be broken down into smaller processes.

Different learning goals call for different instructional approaches. The structure and delivery of learning should be shaped by predetermined goals and outcomes.

In sum, learning is complex and instruction should be adaptable, iterative, goal-focused, and student-centered; in response, the USER method is based on these principles. ID models break a teaching scenario or object into components and provide a template for facilitating learning. ADDIE describes steps in the design process, but it is less a "model" in the formal sense than the framework upon which models are built. Two of the best-known design models are Morrison, Ross, and Kemp's cycle in *Designing Effective Instruction* and Dick, Carey, and Carey's model in *The Systematic Design of Instruction*, while Bell and Shank's BLAAM method is directed toward academic librarians.[11]

DESIGN THINKING IN LIBRARIES

Instructional design methods have existed for decades. The approach initially known as *instructional systems design* was developed during World War II, when rapidly training a large industrial workforce became critical to North American military effort. ID approaches draw on communication studies, systems design, psychology, information technology, and educational theory to identify and solve instructional problems, create learning outcomes, and organize content into teachable units. The related fields of *experience design* and *interaction design* have developed more recently and use design thinking to shape how users interact with physical spaces and interfaces. These relatively young fields share many characteristics with ID, and principles from each inform the USER method. The recommended readings section features suggestions for further study in each of these areas.

In recent years, design thinking has begun to influence library practice. According to Gagné, *learning environments* are constructivist educational spaces that provide the framework for self-discovery, whereas *instructional systems* are behaviorist/cognitivist spaces that "focus on telling . . . learners what they need to know."[12] Increasingly, libraries seek to blend the two to create experiential environments for communication, community building, and "making meaning" that retain elements of our more traditional systems-oriented approach to information access and delivery.[13] As both learning environments and instructional systems, design-focused libraries provide the context for discovery as well as guidance for evaluating and interpreting information. In *Academic Librarianship by Design,* Bell and Shank advocate the use of design principles to facilitate this goal. Whereas blended learning uses face-to-face and online instruction to create dynamic learning environments, the skills of "blended librarianship" leverage instructional design to increase our educational impact:[14]

> The ability to put oneself in the place of the user of the product or service in order to understand how the user can receive the optimal learning experience.

> A willingness to thoughtfully and creatively move through a series of gradual changes in developing a product or service and use this prototyping method to arrive at an optimal experience for the user.

> A commitment to both formative and summative evaluation in determining how well a product or service meets the needs of the user, and then making the necessary adjustments to improve the performance of that product or service to ensure a good library or learning experience for the user.

Other examples of library design methodology emphasize shaping library products based on meaningful user insight, such as Brian Mathews' *Marketing Today's Academic Library*, which offers strategies in "design[ing] media packages that are tangible, experiential, relatable, shareable, and surprising . . . to make the library more visible, engaging, and accessible to our users,"[15] and David Lee King's exploration of library website design, *Designing the Digital Experience.*[16]

JUSTIFYING LIBRARY DESIGN

As the focus on new literacies and the user experience grows, I perceive four justifications for integrating the design approach into library instruction:

Well-designed instruction creates independent learners. Library instruction tends to impart self-sufficient and critical information skills to help users discover and interpret information. Making the most of limited teaching moments can better prepare users for independent research and inquiry.

Library educators face many challenges. In reality, there are many roadblocks between librarians and teaching effectiveness. To keep pace with changing budgets, technology, and user expectations, librarians are involved in a constant process of reorientation. Demonstrating our value requires our teaching and training to have immediate, lasting impact. We need practical strategies for instructional planning and communication with limited resources.

You probably already use design thinking. Many instructional design principles are common best practices among library instructors, such as striving to be a "guide on the side" rather than a noninteractive lecturer. ID has not been an integral element of most library professional education, but you probably already use design thinking every day. Cultivating a commonsense design mindset can improve library education and can expose usability and experience problems in our digital and physical spaces.

Design helps you see teaching as a craft. Design approaches bring an attitude of forethought, flexibility, and continuous improvement that can foster ownership and investment in your instructional work. A Works Progress Administration poster designed by Nathan Sherman in 1937 (figure 7.2) gets at the core of the design mindset—*working with care.* A metaphor for reflective practice, when you teach with care you stay attentive to process as well as outcomes, aware of your skills and potential to impact others.

BALANCING YOUR TEACHING BRAIN

The remaining chapters in this book go into considerable detail about the USER method. It is important to remember as you read through the minutiae that the big picture of instructional design is about more than steps and methods; it is a means of creating balanced instruction. I have observed that people tend to privilege either the left or right side of their brain when they teach or present, which is to say that they are either overly rigid or overly loose. Think of it like this: The left hemisphere of your brain is highly analytical, logical, and systematic, whereas the right is creative, affective, and intuitive.[17] It is never good to let either extreme take over; we have all seen teachers and learning objects with either too much pocket protector or too much thespian.

Few people would record a screencast without thinking about what they plan to say in advance or enter a classroom knowing nothing about the content they are going to cover. In this sense, ID communicates fairly intuitive elements of effective instructional practice. That said, any educator can identify strengths and weaknesses in their planning and execution. In my experience, these strengths and weaknesses tend to be fairly simple, and can often be reduced to left or right hemisphere thinking. The USER method I outline in Part II is a way to keep from privileging one

over the other, a process I think of as balancing your teaching brain. A brain-balanced instructor manages to keep learners engaged with the content while communicating their teacher identity, at once covering the rational and the emotional.

SUMMARY

- **Design thinking** is a creative and systematic process of translating goals into outcomes.
- **Instructional design** is a method and profession for developing solutions to learning-related problems.
- You can use **frustration/flaw/fix** thinking to troubleshoot design issues.
- **ADDIE** (Analyze, Design, Develop, Implement, Evaluate) represents the underlying steps of the universal design cycle.
- **Experience design** and **interaction design** are two alternate and recently developed approaches to ADDIE that can be used in the creation of digital as well as physical spaces.
- Design thinking helps you **balance your teaching brain**.

REFLECTION POINTS

1. If you were not familiar with ID at the outset of this chapter, does it mesh with your expectations? Do aspects of ID appear to offer practical solutions to actual teaching challenges you face?

2. Do you tend to privilege one side of your brain while teaching, either left (order) or right (creativity)? What effect does this have on your pedagogical style, and in turn on the learning experience of your students?

3. Consider an instructional scenario in your past that could have benefited from attention to ADDIE. What parts of the cycle seemed to be lacking?

Figure 7.2
Work with Care, 1937

NOTES

1. Char Booth, "American Automobile Streamlining and Commodified Aesthetic-Technological 'Progress' during the Great Depression," BA thesis, Reed College, 2001.
2. John Heskett, *Design: A Very Brief History* (Oxford: Oxford University Press, 2005), 3.
3. Robert Gagné, Walter Wager, Katherine Golas, and John Keller, *Principles of Instructional Design,* 5th ed. (Belmont, CA: Thomson/Wadsworth, 2005).

4. Heath, Chip, and Dan Heath, *Made to Stick: Why Some Ideas Survive and Others Die* (New York: Random House, 2007), 252–257.

5. FAFLRT, Federal and Armed Forces Libraries Round Table; LSSDDPMAG, Library Service to Developmentally Disabled Persons Membership Activity Group; RTSDCCSSAC, Resources and Technical Services Division Cataloging and Classification Section Subject Analysis Committee (Subcommittee on the Naming of Works of Art, Architecture, and Analogous Artifacts). Watch the ALA Focus "Wheel of Confusion" video at www.alfocus.ala.org/videos/wheel-confusion-2 for an explanation of this last one.

6. Michael Molenda, "In Search of the Elusive ADDIE Model," *Performance Improvement* 42, no. 5 (2003): 34–36.

7. Tom Kelley and Jonathan Littman, *The Art of Innovation: Lessons in Creativity from IDEO, America's Leading Design Firm* (New York: Currency/Doubleday, 2001), 252–257.

8. Steven Bell and John Shank, *Academic Librarianship by Design: A Blended Librarian's Guide to the Tools and Techniques* (Chicago: American Library Association, 2007), 9.

9. Charles Reigeluth (ed.), *Instructional Design Theories and Models: A New Paradigm of Instructional Theory,* vol. 2 (Mahwah, NJ: Lawrence Erlbaum, 1999).

10. Gagné et al., *Principles,* 2–3.

11. Gary Morrison, Steven Ross, and Jerrold Kemp, *Designing Effective Instruction,* 5th ed. (Hoboken, NJ: Wiley, 2007); Walter Dick, Lou Carey, and James O. Carey, *The Systematic Design of Instruction,* 7th ed. (Boston: Allyn and Bacon, 2008); Bell and Shank, *Academic Librarianship.* For additional information on these and other ID models in libraries, consult Valeda Dent-Goodman, *Keeping the User in Mind: Instructional Design and the Modern Library* (Oxford: Chandos, 2009).

12. Gagné et al., *Principles,* 27.

13. Steve Diller et al., *Making Meaning: How Successful Businesses Deliver Meaningful Customer Experiences* (Berkeley, CA: Peachpit, 2008).

14. Bell and Shank, *Academic Librarianship,* 20.

15. Brian Mathews, *Marketing Today's Academic Library: A Bold New Approach to Communicating with Students* (Chicago: American Library Association, 2009).

16. David Lee King, *Designing the Digital Experience* (Medford, NJ: Information Today, 2008).

17. To learn more about left and right brain, I highly recommend watching *A Powerful Stroke of Insight,* Harvard neuroscientist Jill Bolte Taylor's TED talk on her experience of recovering from a massive stroke. See www.ted.com/talks/jill_bolte_taylor_s_powerful_stroke_of_insight.html.

Part II

The USER Method

8

USER and Library Instructional Design

GOALS

- Present an overview of the **USER** instructional design method (Understand, Structure, Engage, and Reflect).
- Discuss **scaffolding** as a means of extending the continuum of learning.

Design models and instructional acronyms can seem like a trite approach to any subject, and have in the past led to a fair amount of eye-rolling on my part. As much as they oversimplify, they also provide reflective, learner-focused frameworks for approaching the complex, nuanced processes of pedagogy and praxis. No book on instructional design would be complete without its own acronym, so it is with only a small amount of irony that I present the USER method (figure 8.1).

When you consider the demands of your day-to-day practice, it might seem like I am advocating for the exact thing I warned against in the introduction: overkill. When I started learning about ID methods, the teaching I was engaged in hardly seemed likely to benefit from such a drawn-out planning process. The first project for which I used a formal design method felt cumbersome, but each time I approached a learning experience systematically I learned to focus more intently on the elements that were productive and less on those that weren't. After several years of experimentation, mashing and changing other models, and gathering feedback from colleagues, USER is the result.

The beauty of an ID model is that it acts as a roadmap rather than a ball and chain; it should point you in the right direction rather than drag you down. I have described USER as either a thought or an action model, able to be flexibly applied to the depth called for in a specific scenario or used to provide metacognitive guidance during an in-progress interaction. Design models outline the elements necessary for effective student-focused instruction and provide a rough guideline for implementation and reflection, and I don't recommend that you follow USER to the letter for every class, tutorial, or subject guide you create. USER is a mental or procedural way to approach the four stages of effective instructional planning—*Understand, Structure, Engage,* and *Reflect*—on your own terms. More than anything, it should remind you to teach simply, reflectively, and with the learner at the center.

USER and Communities of Practice

Libraries are increasingly called on to pursue innovative educational initiatives in order to remain engaged with a user base that is beginning to expect more personalized, mobile, digital, and responsive information services. In this climate, effective library instruction requires embedded, strategic, and situated participation in local communities of practice. Creatively integrating into the pedagogical or learning structure of a campus or community can provide a means of redefining information education and adapting to change. This requires looking beyond the library classroom, anticipating emerging learning needs, and engaging in the productive life of an organization or institution in order to become a more integral pedagogical resource.

USER is both a means of perceiving how you can contribute useful knowledge to local communities of practice, and a method for structuring your response. By engaging productively in the discourse and activities of your user community (a process that conflates embedding and outreach) you become better equipped to discern local educational opportunities when they arise and generate high-impact products. In public librarianship, this can involve keeping tabs on current knowledge areas such as technology literacy training, assistance navigating the growing

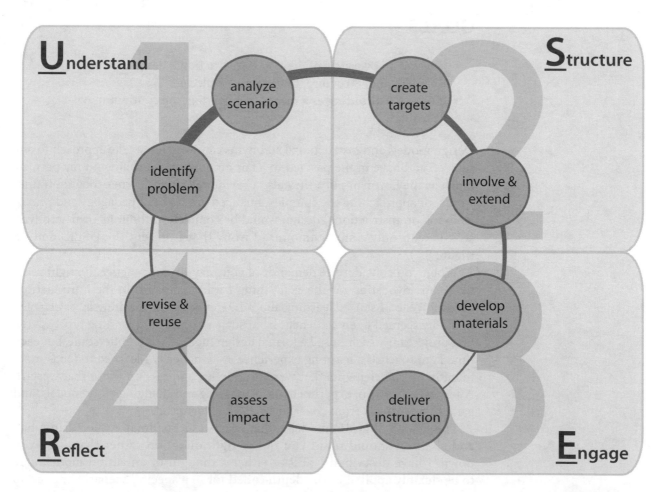

Figure 8.1
USER method

number of e-government sites, or collaborating with community groups to support existing learning initiatives. In higher education, it can involve anything from participating in faculty e-mail discussion lists related to teaching to seeking out campus committees, initiatives, or task forces that deal with topics such as scholarly communication, technology, privacy, literacy, and continuing education. Integrating into the social, working, and learning life of a community or organization is far more productive than expecting it to intuit the value of instructional content that is divorced from its authentic application and sequestered within a library building or site.

An example: As a result of participating in a textbook affordability task force that dealt with open educational content, I perceived campus confusion about digital copyright, and a lack of outreach to faculty about how to provide online course readings from licensed library collections to support fair use and reduce student costs. I created a programmatic "eReadings" initiative in collaboration with the campus educational technology office that sought to raise awareness of making maximum instructional use of digital collections via web-based information, face-to-face education and discussion, "clickable syllabus" review, and train-the-trainer components for library staff, all of which benefited from USER-supported planning. I might have perceived these learning needs without participating in the task force, but I would not have been as connected to stakeholders or the communication infrastructure that allowed me to reach a wider audience.

EXPLORING USER

Speaking from experience, some ID approaches can create unreasonable time and resource demands when applied in the context of library education. In response, the USER method is a streamlined interpretation of ADDIE (Analysis, Development, Design, Implementation, and Evaluation) that focuses on instructional messages, motivation, and the learner/instructor experience while maintaining a realistic concept of constraints and local needs. The acronym is a pedagogical reflection of what I consider to be a central motivation of librarianship: catering to the personal learning needs of a diverse community of patrons with information insight, support, and strategy. Beyond breaking instructional planning into manageable pieces and focusing on

the learner experience, USER is an instructional literacy framework that encourages you to reflect on your process in order to become a "student of learning" as you teach.[1] It can function as a template for design thinking in new scenarios or a benchmark to evaluate your current strategies. You don't have to start from scratch to bring a methodical approach to instructional planning; you can apply USER as a mental checklist as you teach, train, or create learning objects.

USER: STAGES AND STEPS

The following is a description of the four broad phases and eight substeps that comprise the USER method. Although the method is sequential, USER's elements often overlap in practice. For example, as you create targets, you are also thinking through activities and assessment strategies, whereas reflection occurs throughout. You can progress through the model step by step, focus on one area in particular, or jump around to some degree to suit your needs. The most important factor is that each phase and step is considered before a learning interaction occurs. As you read through this brief USER description, think about an instructional scenario or object you are in the process of planning or have recently participated in as a learner. Consider whether you or it progressed through a similar cycle organically, independent of an intentionally design-minded approach.

1. **Understand.**
   In the first phase, investigate the learning scenario.
   a. Start by **identifying the problem** that instruction can solve by asking, *What is the challenge learners face, and how can I help them meet it?*
   b. Follow up by **analyzing the scenario,** or characterizing the qualities and confronting the challenges of each element of instruction: *learner, content, context,* and *educator.* Listing these specifics provides insight into the learning community and how the instructional environment can be shaped to facilitate a positive experience.

2. **Structure.**
   In the second phase, define what you want participants to accomplish and outline the strategies you will use to facilitate learning.

c. Begin by **creating targets**—*goals*, *objectives*, and *outcomes*—that help you organize content and interaction and evaluate the impact of instruction.

d. Identify methods to **involve** learners using delivery techniques, technologies, and activities, and **extend** the interaction by supporting students along the continuum of learning.

3. **Engage**.

In the third phase, create your instructional products and implement the learning interaction.

e. **Develop the materials** of instruction. This involves developing an instructional message, then creating and revising learning objects (e.g., syllabus, handout, or course guide in a face-to-face interaction, or a storyboard, video, or tutorial in a web-based interaction) using a prototyping process.

f. **Deliver instruction** by developing an implementation plan, then capturing and sustaining learner attention throughout the interaction.

4. **Reflect**.

In the fourth phase, consider whether targets have been met and how you might improve and repurpose your instructional product.

g. **Assess the impact** of instruction by investigating the evidence of learning.

h. Finally, consider how you can **revise** and **reuse** content, materials, and strategies in the future.

ON SCALABILITY

Like many librarians, I tend to plan things into the ground. We are a detail-oriented, leave-no-stone-unturned sort of people, often much too thorough for our own good. Instead of making preparing for instruction yet another interminable process, USER actually helps you avoid overplanning by creating reliable strategies and template objects that you can adjust to each scenario. Introducing a new element into your teaching practice can feel like a trial, but after referring to USER on a project or two you will likely start noticing that the process becomes more familiar and that you have more resources to draw from. A fairly simple rule of thumb is this: the more demanding or unfamiliar the scenario, the more detailed a design approach is called for. For example, if you have three

months to plan a large-scale tutorial or credit class, methodical planning and documentation of each step will yield better results. On the other hand, if you have three hours to pull together a workshop you've never taught because a coworker called in sick, USER can serve as an on-the-fly reminder to ask, *Have I identified a central problem that instruction can solve? Does my message speak to the WIIFM principle? Have I included any engaging activities?*

Another aspect of the depth to which you apply USER may be based on your own instructional confidence and familiarity: the newer you are to instruction or the less confident you feel about teaching in general, the more a systematic design method will likely prove beneficial. Experience will help you determine how much energy you devote to different scenarios, and a consistently useful reflective strategy is to maintain awareness of whether scaling back or speeding up might be appropriate. Appendix A provides a template you can use to focus on USER in more rapid planning situations or to help you reflect in longer projects. You can also download this template at www.alaeditions.org/webextras/.

Scaffolding and Extending Learning

The true test of instruction is whether it creates knowledge that can be applied in the future. Intrinsic motivation is higher when learners see that a learning opportunity is immediately useful, but it is not always possible to reach people at this opportune moment. In chapter 6 I discussed extending the learning interaction using instructional technologies, which provide scaffolding opportunities such as recording workshops to distribute online or offering one-on-one chat assistance to students interested in additional help. Instead of confining yourself to a one-off session, tutorial, or training, USER encourages you to be strategic about when and how you engage with learners before, during, and after a face-to-face or virtual interaction, either by building ongoing relationships and ties to a learning community or simply providing avenues for additional assistance.

You probably already support and extend the interaction without thinking about it; you might share your contact information with a class before instruction, join in online discussions or comment on a course blog, or suggest additional sites or resources that a requesting instructor can share with students to prepare them on a given topic. After a session, you might

Table 8.1 JournalTOCs Workshop USER Design Process

1. UNDERSTAND

a. Identify Problem	There are journal table of contents (TOC) feeds and alert services on publisher websites but until JournalTOCs (www.journaltocs.hw.ac.uk) there was no authoritative "clearinghouse" of TOC RSS feeds and associated API. Library staff could benefit from its potential for current awareness, faculty/student outreach, and creating OPAC and other types of mashups.

b. Analyze Scenario:

Learner	*Characterize:* Any library staff can attend, but selectors/liaisons/tech-savvy collections people are more likely to be interested. A quick audience poll during the previous presentation indicated few attendees were familiar with JournalTOCs predecessor, ticTOCs. Turnout and motivation is likely to be relatively high due to expressed interest and timing.
	Confront: Prior knowledge of the subject will be minimal, and participants will represent a wide range of technological skills. Content will need to be pitched generally and simply with plenty of time for independent exploration, questions, and one-on-one support.
Context	*Characterize:* The f2f workshop will be taught solo and will occur in an 18-seat computer classroom equipped with speakers and a projector. Visibility and audibility in the room are decent, and it is a common training space that will not be difficult to book or locate.
	Confront: Request RSVPs in advance to determine if two sessions are needed and to issue a reminder before the session.
Content	*Characterize:* The session will be straightforward and will communicate that the purpose of the class is for attendees to become familiar enough with JournalTOCs to use it comfortably.
	Confront: Make sure not to privilege one discipline or journal type over another; jump around subject areas to draw in multiple perspectives.
Educator	*Characterize:* Speak authoritatively on JournalTOCs due based on experience/research from the prior 6-minute Lightning Talks presentation.
	Confront: Locate more examples of libraries using it for faculty/student outreach and to create current TOC journal listings in OPACs. Research local recording and video hosting options as time permits.

2. STRUCTURE

c. Create Targets	*Goal:* Orient participants to the JournalTOCs journal table of contents service so that they are confidently able and motivated to use it.
	Objective: Learners will discover and track pertinent TOC feeds using their JournalTOCs account.
	Outcome: Attendees will leave the session with fully configured personal JournalTOCs accounts tracking several journals and will be able to name specific ways the service could be used in outreach and OPACs.

(cont.)

Table 8.1 JournalTOCs Workshop USER Design Process cont.

2. STRUCTURE (CONT.)

d. Involve and Extend	*Involve:* Allow participants to work in JournalTOCs to set up accounts, locate journal feeds, and more, and will create structured activities to work through each step.
	Extend: Present myself as a JournalTOCs resource in the future, and encourage participants to indicate whether they would like me to contact them after the session for a follow-up. For future reference and those unable to attend the f2f workshop, post slides to Tech Training site and/or links to supplementary tutorials and follow-up information.

3. ENGAGE

e. Design Materials	*Message:* JournalTOCs is the best method available for discovering and monitoring interdisciplinary scholarly journal TOC feeds, which helps builds current awareness and provides outreach material for faculty and graduate students.
	Objects: Sketch a rough session outline based on learning targets and exercises, and note prerequisite concepts that require explanation (RSS feeds, APIs, email alerts). Design new PowerPoint presentation and handout from existing workshop template handout structured around selection of 3 in-class activities.
f. Deliver Instruction	*Implement:* Publicize session via word-of-mouth, the Tech Training blog, Google Cal, and all-staff announcement.
	Capture & Sustain: Capture learner attention with group introductions and questions and media-rich visuals, sustain attention using a comfortable, conversational tone throughout, hands-on individual and group exercises, and critical dialogue throughout.

4. REFLECT

g. Assess Impact	*Formative:* Monitor attendees during the session through questioning techniques, reading body language and other cues, and observing performance during activities. I will complete a three-question reflection immediately after the session ends to help me remember specific points and observations.
	Summative: Participants will complete a short web evaluation form during the last 5 minutes of class with a few closed- and open-ended questions. After the session, informally checking in with someone within my instructor community of practice will give me an honest opinion of the workshop's effectiveness. If I record the workshop or create a narrated screencast post-facto, I will monitor views, comments, and website analytics to understand its ongoing impact.
h. Revise and Reuse	*Revise:* After reviewing participant feedback and coworker input, make notes of how to adjust the exercises, learning objects, and instructional messages to align with learner expectations for a future class as well as follow up with attendees who indicated their desire for additional one-on-one contact.
	Reuse: Archive the presentation, handout template, and any other instructional objects on my computer and to Google Docs in order to reuse them in the future as the basis for repeat or related classes.

Table 8.2 Example Instructional Scenarios

SCENARIO	1. ONE-SHOT SESSION	2. LMS TRAINING INITIATIVE	3. REVISED CITATION TUTORIAL
Summary	Rapid design process for a face-to-face, course-related research skills one-shot session	In-depth design process for a large-scale faculty and library staff training initiative for the campus learning management system (LMS)	In-depth design process for first creating an interactive Flash tutorial on citation style, and later reviewing it for revision and reuse in another instructional context
Details	I teach many "one-shot" undergraduate course-related workshops in various disciplines. These classes focus on nonstandardized topics and texts, and each research assignment and library session is unique. My planning time for a typical session is about 2–4 hours, depending on course details and my familiarity with the subject matter. This scenario explores a typical 90-minute, 20-student workshop and an online research assignment and guide I developed to accompany it.	I also provide instruction related to the campus learning management and collaboration system, which includes programming face-to-face staff workshops, faculty trainings and online learning interactions/ objects designed to teach instructors and staff to use the system for library and research purposes. This scenario explores the planning process for several learning interactions and objects associated with this initiative.	I hand-coded a large-scale Flash tutorial on citation style as a project for my instructional technology master's degree at Ohio University. This tutorial remained in a relatively rough state and never went live in a professional context, but an ongoing learning need for citation style instruction among undergraduates motivated me to consider the project It for potential updating and repurposing at my current institution. This scenario explores the original tutorial planning process as well as the revision/reuse review.

share the link to a customized online course guide that features content and suggestions or post links to supplementary tutorials to a course management system. Library instruction is often difficult to deploy exactly at the time of need, so this type of supplementary learning support allows the skills and tools you share to be more practically accessible to learners in the future. This strategy mitigates the constraints of teaching in the library world as much as it supports the ongoing, nonlinear nature of information-related and situated learning.

PUTTING USER TO WORK

I consistently relied on USER as I planned and wrote this book, which should indicate its adaptability: broadly speaking, throughout RTEL I try to *understand* my audience and support their practical interests, *structure* my content in a consistent and accessible way, *engage* readers via my ideas and tone as well as my prose, and *reflect* on my impact in order to improve the end product. To demonstrate a more traditional USER experience, consider how I applied it in connection with the Emerging Technology Lightning Talks Pecha Kucha forum I mentioned in chapter 5. At the event's conclusion, attendees evaluated which talks they wanted to follow up on as a means of identifying useful topics for staff training. Several expressed interest in my topic, ticTOCs, a grant-funded free online journal table of contents tracking service and API created by the UK-based Joint Information Systems Committee (now available as JournalTOCs, www.journaltocs.hw.ac.uk). Table 8.1 explains how I applied USER to create a follow-up hands-on workshop.

REAL-WORLD SCENARIOS

Outlining cases like this is a critical aspect of my strategy to encourage you to bring your own actionable insight to instructional design. Because I cannot tell you exactly how to approach USER in every educational setting, considering your own context transforms the process of learning about the method from passive to productive. The reflection points at the end of chapter 7 encouraged you to keep one or several realistic instructional scenarios in mind as you read through each phase and step of the process—this

might be a current or future teaching project, a not-so-successful workshop or course that merits revising, an outreach strategy you hope to refine, or an existing instructional object that should be evaluated. In the final four chapters I outline each USER step in detail. In order to offer the broadest perspective on how design thinking can scalably affect practice, I use examples and vignettes from my own and others' experiences. Rather than give an unbroken and detached narrative of USER's components, I outline the methodology behind each step and point to its application in a variety of common, real-world library education contexts: rapid/in-depth, small-scale/programmatic, face-to-face/digital. The three main scenarios I use are summarized in table 8.2.

At times I compare all three to provide a big-picture view of scalability in action; otherwise I focus on one to examine an issue with more granularity or use another example altogether. To stimulate your thinking about scenarios you might reflect on as you read, consider how the above examples relate to and differ from your own experience. Use the planning template in appendix A to note reflections on how each step might inform your own planning and execution. And now, on to phase 1: *Understand*.

SUMMARY

- The **USER** method (Understand, Structure, Engage, Reflect) is a rapid, scalable, and learner-focused approach to library instructional design.
- USER is a way to **embed**, **extend**, and **scaffold** a learning interaction.

REFLECTION POINTS

1. Imagine a specific instructional scenario that you will soon be planning or would like to revise. Keep this and potentially a few other scenarios in mind as you read through the final four chapters.

2. Examine the scenario you have identified in relation to the USER method. Walk through how you might approach each phase and step by referring to the brief description on pages 95–96 and table 8.1. Refer to the USER Planning/Reflection Template in appendix A or online at www.alaeditions.org/web extras/ and note what about your current approach

seems to reflect or diverge from USER. Do you already follow a similar process when you plan and deliver instruction? If so, are there areas you privilege more than others? What might you do to balance your efforts?

NOTE

1. James Stronge, *Qualities of Effective Teachers* (Alexandria, VA: Association for Supervision and Curriculum Development, 2007).

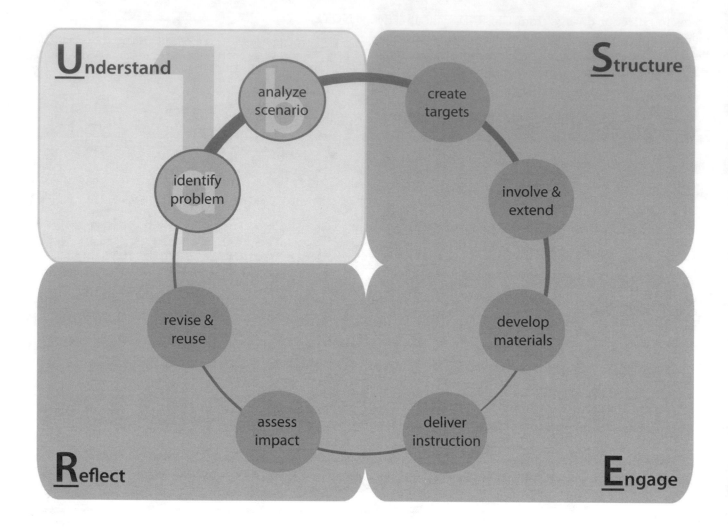

Understand
analyze scenario
identify problem
revise & reuse
Reflect

Structure
create targets
involve & extend
develop materials
deliver instruction
assess impact
Engage

9

Understand

ONE OF THE most consistently challenging aspects of instructional planning is gaining insight into participants and their learning needs. The first USER phase begins with investigating a situation from a learner-centered perspective. In *Understand*, you **identify a problem** that instruction can solve, and then **analyze the scenario** in order to determine an effective solution.

Phase 1: Understand. In the first stage, investigate the learning scenario.	
a. Identify Problem	Find a problem instruction can solve by asking, *What is the challenge learners face, and how can I help them meet it?*
b. Analyze Scenario	Establish needs by **characterizing** and **confronting** each element of instruction: *learner, context, content,* and *educator.*

USER 1a: IDENTIFY THE PROBLEM

The most basic element of a learning scenario or object is its justification, usually referred to in ID literature as the "instructional problem."[1] This is not a problem you anticipate will occur during a learning interaction; rather, it is a problem that instruction can help solve.[2] The instructional problem is a gap in knowledge or understanding in an organization, community, or group, which becomes the foundation upon which you build instructional strategies during the subsequent USER stages. Defining an instructional problem focuses your awareness on the purpose of the interaction or object, and is the quickest route to identifying the intrinsically motivating core of your instructional message.

Identifying instructional problems is rarely difficult—they tend to present themselves regularly. The constant cycle of change that accompanies software, services, and applications in information organizations provides ample opportunities for determining learning needs, which can be as simple as listening to your users and colleagues. If a library plans to redesign its circulation software, staff must learn new workflows to perform their jobs to satisfaction. Explanatory web pages or guides grow out of questions funneled through service points, and challenges are commonly felt and expressed by user types (e.g., citation management for graduate students and faculty, technology instruction for job seekers).

When requests for instruction originate externally, a problem has already been somewhat defined for you—the requestor has identified an issue library instruction can help solve, such as in the first scenario I outlined in chapter 8:

Scenario 1. One-Shot Session	
Instructional Problem	Students need to find subject-appropriate research sources to search, evaluate, and annotate scholarly materials in order to create a class "research archive" and annotated bibliography.
Source	This problem was identified in communication with the course instructor, who submitted her session goals through the web instruction request form.

An external requestor will have their own perspective of the learning problem, which can lead to a differing of opinions on the content that should be covered or to misaligned teaching strategies on your part. Even if the externally defined instructional problem is clear and concise, it is always good practice to communicate strategically with the requestor to learn more about their vision for the interaction. In the one-shot scenario above, the requestor submitted a vaguely defined instructional problem ("they should know

how to use different databases for research and how to get a hold of the materials"). By reading through the syllabus and communicating persistently about what the "research archive" entailed, I was able to refine the problem to include specific discovery skills to support their coursework. If your problem seems too general at first, try a straightforward strategy of refining from the learner perspective to imagine the worst-case outcome if instruction was not provided, such as:

Scenario 1: Students will not develop the necessary research skills and will perform inadequately on course assignments.

Scenario 2: Library staff will remain unaware of the learning management system, and important campus collaborations, content distribution, outreach, and instruction opportunities will not be realized.

Scenario 3: Lower-level undergraduates will lack sufficient knowledge of the characteristics of citation style and resources available to facilitate citation management.

Assessing Needs

Being a useful learning agent in your community requires perceiving and responding to the library, information, and technology needs that you can support. A needs assessment actively identifies the knowledge gaps that confront your organization or learners, in order to identify teaching opportunities that do not originate with an external request. Gary Morrison and his coauthors identify six types of needs that can be assessed: *normative, comparative, felt, expressed, anticipated/future,* and *critical incident.*[3] Table 9.1 provides a brief description of each, examples of when they might arise, and common research or analytical methods for establishing them.

Needs assessments can be in-depth or rapid depending on time and context, and can be conducted formally or informally depending on the scenario. Consider a few informal assessment strategies and the types of need they identify:

Informal Needs Assessments

- Review other libraries' tutorial portals, course schedules, and instructional services pages for instruction ideas. (*comparative*)
- Track student and faculty blogs and Twitter feeds for keywords such as "library," "assign-

ment," and "research" to gain insight into experienced challenges. (*felt*)

- Look for changes in information services and products that could require additional education. (*anticipated*)
- Monitor the economic and social climate in your community to identify the need for adult learning skills such as online job searching and resume writing during a recession. (*anticipated*)
- Identify useful social/technological/productivity tools via gadget and educational technology blogs. (*anticipated*)

Some needs assessments involve more in-depth research. Table 9.2 describes strategies for conducting a more formal needs analysis, many of which can be used for other types of assessment. User research can raise your level of cultural awareness of your learning community. In the Ohio University user study that provided the background for a previous publication, *Informing Innovation* (tinyurl.com/ii-booth), my colleagues and I integrated a learning needs analysis component in our instructional offerings. We found that respondent receptivity to technology-based library tools tended to increase with age and research intensity.[4] Student participants self-evaluated their information skills, rated the effectiveness of features of online tutorials, and noted useful library services. By cross-tabulating these results with demographic characteristics such as major, and enriching this data with open-ended commentary, clear need profiles of different student types emerged that helped instructors question assumptions and identify strategic instructional content areas.

Here are a few suggestions of how you might translate these methods to formal assessments, and the need types they identify:

Table 9.1 Instructional Need Types

NEED	DESCRIPTION	EXAMPLE	REVEALED BY
Normative	Identified by comparing local performance against standardized assessment data	comparing low local SAILS (Standardized Assessment of Information Literacy Skills) or LibQUAL+ scores to national benchmark	• national standards • shared test data
Comparative	identified by less formal comparison of groups	evaluating poor performance of one department versus another in an annual review or workflow assessment	• productivity data • organization insight
Felt	identified as the consciously recognized desire to supplement knowledge or performance	noting responses to a staff survey question "Are there technology topics you wish you were more familiar with?"	• surveys • questionnaires • observation
Expressed	identified by the action-based pursuit of felt needs	tracking registrants for an online workshop on instructional design	• participation • feedback
Anticipated	identified by anticipating knowledge gaps based on future changes	scheduling staff training in a new operating system that will be installed in a number of months	• observation • questionnaires
Critical Incident	related to emergencies or disasters	fire evacuation plan based on local protocol	• risk assessments • organizational mandate

Formal Needs Assessments
- Conduct focus groups with library users to pinpoint trouble areas in the search and research process. (*felt*)
- Examine web analytics and perform usability testing to identify problematic online procedures that could be addressed by digital learning objects. (*anticipated*)
- Use Standardized Assessment of Information Literacy Skills (Project SAILS) or other standardized benchmark data to identify areas of information literacy deficiency. (*normative*)
- Collaborate with faculty to examine learning outcomes within a defined curriculum for research-related needs. (*comparative*)
- Survey library staff to gather suggestions for useful technology learning topics. (*felt*)

In planning the interactive tutorial in scenario 3, I conducted interviews and focus groups with

Table 9.2 Needs Assessment/User Research Strategies

	DESCRIPTION	STRENGTHS	LIMITATIONS
Focus Groups	guided discussion among 6–10 participants to gauge attitudes and beliefs	• provokes in-depth conversation • more efficient than individual interviews	• outside facilitator may be necessary for objectivity and quality
Ethnography/ Participant Observation	close study and/or recording of subjects engaged in tasks or using services in natural environments	• low intrusion on participants • realistic picture of user behavior • produces rich immersive descriptions	• observer can impact participant behavior • not all tasks can be easily observed • time intensive • difficult to collate observer data
Interviews	structured communication typically with one subject	• produces personal, detailed feedback • can allow for flexibility and greater depth of information	• time intensive • low participation levels • hard to interpret and analyze • interviewer can influence response
Case Studies	long-term observation of a single population or case	• provides in-depth information • change over time • offers multiple perspectives	• potentially expensive • long-term commitment • limited generalizability of results • narrowly focused
Questionnaires and Surveys	online, onsite, or telephone surveys using closed and open-ended questions	• large sample size • easy to analyze • produces consistent results	• impersonal • difficult to achieve desired response rates • may require incentives
Formal Action Research	problem-based reflective process of data gathering and analysis	• dynamic and results-driven • productively focused • involves multiple research techniques	• complex process • involves multiple stakeholders and teamwork

Source: Adapted from Char Booth, *Informing Innovation: Tracking Student Interest in Emerging Library Technologies at Ohio University* (Chicago: Association of College and Research Libraries, 2009), www.ala.org/ala/mgrps/divs/acrl/publications/digital/ii-booth.pdf, 31.

undergraduates to establish their learning needs related to citation and style guides. Often, formal and informal assessment methods overlap in a single project. In scenario 2, in addition to on-the-fly information gathering and observation, I administered an online survey that gauged staff proficiency with and interest in the Berkeley learning management system (bSpace). Results provided perspective on attitudes and experiences using the LMS in instruction and collaboration, and insight into training formats and learning goals (figure 9.1).

Useful feedback such as "I would like to have a better understanding of how students and faculty are using bSpace, and how the library can infiltrate" to "interesting ideas for how library instructors can better integrate into bSpace without taking hours and hours" outlined clear knowledge gaps and provided rich content detail for training. I grouped common responses and specified three main instructional problems that could be addressed by workshops, consultations, and digital learning objects:

Scenario 2. LMS Training Initiative	
Instructional Problems	Library staff require proficiency in the campus LMS in order to use it more effectively in 1) course-related/integrated instruction, 2) faculty outreach, and 3) organizational collaboration.
Source of Need	Online survey and informal observation identified consistent felt and anticipated needs among staff to learn more about features and functionality.

USER 1b: ANALYZE THE SCENARIO

Even if two classes or trainings cover the same subject, slight differences in the elements of instruction—such as time of day or e-learning platform—can interact to create an entirely new learning dynamic. Gaining perspective on the distinguishing aspects of a scenario is a method of understanding how it lends itself to customization. This is the goal of the second USER

step, *Understand* 1b. After determining the problem that learning can address, you analyze the scenario by considering the four elements of instruction: *learner, content, context,* and *educator.* Scenario analysis continues the information-gathering focus of the needs assessment, but hones in on practical details that allow you to develop an informed response.

In business, a SWOT analysis is a method of identifying strengths, weaknesses, opportunities, and threats related to a venture. Analyzing an instructional scenario is similar, but is simplified to *characterizing* and *confronting* each instructional element. Characterization establishes basic, objective qualities (e.g., how many participants, topics to be covered), while confrontation imagines any challenges that might occur (e.g., browser incompatibilities, lack of motivation). By the end of this step, you will have hammered out instructional specifics at the same time that you have anticipated problems. Characterization and confrontation can be accomplished by asking a straightforward question about each element at the outset of this step. I provide examples of this in each scenario analysis subsection below.

Element 1: Learner Analysis

The more insight you gain into your participants, the more prepared you will be to share information that benefits them. The assessment methods you used to define an instructional problem in USER 1a can easily support this process. For example, in the scenario 2 staff survey I used to establish instructional problems related to the LMS, I also asked questions related to attendees' backgrounds, frustrations they endured with the system, learning objects and topics that would interest them, and goals they had for improvement.

Characterize Learners: *What are my participants' needs and potential areas of motivation?*

The Ohio University research project I mentioned earlier in the chapter revealed interesting distinctions between learner populations. For example, whereas a large number of undergraduates indicated that it would be useful for them to use library tools in the course management system, far fewer graduate students indicated the same. The survey also revealed motivational differences among learners based on their characteristics; some were more intrinsically interested in in-depth learning opportunities and technologies. Staff were able to use this data to strategically highlight the most useful skills and services during instruction and marketing.

According to Harold Gardner, "Because of their biological and cultural backgrounds, personal histories, and idiosyncratic experiences [learners] possess different kinds of minds, with different strengths, interests, and modes of processing information."[5] Effective instructors recognize that people learn differently, and that not all participants will benefit from every strategy they present or dialogue they facilitate. There are several schools of thought on this concept, all of which focus on the same core idea: people have styles and preferences around learning, which requires responding with differentiated instruction. *Multiple intelligences theory* isolates eight distinct intelligences: linguistic (writer), logical-mathematic (engineer), spatial (architect), musical (composer), bodily-kinesthetic (athlete), naturalist (zoologist), interpersonal (psychologist), and intrapersonal (self-insight).[6] Although educators tend to reflect their own strength areas pedagogically, making an effort to address each category provides a useful framework for differentiation. Gardner recommends using six "points of entry" to span multiple intelligences during instruction:[7]

Narrational: Appeals to learners who are engaged by stories and narratives. Strategy: Use personalized and vivid allegories and examples.

Quantitative/numerical: Appeals to learners who are interested in numbers and empirical conclusions. Strategy: Use statistical, logical, or data-driven examples.

Foundational/existential: Appeals to philosophical or big-picture thinkers. Strategy: Pose challenging and critical questions.

Aesthetic: Appeals to visually oriented learners. Strategy: Use images, multimedia, and reliable visual design strategies.

Hands-on: Appeals to learners engaged by activity. Strategy: Use multiple exercises to break up a learning interaction.

Social: Appeals to learners who prefer interpersonal engagement. Strategy: Incorporate learner/instructor interactivity and group engagement.

To facilitate reaching several points of entry in a brief learning scenario, select fewer topics and examine them in more depth, and communicate your instructional message from multiple perspectives. An approach known as *universal design for learning* presents three simplified differentiation strategies:[8]

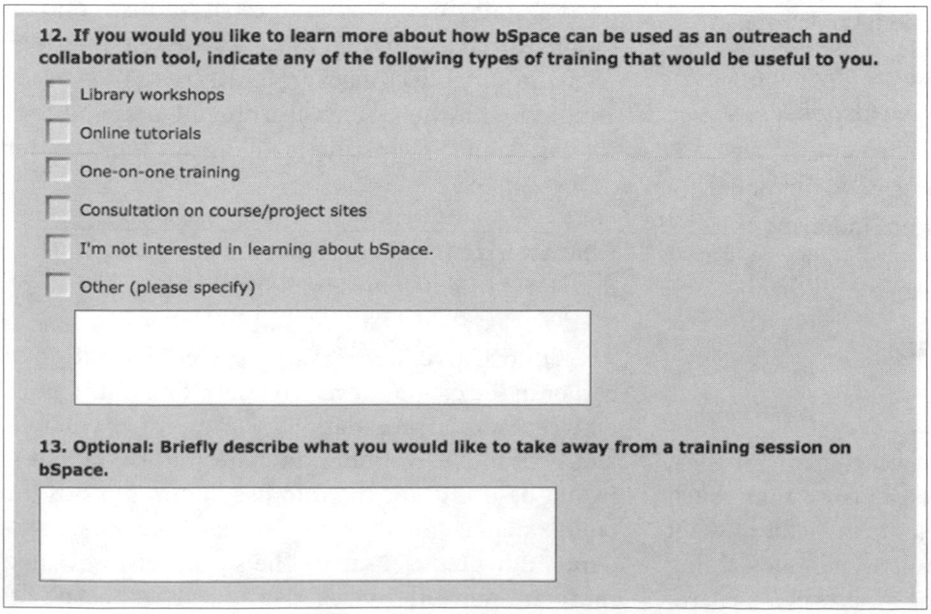
12. If you would you like to learn more about how bSpace can be used as an outreach and collaboration tool, indicate any of the following types of training that would be useful to you.

- Library workshops
- Online tutorials
- One-on-one training
- Consultation on course/project sites
- I'm not interested in learning about bSpace.
- Other (please specify)

13. Optional: Briefly describe what you would like to take away from a training session on bSpace.

Figure 9.1

Staff LMS survey (detail)

Activity 9.1 **Barriers to Learning**			
Example: Staff LMS training	feeling of information overload or lack of relevancy	low morale due to frustration with new workflows and tasks	attendees confused by disciplinary-specific language or assumed knowledge
1)			
2)			

- Provide multiple and flexible methods of **presentation** to give students with diverse learning styles equivalent opportunities to engage with the material.
- Provide multiple and flexible means of **expression** to provide diverse students with alternatives for demonstrating what they have learned.
- Provide multiple and flexible means of **engagement** to tap into diverse learners' interests, challenge them, and motivate them.

Confront Learners: *What are my participants' potential barriers to learning?*

Just as individuals have preferred learning styles, we also have unique learning barriers. If you teach or present, it is likely that from time to time (or perhaps perpetually) you sense that participants are struggling or not as attentive as you would like, or you might receive feedback that some aspect of instruction was off the mark or difficult to grasp. At these times, I try to reflect on my own less-than-ideal learning experiences to better identify with frustrated or bored learners. I can recall many instances where one thing or another worked against my own attention or motivation during an interaction. Learning barriers can be inherent (a learning disability), developmental (teen angst), temporal (a hard day), or situational (technophobia). These are the internal and external issues, distractions, complexes, and perceptions that keep all of us from engaging with an instructor or learning object. Some learning barriers are independent of instruction, while others are created by teachers and designers—you might unintentionally sequence information out of logical order, or speak too rapidly for an audience to follow.

I have observed that effective educators tend to anticipate and break down learning barriers among their audiences with simple contingency planning. In activity 9.1, think about a learning situation or

two you have participated in or are planning for and imagine three associated barriers. In this example, I list three potential issues associated with scenario 2 trainings. If you are not yet actively teaching, list barriers to learning you yourself have experienced. You can use this foresight to address barriers during later stages of planning.

If recording your design process is productive, you can collect your thoughts in a simple grid as you characterize and confront each element of instruction. Table 9.3 outlines brief learner analyses of my first two instructional scenarios.

Element 2: Context Analysis

Context analysis involves surveying the environment of instruction. This type of analysis will vary depending on the scope of the learning interaction, but is always oriented toward covering your logistical bases and thinking through their best arrangement both physically and digitally. Determining contextual characteristics is aided by experiential investigation. Meeting collaborators or requestors in person or via phone, testing an e-learning platform, or physically taking stock of a presentation or teaching room are all methods of understanding the learning environment to establish a comfort level prior to the interaction.

Characterize Context: *What do I know about the instructional environment, and how can it be shaped to create a positive learning experience?*

Once you have established the instructional problem and performed learner analysis, you will be in a better position to determine a suitable response in terms of the context and resources available. If you are embarking on a larger or programmatic project, this requires considering staff coordination, timeline, scope, team dynamics, and other specifics. In a one-shot workshop, this is the time to make sure you have the syllabus or research assignment well beforehand, your

Table 9.3 **Learner Analysis Grid**				
	ATTRIBUTES	**MOTIVATION**	**PRIOR KNOWLEDGE**	**BARRIERS**
Scenario 1	• 20 1st-/2nd-year undergrads • non–major specific • "pretty quiet"	• understand and complete assignment for credit • low intrinsic motivation	• minimal library experience • in-class discussion of research process	• low prior experience with college-level research • potential preconception of proficiency
Scenario 2	• library staff, selectors/liaisons • various levels of technical proficiency	• use the LMS for faculty/student outreach, instruction, e-reserves • high intrinsic motivation	• extremely varied levels of LMS use • basic awareness of bSpace as campus system	• low perceived daily relevance • perceptions of outreach challenges among faculty • technology fatigue

room is booked, you have what you need in terms of computers, etc. When characterizing the context for the series of staff trainings in scenario 2, I used the information from the employee survey on preferred instructional formats (face-to-face workshops and online learning objects) to consider the practical elements of *space*, *technology*, *collaboration*, and *marketing* required for the series of face-to-face workshops and supplementary e-learning sites. From this, I was able to list the necessary contextual steps for shaping the learning environment.

Scenario 2: LMS Staff Workshop Context Characteristics

Spaces

- Book training rooms based on expected attendance (8–15 per session).
- Check and confirm RSVPs.

Technology

- Check software on instructor/learner computer stations.
- Create project sites for each workshop.
- Pose forum questions for learners to consider before workshop.

Collaboration

- Work with educational technology services staff to vet content.
- Ask for development feedback from attendees within my department.

Marketing

- Identify staff e-mail lists to post workshop list and times.

- Use word-of-mouth to increase interest.
- Develop half-sheet handout of workshops and times to distribute at meetings and via e-mail.

Surveying the context of instruction helped me realize that I could use the LMS to foster a blended learning environment by creating "project sites" for each workshop that allowed me to communicate with participants before the interaction, share content, and provide a backdrop during live instruction. Moreover, these sites doubled as an authentic demonstration of the LMS user experience for training attendees.

Confront Context: *Does additional troubleshooting or information gathering need to occur?*

Troubleshooting problems in the learning environment is usually spread over the entire planning and delivery process, but anticipating issues early helps prevent the most avoidable. Even when the teaching or design is a solo endeavor, this often entails some degree of collaboration, as in coordinating with an instructional requestor or IT staff to square things away. On the technological side, contextual troubleshooting requires considering disability access, updates, and installations prior to an interaction. At its simplest, this step is a good point to list contingencies that will reduce the likelihood of misfires.

Scenario 2: LMS Staff Workshop Context Contingencies

- Touch base with participants after their RSVP to make sure they are able to log into the system without issue.

- Remind attendees about workshop the morning of via email.
- Arrive in the classroom at least fifteen minutes early to test equipment, connections.
- Review workshop site prior to live instruction to make sure it is functioning/displaying correctly.

Element 3: Content Analysis

Analyzing the content of instruction requires you to broadly characterize the knowledge, skills, and attitudes (KSAs) you want participants to gain from the interaction, as well as confront the prerequisites required of them to be able to do so.[9] At this point, you reconsider your instructional problem balanced against the characteristics and needs of your audience, established earlier in the *Understand* phase.

Characterize: *What are the KSAs I want to result from instruction?*

Determining KSAs should be relatively straightforward; they are the basic, need-to-know aspects of your scenario that provide the solution of your instructional problem. Consider, in an ideal world, the knowledge and skills learners would gain as a result of participating in the experience, and how you hope influence their attitudes. In the next USER phase, *Structure,* creating targets (goals, objectives, and outcomes) and designing activities helps you translate these KSAs into more teachable form, so it is not necessary to worry about being overly specific at this point. Consider the KSAs I identified for scenario 1:

Scenario 1: One-Shot Session

Knowledge. Difference between peer-reviewed and popular literature. Organization of information resources within the library website. Familiarity with the process of annotating a research source.

Skills. Finding scholarly information through library and web interfaces. Evaluating an article for its relevance to a given research topic. E-mailing, downloading, and saving articles and citations. Creating a bank of searchable keywords.

Attitudes. Libraries are navigable and useful. Librarians are savvy, challenging, and approachable. Finding and evaluating resources is doable, even when I start from

Google. Research is interesting, or at least necessary.

Confront: *Is there prerequisite knowledge in this scenario?*

You should also consider what prior knowledge and skills are essential for participants to engage successfully with the content of instruction. Considering this contingency is an excellent means of analyzing your content from the learner's perspective prior to the next step, when you begin to design learning materials in earnest. The rule of scalability applies in this case, as well. Advanced instructional design training requires some knowledge of the theoretical concepts covered in chapters 4–6. If a learning interaction is more basic, its prerequisites will likely also be basic.

Scenario 1: One-Shot Session

Prerequisites. Familiarity with course texts and assignment. Facility with computers and browsers. Awareness of research topic and tacit understanding of types of research materials.

Element 4: Educator Analysis

Of all the elements in the scenario analysis process, this is the one I find the easiest. Educator analysis is geared toward recognizing your own resources and constraints by identifying template learning objects that are available to streamline subsequent design steps and determining if you need to supplement your own KSAs prior to instruction.

Characterize: *What resources can I review and reuse to assist me with this project?*

Educator analysis helps you, in essence, recycle. By reviewing information sources related to your subject and evaluating existing learning objects, you identify time-saving elements you can bring into the planning process. In chapter 3 I discussed maintaining a gleaning orientation to your environment; deft instructors recognize ways to streamline their pedagogy by (respectfully and consensually) incorporating external objects and reusing their own adaptable resources. This could involve anything from asking a colleague who had designed a successful tutorial for her source files, to embedding a video from another library into a local online course guide (this type of reuse mentality is the final step of *Reflect*, in order to encourage the process of designing with an eye to the future).

The resources you identify will differ significantly depending on the situation, clearly demonstrated by comparing my three example scenarios:

Scenario 1: One-Shot Session

- Duplicate a prior online course guide and replace outdated content with new workshop-specific elements.
- Use a handout template to customize exercises and language to better match subject area content.

Scenario 2: LMS Training

- Look over predecessor's related training materials and consider the success of her approach.
- Ask educational technology services staff for their workshop slide and image templates to maintain consistent branding.
- Create workshop collaboration site and in-class handouts in modifiable form; revise for each new workshop.

Scenario 3: Revised Citation Tutorial

- Consult updated citation style tutorials and guides for ideas and inspiration.
- Review other instructional objects for branding, stock campus images, resource screenshots, etc. to bring into existing navigation, image, and design elements.

Confront: *Are there knowledge, skills, or attitudes that I need to acquire?*

In this final aspect of scenario analysis, reflect on your own knowledge, skills, and attitudes in order to confront whether you need additional preparation. It may seem obvious, but you should know your content and teaching technologies well enough to be able to function confidently during instructional design and delivery. In a fast-changing profession, this is easier said than done. Because it is continually challenging to develop new expertise when you teach and train frequently, approaching your own KSAs on a case-by-case basis is a more resource-conscious way to prepare.

In scenario 2, at the time of developing the training initiative I knew relatively little about bSpace, having only recently arrived on campus. I knew that it would take time to become truly expert with the system, so I found that it was useful to identify specific functional areas to focus on for each workshop based on their topical coverage. In my content analysis phase I determined that several of the learner KSAs involved document uploading and linking options within the LMS. I therefore had to identify all of the available methods for posting content within the LMS, which included uploading PDFs, linking to subscription resources, batch uploading using an FTP site, creating a "citation list" via Google Scholar, and importing references from RefWorks or Zotero.

At times this will require the input of external collaborators. Confronting my own KSAs in the LMS training scenario also required consulting with *subject matter experts* in several ways. In formal instructional design models, the subject matter expert plays a central role. Often, professional instructional designers are hired to create learning materials in complex technical fields in which they themselves have no training, meaning that relying on the input of local experts becomes key to understanding instructional needs and content.[10] In USER, the subject matter expert plays a less prominent role based on the rapid, embedded, and/or resource-scarce nature of the teaching and training we tend to deliver, but it is still critical to evaluate external human resources that can provide guidance. These are individuals that may or may not be your primary co-teachers or collaborators, but who have greater topical insight and can identify issues in your instructional materials or suggest how you might shore up your content knowledge. In the same scenario, I ran my template exercises, workshop sites, and outlines past trainers in the Educational Technology Services office for their feedback, and asked them to sit in on my workshops to triage any misinformation I unwittingly shared and answer participant questions that were beyond my depth.

To identify instructor KSAs, review your learner, content, and context analyses to identify specific areas in which you could benefit from greater understanding. To illustrate how this can differ in rapid and in-depth instructional planning, compare my requisite KSAs in the tutorial scenario compared to the one-shot scenario:

Scenario 3: Flash Citation Tutorial

- Become more conversant with ActionScript 3.0 and find a quality Flash hacks book.
- Review process for importing .wav files and creating looping sound effects.
- Look into scripts and events for importing external video.

- Search for new developments on Flash accessibility; consider transcription or other methods that could make content more usable for the visually impaired.

Scenario 1: One-Shot Session Instructor KSAs

- Familiarize myself with assigned course texts.
- Read documentation on using the LMS forums tool for class discussion exercise.
- Brush up on theater/fine arts article databases.
- Run a few canned searches as backups if learner-suggested searches fall flat.

A closing thought on the value of confronting instructor KSAs: Beyond shoring up skills and knowledge, it can be extremely productive to examine any extant or potential negativity in your attitudes toward an instructional interaction; any number of internal and external conflicts can derail an otherwise sanguine planning process. Critically examining anxiety, frustration, or antipathy associated with an instructional project becomes a conscious step in the process of overcoming it. The second USER phase, *Structure*, is the point at which design begins in earnest—if you enter it with understanding as well as positivity, planning will proceed with greater ease.

PHASE 1: UNDERSTAND SUMMARY

- The first phase of the USER method, **understand**, consists of two steps: (a) **identifying a problem** that instruction can solve, and (b) **analyzing the scenario** to determine how to create an effective solution.
- An **instructional problem** is the fundamental knowledge gap that can be addressed by learning.
- Performing a **needs analysis** is a means of identifying instructional problems.
- Analyzing the scenario consists of **characterizing** and **confronting** each element of instruction—learner, content, context, and educator—in order to understand instructional needs and engage in contingency thinking.
- Identifying **learning barriers** helps you anticipate and troubleshoot obstacles to understanding and engagement.

- **Differentiated instruction** appeals to multiple intelligences and learning styles.
- **Subject matter experts** are individuals better versed in topical content who can assist in identifying your own knowledge gaps.

REFLECTION POINT

1. You've been hired straight out of library school to work for the instructional services department in a main library at a large research university. A budget crisis is looming, the department is two teachers down, and everyone is complaining about the crazy amount of work. Even though you just arrived, your colleagues have asked you to jump in immediately as an instructor in basic information literacy classes for a required freshman English course. This means you're going to have analyze the scenario, fast. Where do you start? List a few resources that might help you rapidly gather information on each factor of instruction: learner, context, content, and educator. If it is useful, use step 1b of the USER template in appendix A to record your ideas.

NOTES

1. Gary Morrison, Steven Ross, and Jerrold Kemp, *Designing Effective Instruction*, 5th ed. (Hoboken, NJ: Wiley, 2007), 31.
2. Robert Gagné, Walter Wager, Katherine Golas, and John Keller, *Principles of Instructional Design*, 5th ed. (Belmont, CA: Thomson/Wadsworth, 2005), 23.
3. Morrison, Ross, and Kemp, *Designing Effective Instruction*, 33–36.
4. Char Booth, *Informing Innovation: Tracking Student Interest in Emerging Library Technologies at Ohio University* (Chicago: Association of College and Research Libraries, 2009), www.ala.org/ala/mgrps/divs/acrl/publications/digital/ii-booth.pdf.
5. Harold Gardner, "Multiple Approaches to Understanding," in Charles Reigeluth (ed.), *Instructional Design Theories and Models: A New Paradigm of Instructional Theory*, vol. 2 (Mahwah, NJ: Lawrence Erlbaum, 1999), 69–89.
6. Ibid., 78.
7. Ibid., 81–82.
8. National Universal Design for Learning Task Force, "Universal Design for Learning," 2007, www.advocacyinstitute.org/UDL/.
9. Gagné et al., *Principles*, 25.
10. Morrison, Ross, and Kemp, *Designing Effective Instruction*, 18.

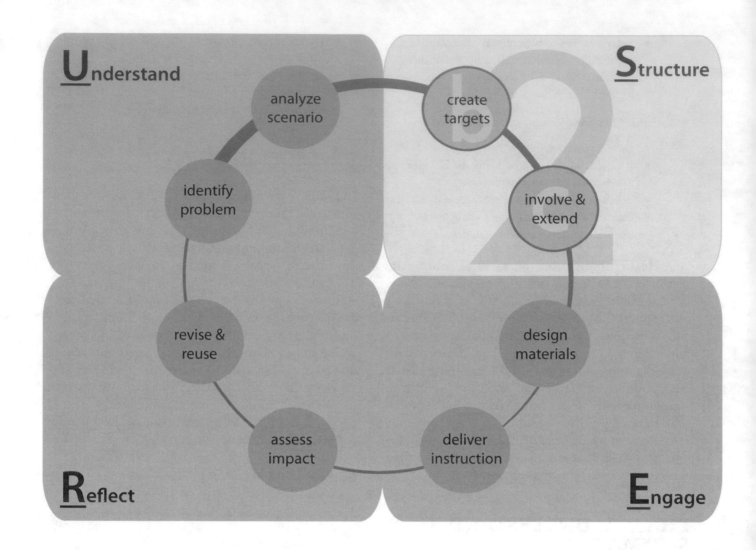

Structure

IN THE SECOND phase of USER, *Structure*, you focus on outcomes and activities to translate the information gathered during the previous phase into a measurable and interactive experience. Charles Reigeluth and James Moore recommend considering the *type, focus, control, grouping, interactions,* and *support* for learning during instructional planning.[1] These elements provide a backdrop for the two steps in this phase: (c) **creating targets** determines the type and focus of learning, and (d) **involving participants** addresses the control, grouping, and interactions, while **extending the interaction** determines the support.

Phase 2: Structure. Specify the content of learning and create engagement and support strategies.	
c. Create Targets	Define **targets** in the form of goals, objectives, and outcomes that organize content and provide a backdrop for learner evaluation.
d. Involve and Extend	Determine ways to (a) **involve learners** using differentiated delivery techniques, technologies, and activities, and (b) **extend the interaction** through scaffolding and support along the continuum of learning.

USER 2c: CREATE TARGETS

Questions to Consider

Type of Learning. Does the content of instruction lend itself to memorization, skill application, relationship understanding, and/or critical inquiry?

Focus of Learning. Is the focus of the session interdisciplinary, topic, problem, or domain knowledge?

Creating targets—*goals*, *objectives*, and *outcomes*—is essential to design because it allows you to imagine the impact of instruction from the perspective of the educator (goals) and the learner (objectives and outcomes). Targets organize the knowledge, skills, and attitudes specified in the *Understand* phase into content units and instructional strategies, and provide the criteria to assess learning during and after instruction. They are also a framework for guiding student understanding and metacognitive awareness.

Knowledge Dimensions

Instructional design operates on the premise that different kinds of knowledge construction are supported by different teaching strategies, and that it is important to use targets that align the two. Creating targets begins by examining the types of knowledge learners will build during the interaction. One approach to this process is to divide the KSAs you specified in *Understand* 1b into one of four *knowledge dimensions*: factual, procedural, conceptual, or metacognitive (table 10.1).[2] Facts and procedures represent lower-order thought or "simple recall of information," whereas concepts and metacognitive/reflective strategies represent higher-order thought, or "intellectual activity." Most of your KSAs can be readily identified among these categories, from the procedure of locating a database or conducting an advanced search, to the fact of a proxy URL, to the concept of evidence-based practice. Different pedagogical methods are better suited to each dimension: facts and processes are effectively taught using direct instruction with elements of active learner participation and reinforcement; concepts and metacognitive strategies are better acquired through critical questioning, problem scenarios, and discovery learning.

Linking KSAs to knowledge dimensions is particularly useful in structuring tutorials and other types of e-learning objects. For example, one of the

Table 10.1 **Knowledge Dimensions**				
	DEFINITION	**EXAMPLE**	**COGNITIVE LEVEL**	**STRATEGY**
Factual	declarative associations between pieces of information	the Learning Commons is open 24 hours.	lower-order	• mnemonics • direct instruction • repetition
Procedural	a series of steps undertaken to achieve a specific result	to log in, click the MyAccount link and enter your library ID and password.	lower-order	• problem-based or authentic learning • demonstration and active learning
Conceptual	qualities, attributes, or characteristics shared by a group of entities, or that create links between concepts	information sources should be evaluated to establish their credibility, relevance, and reliability.	higher-order	• deduction (rule-example) • induction (example-rule) • problem-based or simulation
Metacognitive	reflective awareness of performance, preference, and thought processes	I should cite sources in order to avoid plagiarism.	higher-order	• problem-based or simulation • questioning

components of scenario 2 is a faculty-focused online course space that profiles different methods of providing access to online course readings. In addition to developing conceptual awareness of copyright regulations and the "four-factor analysis" that helps determine fair use, linking and uploading involves procedures such as finding stable URLs in article databases and metacognitive skills such as self-awareness of intellectual property infringement. In table 10.2, I organize the KSAs from this aspect of scenario 2 by knowledge dimension as a precursor to writing targets.

Task Analysis

Many of the skills outlined in your KSAs likely fall into the procedural knowledge category, which is almost inevitable in our navigation and discovery-heavy line of teaching. You can conduct a *task analysis* to plot out the series of steps required for a learner to master a skill. Task analysis is primarily a way to familiarize yourself with the progression of action and thought behind a skill from the learner's perspective, which reduces the risk of incorrectly assuming prior knowledge and supports your ability to demonstrate processes clearly in analog interactions and digital learning objects. In the scenario 2 course space I described in the previous section, the procedures column in table 10.2 identifies the four "tasks" (e.g., procedures or skills): (1) locate stable URLs, (2) link to subscription resources, (3) create accessible digital documents, and (4) upload files to the resources area. A sample analysis of the fourth task:

Task 4: Upload files to the resources area.

> Step 1. Navigate to bspace.berkeley.edu.

> Step 2. Log into the course management system using your campus ID.

Step 3. Access the appropriate course site by clicking on its named tab in your personal workspace.

Step 4. Click the "Resources" link from the "Course Tools" menu on the left-hand side of the course site interface.

Step 5. Locate the "Add" drop-down menu in the resources file structure.

Step 6. Select the "Upload Files" option.

Step 7. Browse the desktop or other directory for the file to be uploaded.

Step 8. Click "Open" to select the appropriate file.

Step 9. Edit the document display name.

Step 10. If desired, use the drop-down box on the confirmation screen to indicate the copyright status of the document.

Step 11. Click the "Upload Files Now" button.

Your procedural steps should be able to double as how-to instructions on a help or FAQ page. A task analysis can also easily be scaled up or down for rapid or in-depth contexts. In rapid planning situations, break each task down into a numbered list in order to perceive the progression of steps required of the learner to successfully perform the skill: For more in-depth or complex planning contexts or in cases where the learner simply needs more detail, tasks can be broken down into subtasks, steps, and substeps ad infinitum.

Scenario 2, Task 1 Subdivision: Locate stable URLs.

- Subtask A. Navigate to the library website and click on the "Articles" link.

> Step 1. Open a web browser.

Table 10.2 **Course Content by Knowledge Dimension**			
FACTS	**PROCEDURES**	**CONCEPTS**	**METACOGNITION**
• file size limits • proxy address • licensing specifications	• locate stable URLs • link to subscription resources • create accessible digital documents • upload files to the Resources area	• library linking • intellectual property • ADA accessibility • four-factor analysis	• awareness of "golden rule" of fair use • personal liability and risk assessment • commitment to open content

Substep a. Double-click on the Firefox, Internet Explorer, Safari, etc. icon on your desktop or dock (Mac), or in your lower-left hand Start menu under the Internet heading (Windows).

Step 2. Enter www.lib.berkeley.edu in the navigation bar.

Step 3. Etc…

- Subtask B. Select a subscription database using the subject or alphabetical listing.
- Subtask C. Enter search terms and execute search.
- Subtask D. Scan results list for citation and click title to navigate to the item record.
- Subtask E. Determine if the article is available in full-text PDF or HTML.
- Subtask F. Scan record for stable linking language such as "persistent URL," "stable link," or "link to this article."

Write Targets

After considering the knowledge dimensions and potentially conducting a task analysis (or neither if you are in a rush), you are ready to create targets. Each target is a guide for intentional practice; instead of simply assuming that learning will occur, you use goals, outcomes, and objectives to encourage and measure it. Approaches to creating targets vary greatly in the education literature; mine is comparatively simple and flexible. In the USER method, *goals* focus you on your instructional role; *objectives* organize content into activities and content units; and *outcomes* describe how participants are substantively different because of the knowledge they have gained. In terms of scalability, objectives are the most essential target because they are highly functional in subsequent USER steps. In an in-depth scenario, you can create a detailed series of goals, objectives, and outcomes related to each topical area; in a rapid scenario you can limit yourself to three quick objectives that you communicate to students at the outset of the interaction as an advance organizer or during your instructional message.

GOALS

Goals are straightforward and should be written from your perspective. Consider the aspirations for the object or interaction by asking yourself reflective questions: *What do I hope to achieve in this interaction?*

What is the value of the instruction for participants, my organization, and myself? What will help me focus on the core of my message and minimize digressions? What instructor characteristics will encourage meaningful learning? Work elements into your goals that help you reflect as you develop learning objects and deliver instruction. For example, my goals for the faculty course space in scenario 2:

LMS Course: Goals

1. Translate the complicated linking and uploading options into a viable online access strategy.

2. Reduce the financial and environmental waste associated with physical course packets and increase use of library licensed content.

3. Raise instructor awareness of copyright and fair educational use standards.

OBJECTIVES

Objectives often require more thought than goals or outcomes, because they provide the framework for lessons and activities in the next step and suggest the criteria for learner assessment in the final phase (chapter 12). Thorough objectives are learner-focused, action-oriented statements that provide the concrete criteria to evaluate if learning has occurred. *Bloom's taxonomy* is the de facto approach to creating educational objectives, and is somewhat similar to the process of considering knowledge dimensions outlined earlier in the chapter. The taxonomy divides learning into three domains: *cognitive, affective,* and *psychomotor.*[3] Affective (emotional) and psychomotor (kinesthetic) learning tend to fall outside the scope of library instruction; I focus here on the cognitive (thought) domain.

Within the cognitive domain, Bloom classifies six levels of thinking skills: *knowledge, comprehension, application, analysis, synthesis,* and *evaluation.* Lower-order thinking occurs in the first three levels (*knowledge, comprehension,* and *application*); higher-order thinking occurs in the last three (*analysis, synthesis,* and *evaluation*).

In 2001, Lorin Anderson and David Krathwohl published a "revised" taxonomy that gives a more contemporary and active focus to Bloom's original categories, shown in table 10.3.[4] The higher a task falls on the scale, the more cognitively immersive it becomes; it

Table 10.3 **Bloom's Revised Taxonomy**	
Lower-Order	1. *Remembering:* Retrieving, recognizing, and recalling relevant knowledge from long-term memory
	2. *Understanding:* Constructing meaning from oral, written, and graphic messages through interpreting, exemplifying, classifying, summarizing, inferring, comparing, and explaining
	3. *Applying:* Carrying out or using a procedure
Higher-Order	4. *Analyzing:* Breaking material into constituent parts, determining how the parts relate to one another and to an overall purpose through differentiating, organizing, and attributing
	5. *Evaluating:* Making judgments based on criteria and standards through checking and critiquing
	6. *Creating:* Putting elements together to form a coherent or functional whole; reorganizing elements into a new pattern or structure through generating, planning, or producing

takes much deeper intellectual activity to storyboard an instructional video (*creating*) or critique a colleague's instructional performance (*evaluating*) than it does to memorize the phases and steps of USER method (*remembering*). Factual learning occurs at the lower classification levels of *remembering* and *understanding*, procedural and critical thinking tends to occur at the mid-range *application* through *evaluation* levels, and theoretical and creative applications tend to occur at the higher levels of *evaluation* and *creation*. You can draw on specific action verbs at each cognitive level to assist you in creating corresponding objectives:

Remembering: define, list, state, list, memorize, recall, repeat, duplicate, reproduce

Understanding: discuss, classify, describe, explain, identify, locate, paraphrase, label

Applying: choose, find, select, demonstrate, employ, illustrate, interpret, operate, solve, use

Analyzing: differentiate, appraise, compare, contrast, discriminate, distinguish, examine

Evaluating: appraise, critique, review, evaluate, argue, defend, judge, support

Creating: assemble, produce, remix, construct, create, author, design, develop, formulate, write

Jerilyn Veldof recommends that objectives contain three elements—a condition for the action to take place, an action, and a performance standard related to the action.[3] The three following examples are written highlighting each of these elements, a *condition* (*italics*), one or more **actions (bold)**, and a performance standard (underlined):

LMS Course: Objectives

1. *Given access to bSpace and a computer,* the faculty member will be able to **upload** ADA-accessible files to the Resources area of a course site. (taxonomy level: Understanding, Applying)

2. *Provided access to a library subscription database,* the faculty member will be able to **locate and link** to stable URLs in the Resources area of a course site. (taxonomy level: Applying, Analyzing)

3. *When confronted with an online course materials use case,* the faculty member will be able to **execute** a four-factor analysis of a given e-text and **defend** its acceptance or rejection as fair educational use based on that analysis. (taxonomy level: Analyzing, Evaluating)

Although Bloom's taxonomy is successive, meaning that learners progress from one level to the next as expertise is gained, aiming for the "top" is not the end goal of learning classification. A learning interaction or object should blend lower- and higher-order content to step learners from one level to the next, and need not span all levels to be effective. A simple method for differentiating instruction is to create objectives that involve higher-order as well as lower-order engagement and appeal to different learning styles. Think about strategies along the taxonomy for teaching the concept of peer review to lower-level undergraduates in a one-shot session. On the one hand, you could list the characteristics of a scholarly article via a slide-assisted lecture or other method and ask learners a few questions at the end of the lesson to gauge their comprehension (understanding), then later evaluate recall of these characteristics using an item or two on multiple-choice assessment at the end of the session (remembering). On the other hand, you could facilitate a critical discussion exploring the difference between scholarly and popular literature (understanding), then ask students to work in pairs to identify examples of scholarly and nonscholarly articles (analyzing) *without* using the "limit to peer review" function in a given database (applying), and then support their rationale as they demonstrate article choices to the entire group (evaluating). These two examples ostensibly achieve the same concept knowledge, but the former is a direct approach rooted in lower-order functions, whereas the latter is discovery-based and creates a more cognitively engaged interaction.

OUTCOMES

Outcomes are as similarly straightforward as goals. They are the actionable, real-world result of the interaction, which I find are often my own goals mirrored from the learner's perspective. To determine outcomes, consider how the knowledge, skills, and attitudes of instruction will carry into authentic contexts continuing with the prior example from scenario 2.

LMS Course: Outcomes

1. Faculty will provide more online course material through open access and library subscriptions.

2. Faculty will more consistently provide low-cost course readings.

3. Faculty will make informed decisions around fair educational use standards.

USER 2d: INVOLVE AND EXTEND

Questions to Consider

Control of Learning. Which areas of the interaction will be teacher centered (direct instruction), and which will be more student centered (discovery instruction)?

Grouping for Learning. Will you ask learners to work as individuals, pairs, teams, or groups?

Interactions for Learning. Will you create learning interactions that are human (student/teacher, student/student, other) or nonhuman (student/tools, student/information, student/environment, other)?

Support for Learning. Will you provide cognitive support or emotional support?

In the second step of the *Structure* phase (USER 2d) you construct your lesson by choosing the techniques and technologies you will use to **involve learners** and **extend the interaction**. You already have a solid sense of the elements of instruction from the *Understand* phase and a sense of your targets from the previous *Structure* step; you now select pedagogical methods and student-focused activities that differentiate instruction and create a delivery approach (*Engage*) and assessment plan (*Reflect*).

Involve: Choosing Strategies

Much of the instruction you engage in will involve direct methods, but you should be cognizant of involving your participants in the interaction through active learning and critical engagement whenever possible. Designing learning activities is one of the most challenging aspects of instruction, and it is important to use gleaning and collaboration for inspiration during this phase. There are many resources that suggest proven lessons and active learning strategies, including Ryan Sittler and Douglas Cook's *Library Instruction Cookbook,* a collection of close to one hundred "recipes" from actual library instructors on topics ranging from basic skills to topics in technology.[6] John Keller's Attention, Relevance, Confidence, and Satisfaction (ARCS) model is a widely cited method for addressing learner engagement, which can provide a useful backdrop as you consider learning activities.[7] Keller and Katsuaki Suzuki outline each element of ARCS:[8]

Attention

Perceptual arousal: Gain and maintain student attention by the use of novel, surprising, incongruous, or uncertain events in instruction.

Inquiry arousal: Stimulate information-seeking behavior by posing, or having the learner generate questions or a problem to solve.

Variability: Maintain student interest by varying the elements of instruction.

Relevance

Familiarity: Adapt instruction, use concrete language, and use examples and concepts that are related to the learner's experience and values to help them integrate new knowledge.

Goal orientation: Provide statements or examples that present the objectives and utility of the instruction, and either present goals for accomplishment or have the learner define them.

Motive matching: Adapt by using teaching strategies that match the motive profiles of the students.

Confidence

Expectancy for success: Make learners aware of performance requirements and evaluative criteria.

Challenge setting: Provide multiple achievement levels that allow learners to set personal goals or standards of accomplishment and performance opportunities that allow them to experience success.

Attribution molding: Provide feedback that supports student ability and effort as the determinants of success.

Satisfaction

Natural consequences: Provide opportunities to use newly acquired knowledge or skills in a real or simulated setting.

Table 10.4 Involving Learners

OBJECTIVE	(A) Strategy	(B) Activity	(C) Characteristics
Scenario 1: After defining a preliminary paper topic, students will successfully identify 2–3 core research elements within it and list two alternate keywords or search terms for each.	*Direct/Discovery:* instructor demonstration of exercise, Visual Thesaurus, and Wordnik (5 min) followed by activity described on class handout (10 min)	• model example using questioning and discussion methods • pair and share activity using visual thesaurus to identify keywords; half of class uses Visual Thesaurus, half uses Wordnik	• *Control:* a) instructor and b) student • *Grouping:* a) full class and b) pairs • *Interactions:* human a) teacher/student b) student/student
Scenario 2: Given access to bSpace and their personal computer or laptop, the faculty member will successfully upload ADA-accessible files to the Resources area of their course site.	*Direct:* step-by-step screencast demonstration of uploading procedure with audio narration (2 min)	• some navigation and sound interaction • graphic design elements to capture attention • invite viewer to follow outlined steps at their own pace	• *Control:* viewer can adjust speed and replay using taskbar • *Grouping:* individual • *Interactions:* nonhuman, learner/tool
Scenario 3: Based on their assignment specifications, students will accurately create in-text citations and works cited lists formatted according to a specific citation style.	*Discovery/Direct:* series of interactive modules on different aspects of citation style and formatting (2-3 mins each, total of 10-15 mins)	• animated graphics and on-screen response elements throughout • evaluation questions at end of each module assess learning and progress tutorial	• *Control:* interactive navigation menus allow viewer to adjust speed, move back, and jump forward as needed • *Grouping:* individual • *Interactions:* nonhuman, student/tools

Positive consequences: Provide feedback and
reinforcements that will sustain the desired
behavior.

Equity: Maintain consistent standards and
consequences for task accomplishment.

The goal of determining how to involve learners
should be to say as little as possible while inviting
as much interaction as the situation permits. Direct
strategies can be interspersed with immersive peri-
ods of activity that reflect the authentic context of
the learner, while you provide modeling, coaching,
and scaffolding as support.[9] Chunking a workshop
or webcast into direct lessons or content units of
no more than ten to twenty minutes bracketed by
activities that allow participants to apply skills and
knowledge immediately encourages a more balanced
dynamic between lower-order and higher-order cognitive activity. In self-guided e-learning, the same
basic rule applies: modules exist as separate units
and should be limited in duration, and if cohesive,
should be broken by practice elements to keep viewers engaged.

One method of defining modules of instruction
that involve learners is to list each of the objectives
you created in the previous step and specify (a) an
instructional/technological strategy and timing, (b) a
corresponding engagement activity, and (c) the control, grouping, and interaction characteristics related
to each objective (see Reigeluth's list at the beginning
of *Structure* 2d, p. 117). Table 10.4 provides examples
from scenarios 1, 2, and 3.

By associating strategies and activities with content
and objectives, it becomes possible to create a balanced and active learning interaction that does not
tax cognitive load. Items in the activity column do
not have to be extremely in-depth; using discussion or
questioning instead of an exclusively one-sided lecture
achieves learner involvement.

Extend the Interaction

In chapter 6, I discussed the idea of "teaching naked"—using social tools and online learning objects to
prepare a student prior to a synchronous interaction,
which leverages the potential of instructional technology while making the focus of face-to-face interaction
more human-centered. Chapter 6 also introduced
the toolkit evaluation for identifying instructional
technology affordances. In the final component of
the *Structure* phase, you combine these approaches to
imagine how you can extend the impact of a typical

training, workshop, or tutorial by providing analog or
technology-facilitated support prior to, during, and/
or after the interaction. The goal is to use technology
to supplement brief or poorly timed interactions, integrate more effectively into a participant's productive
context, and offer assistance when additional learning
needs arise.

Extending the interaction most frequently involves
two things: embedding instructional materials in other objects, and using social and communication technologies to make yourself available for personalized
support. The former includes approaches like adding
links to library-created tutorials in a course management system, sharing online course guides, setting up
a course-specific Yahoo Pipe (http://pipes.yahoo.com)
that feeds the contents of search alerts and blog feeds
into one centralized resource, or maintaining a list of
Delicious links. The latter can be direct, as in inviting
learners to submit follow-up questions via e-mail,
SMS, or chat, or indirect, as in suggesting additional
resources that build on the information you present
during an interaction. Extending the learning interaction can also occur through strategic communication
with an instructional requestor (faculty member, library staff contact) to explore opportunities to embed
into a course or department.

To extend the interaction, brainstorm ways you
might provide additional support before, during, and
after instruction. A few examples applicable to in-
person instruction in scenarios 1 and 2:

Before Instruction

- Send introductory communication
  recommending a list of readings or sites to
  review.
- Suggest links to tutorial or other digital
  learning content for prior viewing.
- Send a problem, question, or scenario for
  learners to consider prior to the interaction.

During Instruction

- Provide examples of blogs, websites, Twitter
  feeds, and other resources that feature
  supplementary information.
- Suggest links to tutorials or other digital
  learning content to the instructor.

After Instruction

- Distribute contact information and encourage
  participants to get in touch for additional help.
- Follow up personally on student questions
  that went unanswered during the learning

interaction or by creating and posting a generalized online response.

- Create a Doodle poll (www.doodle.com) to allow learners to set up face-to-face or virtual appointments during specified "office hours."
- Embed a questions and comments form in an online course guide and respond to learner queries directly or on the guide itself.

PHASE 2: STRUCTURE SUMMARY

- The USER **Structure** phase helps you determine the type, focus, control, grouping, interactions, and support for learning.
- This process begins by **creating targets** in the form of goals, objectives, and outcomes.
- You can classify KSAs into **factual, procedural, conceptual**, or **metacognitive** knowledge dimensions.
- A **task analysis** is a method of plotting the steps involved in skill-based and procedural learning.
- **Bloom's taxonomy** of the cognitive domain suggests action terms that classify knowledge and assist in writing objectives.
- Connect objectives with instructional strategies and activities that **involve participants**.
- Determine how you can **extend the interaction** using technological and analog support methods.

REFLECTION POINTS

1. Reflect on a face-to-face or digital learning interaction you have recently designed or participated in.

How many levels of Bloom's revised Taxonomy (table 10.3) did it span?

2. Identify methods you already use to extend learning interactions.

NOTES

1. Charles Reigeluth and James Moore, "Cognitive Education and the Cognitive Domain," in C. Reigeluth (ed.), *Instructional Design Theories and Models: A New Paradigm of Instructional Theory* (Mahwah, NJ: Lawrence Erlbaum, 1999), 56.
2. Gary Morrison, Steven Ross, and Jerrold Kemp. *Designing Effective Instruction* (Hoboken, NJ: Wiley, 2007), 105.
3. Benjamin Bloom, *Taxonomy of Educational Objectives, Handbook 1: Cognitive Domain* (New York: Longman, 1956).
4. Lorin Anderson and David Krathwohl (eds.), *A Taxonomy for Learning, Teaching and Assessing. A Revision Of Bloom's Taxonomy of Educational Objectives* (New York: Longman, 2001), 67–68.
5. Jacqueline Veldof, *Creating the One-Shot Library Workshop: A Step-by-Step Guide* (Chicago: American Library Association, 2006), 66.
6. Ryan Sittler and Douglas Cook, *The Library Instruction Cookbook* (Chicago: Association of College and Research Libraries, 2009).
7. John Keller, "Strategies for Stimulating the Motivation to Learn," *Performance and Instructional Journal* 26, no. 8 (1987): 1–7.
8. John Keller and Katsuaki Suzuki, "Use of the ARCS Motivation Model in Courseware Design," in D. H. Jonassen (ed.), *Instructional Designs for Microcomputer Courseware* (Hillsdale, NJ: Lawrence Erlbaum, 1988).
9. Jean Lave and Etienne Wenger, *Situated Learning: Legitimate Peripheral Participation.* (Cambridge [England]: Cambridge University Press, 1991).

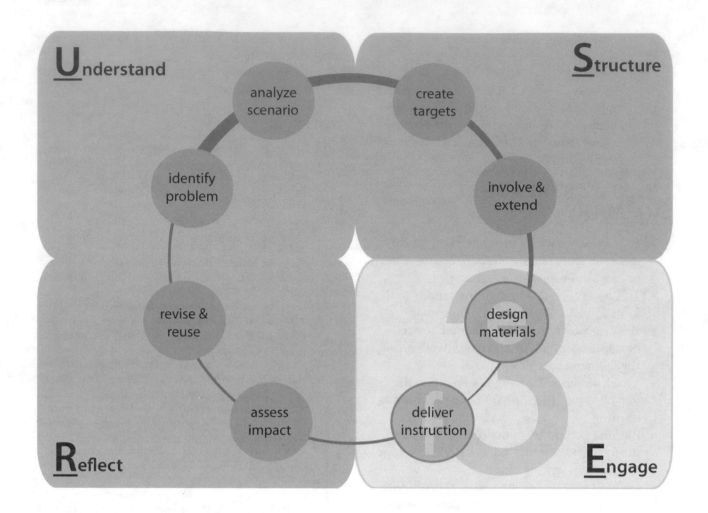

11

Engage

IN THE THIRD USER phase, *Engage*, you **design materials** to support learning in the physical or digital learning environment and **deliver instruction** to its intended audience. These steps focus on communicating clear and appealing instructional messages and objects.

Phase 3: Engage. Create your instructional objects and deliver the learning experience.	
e. Design Materials	Create the **message(s)** and **object(s)** you will use to facilitate learning. This begins with developing prototypes, gathering feedback, then revising and finalizing.
f. Deliver Instruction	Deploy the learning object or interaction by creating an **implementation** plan, **capturing attention**, and **sustaining interest**.

USER 3e: DESIGN MATERIALS

After structuring lessons, strategies, and activities, you are prepared to develop the materials that support instruction. Some instructional materials are intended solely to provide scaffolding for you in the learning interaction (e.g., notes and outlines), while others are created for learner consumption (e.g., podcasts, handouts, and course guides). The latter category is the focus of this USER step. There are two sides to designing materials—creating instructional *messages*, which are communicated through learning *objects*.

Crafting Your Message

Before developing your learning objects, it is critical to create a compelling instructional message. A well-crafted message is essential to engaging delivery, and is the place where learner insight, targets, and teacher identity collide. The instructional message is all about adjusting expectations in order to manage attention and motivation, whether communicated during in-person delivery or woven into noninteractive learning objects. If students come to a learning interaction with low expectations, these can either be challenged or confirmed by your message, which is profoundly important in gaining learner attention and creating positive expectations.

The golden rule of crafting an effective message is *simplicity*: Your message is a student-centered abstract of the entire learning interaction, an elevator pitch for a potential workshop attendee, or how you would tweet the topic of a webinar in 140 characters. It should not only get to the point of the learning interaction, but interest people in pursuing that point. I have discussed instructional messages several times in previous chapters; never underestimate the power of getting up on your soapbox (chapter 1), the SUCCESs method (introduction), or the WIIFM principle (chapter 1). If there is anything that makes people engage with a library learning object or interaction, it's hearing something that will obviously make their life easier, communicated in a not-so-boring way. Revisit the instructional message from the Journal-TOCs training example in chapter 8:

> JournalTOCs is the best method available for discovering and monitoring interdisciplinary scholarly journal TOC feeds, which helps builds current awareness and provides outreach material for faculty and graduate students.

A similarly succinct message can be developed for every class, tutorial, or module of instruction, which can help address learner self-interest and focus instructional delivery.

The Prototyping Process

Once you have created your message, you develop the instructional objects you will use to facilitate learning through *prototyping*. A fundamental aspect of developing learning objects is testing and revising them before you actually deliver instruction. Bell and Shank outline the four stages of this process: prototype,

create/build, formative evaluation, and revision.[1] Creating a mockup of instructional materials or conducting a pilot run of a session or exercise allows you to assess their effectiveness, whether among your community of practice or a group of test participants from the target audience (e.g., quick student usability trials of an online course or tutorial). This formative or in-process evaluation (a type of assessment further discussed in chapter 12) can be quite informal, even a quick once-over from the first colleague you can grab. Based on the input you receive, you will invariably be better equipped to triage unforeseen problems or correct linguistic or aesthetic flaws, sometimes vastly improving its effectiveness and appearance. You may also find that you receive positive feedback on your design, which can generate much-needed instructor motivation or even produce future collaboration and gleaning opportunities. Consulting colleagues on prototype designs is one of the fastest ways to create a de facto community of practice.

As a working example of prototyping, consider how significantly the USER method itself transformed as I planned and wrote this book. After thinking through its underlying structure I sketched several mockups of the model by hand to visualize my approach, then developed a digital prototype early in the writing process using Adobe Illustrator (figure 11.1—note the considerably less catchy "ADDD" acronym at this early stage). I subsequently tweaked and revised drafts of this original as I tested it live and gathered external feedback on its layout, theoretical base, real-world applicability, and the functional progression of each phase and step. I arrived at the final design model almost a year into my writing process, while part II and appendix A planning template continued to undergo substantial revisions even in the latest stages of editing. Comparing USER's initial and final versions, I see plain evidence of community input and my own problem-solving as I encountered logical and execution difficulties within the method, a combination that resulted in a far more developed, flexible, and universal design.

Visual Literacy and Learning Design

Educators frequently use imagery and visual design in learning object creation to communicate information, share insight, and forward knowledge-building.[2] Visual literacy is "the ability to understand and use images, including the ability to think, learn, and express oneself in terms of images,"[3] which in instruction becomes a high-stakes method of more deftly engaging the interest and information processing capacity of your audience. Creating effective instructional visuals is challenging because it involves both abstraction and representation—translating ideas into a form you hope will be comprehensible to others—and because it is simply not as intuitive as other types of communication.

As challenging as it might be, universal design principles can be used to create graphical messages that have more impact. Half of the human cerebral cortex is devoted to processing images. Because so much of our mental energy is devoted to the visual, poor graphical communication is one of the surest ways to disengage or squander attention among sighted learners.[4] Visual design encompasses textual layout as well as imagery and graphics, meaning that everything outside of totally sound-based instructional objects can benefit from graphic design strategies. Richard Mayer lists seven such strategies that make more efficient use of cognitive processing capacity in instructional interfaces, materials, and graphics.[5]

Concentrated: Core ideas are emphasized via highlighting, bolding, and other strategies.

Concise: Brevity and simplicity are achieved by eliminating extraneous text and images.

Correspondent: Pictures, charts, and tables and their captions are placed close to one another.

Concrete: Images provide clear visualizations of the subjects in question.

Coherent: Picture choices are logical and correspond with narration, captions, or surrounding text.

Comprehensible: Graphics and text or narration reflect the prior knowledge of the viewer.

Codable: Graphics and text or narration lend themselves to being integrated into memory.

Universal Design Strategies

No matter the type of instructional object you create, simplicity should again be your guiding strategy. Information designer Edward Tufte famously campaigns against "chartjunk," or extraneous elements that have no relationship to the message or content. The harder someone has to work to interpret blocks of unbroken text on a slide, the more colors and fonts their brain has to process, or the more distracting, erratically spaced, or cutesy images they are required to sift through, the less relevant information they will be able to transfer from working to long-term memory. The same goes for endless Curse of Knowledge lecturing; all tax the cognitive load, causing motivation and attention to wander. The cleaner, clearer, and more to the point you can be in a given learning object or interaction, the better.

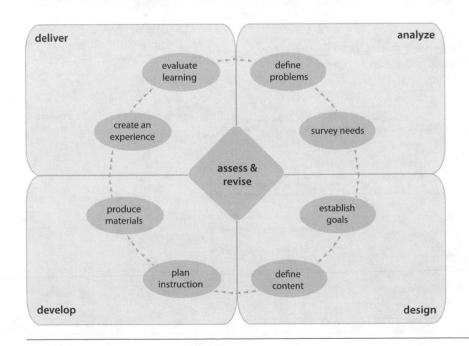

Figure 11.1
Prototype USER method

Simplicity and clarity in learning object design can be achieved by consulting a series of universal design strategies. Linda Lohr recommends considering principles, actions, and tools (PAT) when creating instructional objects.[6] Principles are the cognitive functions that guide how we process and make use of instructional visuals: *selection*, *organization*, and *integration*. Actions are structural design elements: *repetition*, *proximity*, *alignment*, and *contrast*. Tools are the most basic aesthetic building blocks: *typeface/ font*, *color*, *shape*, *depth*, and *space*. In this section, I detail each element in the PAT approach.

PRINCIPLES

Principles are broad elements of design that reflect information processing capacity.

Selection: Selection is the mind's capacity to discern significance, which is guided by the *figure/ground principle*. Figure/ground "explains how the limited information processing capacity of the human mind forces people to focus on one stimulus at a time rather than several. Figure-ground essentially names the two types of attention: (1) what the learner is paying attention to, or *selecting* (the figure), and (2) what the learner is not paying attention to (the ground)."[7] The more elements you integrate, the more difficult it becomes to distinguish the figure (what is relevant) from the ground (what is irrelevant). To determine selection, ask yourself: *What do I want learners to notice?*

Organization: Organization is how learners mentally arrange instructional material and integrate new information into existing schemata. It is essential to help learners see "pathways" through an object, which is achieved by using and clear and consistent navigational elements, chunking information into content units that reflect instructional objectives, providing scaffolding in the form of assistance and support, and incorporating hierarchical elements such as lists, charts, and outlines that suggest relationships. To determine organization, ask yourself: *How can I suggest the structure of information?*

Integration: Integration is what occurs when selection and organization produces results—the action of building knowledge by interpreting instructional objects. Sensory registers process communication modalities information in different areas of memory. By using more than one modality (e.g., verbal narration in a tutorial) you can encourage better integration of instructional materials. To determine integration, ask yourself: *How do I help learners make connections?*

ACTIONS

The PAT method becomes increasingly specific in the techniques it suggests; whereas principles are broad best practices in learning design, **actions** are four functional visual strategies: *repetition*, *proximity*, *alignment*, and *contrast*. I highlight each action in a screenshot taken from the scenario 3 Flash tutorial [Figure 11.2]:

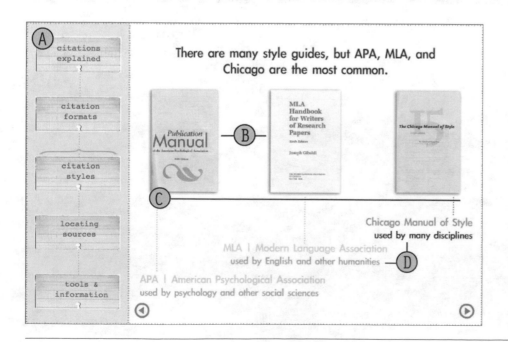

Figure 11.2
Design actions identified

A. *Repetition* manages cognitive load through continuity of navigational structure, bounding elements, and a limited number of new visual and auditory elements introduced throughout a learning object. Consistent design choices such as font, color, and images impart a feeling of unified predictability; the left-hand menu and icons are identical throughout, allowing the learner to devote more processing capacity toward content and less towards orienting to a changing navigational structure.

B. *Proximity*, the distance between objects, indicates their relationship to one another through tacit association; the closer objects are, the greater their connection. If elements are grouped too closely they become difficult to distinguish, thus placing a strain on information processing capacity. In figure 11.2, image thumbnails are placed close enough together to indicate similarity, but not so close as to give the sensation of being crowded. Distance indicates the conceptual separation of content "chunks" at the same time it makes them more pleasant to observe.

C. *Alignment* is the consistent placement of elements along an invisible grid or axis, which also indicates a relationship. Alignment of framing and navigation elements is similarly crucial to focusing viewers on content rather than structure; even small visual differences can create significant cognitive dissonance and draw the eye toward elements that appear misaligned.

D. *Contrast* is the distinction in color, shade, hue, or other means of visual differentiation, a useful strategy for calling attention toward figure and away from ground. To focus viewers briefly on the caption under the Chicago Manual icon (the *figure*) in figure 11.2, I increased the transparency of the captions under the other icons (the *ground*). The use of italics on two words in the previous sentence indicates that they are emphasized and thus deserving of particular attention, another use of textual contrast to indicate significance.

TOOLS

Tools like *type, color, shape, depth,* and *space* are the simplest and most intuitive strategies for creating streamlined and consistent learning object layouts. Figure 11.3 also shows working examples of each tool in the scenario 3 tutorial:

E. *Font* and *typeface* determine legibility (the ease of understanding short blocks of text such as captions or bullet points) and readability (the ease of reading lengthy passages of text). Simple sans-serif fonts, those with no squiggly or curved lines at the ends of characters, are used throughout the tutorial for captions, whereas traditional serif fonts are a stylistic choice that lend citations and catalog cards a feeling of authenticity.

F. *Color* is instrumental to setting mood and feel and can also indicate relationships and emphasis, but it should not be relied upon too heavily in e-learning, due to display differences among technology formats as well as the potential for colorblindness or other visual impairments among users. In this example,

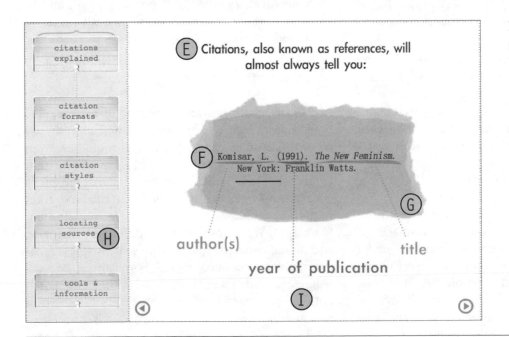

Figure 11.3

Design tools identified

primary colors distinguish the parts of the citation, and a bright, simple scheme with no more than five colors total is used to capture attention and simplify the user experience. Although the images in this book are not rendered in color, figure 11.3 illustrates how gray-scaled objects can employ a complementary strategy through hue and contrast.

G. Symmetrical *shapes* create a sensation of balance, asymmetrical shapes of imbalance; both can be useful in the appropriate context. The shape of the images used in this screen—catalog card navigation icons as well as the torn citation paper—are consistent and roughly rectangular and therefore "fit" within the tutorial frame to achieve a sense of structural balance.

H. *Depth* often involves details that indicate texture and feel as well as those that indicate dimensionality, all of which can be used for emphasis and to make images more or less prominent in relation to those around them. The shaded, torn edges of the catalog cards indicates depth, a stylistic choice that lends the images visual appeal and realism.

I. *White space,* also known as negative space, is the unbroken distance between objects critical to managing cognitive load and making instructional materials from slides to handouts more pleasant to view. Sufficient negative or white space enhances efficiency, enforces simplicity, and is a reliable strategy for emphasizing the figure over the ground.

Multimedia Instruction

Visual communication is only one aspect of creating effective instructional messages. As the learning pyramid deconstruction in chapter 4 revealed, neither hearing, seeing, nor doing is categorically the best way to learn, and many among us are sight or hearing impaired or otherwise differently abled. We increasingly hybridize media and messages as information consumers and producers, and mobile, surface, and gesture interfaces are transforming the affordances of instructional media. Truly learner-centered instruction therefore aims for universality by engaging interaction across a number of communication forms: kinetic, affective, textual, auditory, and visual.

Multimedia instruction has a simple definition: using a combination of text, sounds, and images in learning materials. This can involve "delivery *media* (e.g., amplified speaker and computer screen), presentation *mode* (e.g., words and pictures), or sensory *modalities* (e.g., auditory and visual)."[8] Because the layout and organization of visuals, vocals, and text have so much influence over cognitive capacity,

multimedia design strategies are firmly based in information processing theory. Multimedia integration in instruction is a widely recognized cognitive load management strategy, and is based on the deceptively simple principle that combining words, pictures, and/ or sounds (but not necessarily all three) encourages more effective transfer and recall, particularly for learners with low prior subject matter knowledge.[9] Mayer offers ten multimedia design principles:[10]

Coherence: Extraneous words, sounds, and pictures are minimized.

Modality: Narration occurs as speech rather than printed text in multimedia presentations.

Personalization: Narration occurs in conversational rather than formal style.

Pretraining: The learner knows the names and characteristics of the key concepts.

Redundancy: Animation and narration are preferable in multimedia presentations over animation, narration, and on-screen text (to reduce cognitive overload).

Segmenting: A fast-paced, complex multimedia lesson is presented in user-paced segments rather than as a continuous presentation.

Signaling: The essential material is highlighted.

Spatial contiguity: Corresponding words and pictures are presented in proximity to one another on a page or screen.

Temporal contiguity: Corresponding words and pictures are presented simultaneously rather than successively in time.

Voice: Narration occurs in a friendly human voice rather than a machine voice.

In other words, images and words should appear at the same time and close to one another, narration should be inviting and conversational, users should be given control over pacing in complex lessons, important content should be familiar and emphasized, and either vocal or on-screen text is preferable to dual narration (although vocal is a more effective accompaniment to images). While they manifest differently in analog and digital contexts, many of these principles translate across instructional media. For example, Mayer's *redundancy* mirrors the familiar adage that one should not read presentation slides verbatim.[11] If both vocal narration and text accompany images, each should supplement visual information while remaining distinct.

Evaluating Instructional Objects

To enhance the prototyping process it is useful to have a few simple, rational rules you can use to judge the effectiveness of the materials you create. The pillars of learning design evaluation are *effectiveness,* qualities that help an object achieve its purpose; *efficiency,* qualities that make an object more understandable; and *appeal,* qualities that make an object more attractive. Lohr recommends asking yourself and those you ask to review your learning materials a series of questions that evaluate their overall "learner-friendliness," modified here slightly to include the widest range of instructional formats:[12]

Effectiveness

- Does the learning object cover the correct content?
- Does the learning object cover an optimal amount of information (not too much and not too little content)?
- Does the learning object "work" instructionally?

Efficiency

- Does the learning object make important information (selection) easy to perceive?
- Is the learning object organized (organization) so that information is easy to access?
- Does the learning object help the user relate the information to the overall instructional or performance target (integration)?

Appeal

- Does the design of learning object motivate the user to engage with it?
- Is the information in the learning object relevant and important to the user in the instructional context?
- Is the learning object clear enough to convince users that they will understand it?

Creating functional and attractive instructional materials takes skill acquired through gleaning and practice and dedication inspired by refining a personal sense of style. A useful reflective strategy is to consciously take note of what is effective, efficient, and appealing about the learning objects and messages you encounter in your environment. For additional reading on design strategies, William Lidwell and coauthors' *Universal Principles of Design* provides a comprehensive visual design overview, while Ruth Clark and Chopeta Lyons's *Graphics for Learning* and Lohr's *Creating Graphics for Learning and Performance* provide excellent insight into the role of principles, actions, and tools in instructional objects.[13] Edward Tufte's many works feature beautiful information graphics and thought-provoking critical discussions on effective visual communication.[14]

USER 3f: DELIVER INSTRUCTION

After you design learning materials, it is time to actually deliver the instructional product. In real-time scenarios, this is the point at which you lead a class, workshop, or presentation; in an asynchronous digital instruction this is the moment when you embed or release the tutorial, web-based course, podcast, or video. This USER step is arguably the most dynamic, depending as much on the contributions of participants as on the thought you have given to previous steps. Although you're largely on your own during instructional delivery, a positive instructional dynamic in both real-time and asynchronous interactions can be fostered by developing an *implementation plan,* considering the sequence of instructional events, and communicating your *pitch* and *persona* in order to capture and sustain learner attention.

Implementation Plan

Part of ensuring successful delivery is considering how to use communication, marketing, and technology tools to create a more receptive and reliable learning environment. Implementation plans vary widely depending on audience and delivery method and often overlap with your attempts to extend the interaction prior to instruction. In an elective learning scenario such as a drop-in workshop or point-of-need tutorial, your marketing strategy might include highlighting a new product on a library website, sending announcements to email lists or individuals, spreading the word via social networking sites, and building ground-up support by securing incentives for participation. In course-integrated sessions and trainings, this process will look a bit different considering that you already have something of a captive audience, but you might prepare participants by sending a link to a customized guide or introduce yourself to the class via a video message or other means of pre-personalizing the interaction. A few more implementation strategies from different learning interactions:

Unconference: Clearly communicating guidelines for participation and ground rules.

E-Learning Objects: Increasing the findability of digital learning materials on a library website as well as announcing via different channels.

Web-Based Training: Testing the technical stability of synchronous learning delivery platforms.

Capturing and Sustaining Attention: Gagné's Events of Instruction

In the *Structure* phase, you considered instructional content and identified delivery methods and activities to facilitate engaged learning. During instructional delivery, you need a framework through which to reliably step through each lesson and activity in a way that enhances attention, transfer, and recall. Gagné's "Nine Events of Instruction" are a series of implementation steps that organize the effective progression of instructional events. The events are themselves scalable and format independent, and, similar to the PAT visual design approach, focus on universal delivery elements that create the conditions for lasting learning.[15] The Events of Instruction are a particularly useful template for ordering the presentation of content in the brief face-to-face interactions or digital learning objects typical to library educators. If your planning time is minimal, you can use Gagné's Events as a fast framework for workshop delivery or on-the-fly screencast scripting. They are also a reflective base for considering consistent delivery pace, content communication, activity deployment, and assessment strategy during a synchronous interaction.

Gagné's Events of Instruction

1. Gain attention.

2. Inform learner of objectives.

3. Stimulate recall of prior learning.

4. Present stimulus material.

5. Provide learner guidance.

6. Elicit performance.

7. Provide feedback.

8. Assess performance.

9. Enhance retention transfer.

In in-depth planning, the Events can assure you deliver instruction in a way that interactively incorporates prior USER elements and doubles as a checklist for reviewing each lesson or unit. In scenario 3 I used the Events to support my tutorial storyboarding process, laying out the pedagogical strategy and on-screen progression of each of the five modules:

Module 1 Events (Citations Explained)

1. *Gain attention:* Open on a stylish and minimalist tutorial window. First frame of module: Use old-school catalog card image and typing animations with added sound to catch the eye. Also, title tutorial provocatively ("WTF Is a Citation?") and use creative/interesting reference examples.

2. *Inform learner of objectives:* Communicate first module objective ("given a bibliographic citation, students can correctly name the constituent parts of the citation"), translated into informal language and delivered via a similar catalog card animation.

3. *Stimulate recall of prior learning:* Provide series of content frames that indicate where users have previously used and relied on citations.

4. *Present stimulus material:* Deliver series of content frames, first defining and providing examples of the parts of bibliographic citations using working examples, text captioning, narration, interactivity, and images to stimulate multiple sensory modalities.

5. *Provide learner guidance:* Use an instructional message that explains clearly why understanding citations is important to research and writing. Provide self-directed navigation elements that allow users to move at their own pace.

6. *Elicit performance:* Require users to complete a short multiple-choice quiz item at conclusion of the module that covers key content points (the characteristics, parts, and uses of citations).

7. *Provide feedback:* Quiz includes reinforcement and commentary for both correct and incorrect answer choices.

8. *Assess performance:* Tabulate and display correct and incorrect responses, which can

also be sent to the learner/instructor at the end of the tutorial, if desired.

9. *Enhance retention transfer:* At the end of the entire tutorial, revisit the performance objective for each module via a general summary.

Pitch and Persona

In the previous *Engage* step, you defined an engaging instructional message. When delivered, the message consists of two parts: *pitch,* how you communicate content so that learners make sense of and identify with it; and *persona,* the personality you bring to the interaction.

Pitch. In chapter 2, I described a metacognitive questioning exercise I often use at the beginning of face-to-face undergraduate classes. I ask attendees to introduce themselves, describe their research topic if they have one, make an observation about libraries, and name one thing they would like to get out of the class. The most important teaching moment of the session occurs immediately after this exercise, when I have the opportunity to make my pitch. A pitch is the part of the instructional message that captures participant attention and communicates objectives coded in WIIFM language. I sometimes set up my pitch with critical dialogue about librarianship, which I think of as "What is a librarian, anyway?" With undergraduates, it usually goes something like this:

Me (to the room): "So, who can tell me what I had to do to become a librarian?"

(Long pause, mumbles) "Um, you studied information? Like you got a certificate or something?"

Me: "Something exactly like that, which believe it or not requires a master's degree (eyebrows always raise here). What, exactly did I study about information?" . . .

(wheels turning) " . . . like how it is organized?"

Me: "Right! And why would I need to do that?"

"Wait, because . . . there are so many kinds of it?"

Me: "Bingo. And, so what? Why am I up here talking to you about this? What exactly do I do?"

(any number of responses, ranging from earnest to clueless)

And so forth. This interplay sets me up for delivering my message with personal credibility and a sense of audience investment. The SUCCESs model (see p. 12) often helps me structure my pitch:

I'm here to help you figure out how to [complete your assignment, learn how to use Prezi, etc.], (Simple), and I'm not going to be a boring caricature of what you think a librarian is (Unexpected). When you leave, you will have a better handle on [your annotated bibliography/Zotero/fair use/etc]. (Concrete). I work with learners in your situation all the time and I have a couple of master's degrees, which means I'm relatively likely to know something about what I'm talking about (Credible). Moreover, I'm here because being a librarian is something I love to do (Emotional). Now, let me tell you exactly how you can put what we're about to examine to good use (Stories).

When I really feel like pulling out my rhetorical guns, I throw in a bit about libraries being essential to a representative society and intellectual freedom, and that they act as an *indicator species*—one of the first things to be attacked (Library of Alexandria) or show signs of decline (de-funding) when something is amiss in a given culture or context (war, budget crisis). Pitch is a reflective delivery technique you can use to stimulate learners to consider your motivation for being in front of the room, the qualifications that make you worth listening to, and why libraries are worth caring about, all in a way that speaks to their self-interest. I use this technique for faculty audiences and another for staff, because each audience type has its own characteristics. Pitches are not limited to face-to-face teaching and training; they are just as crucial in digital learning objects. Learners naturally make judgments about the content, medium, and individuals *behind* instruction; using this technique, you can help create audience perceptions about who you are and what role you play in their learning and research process.

Persona. In the example above, I show learners my persona: the aspects of my personality and professional interests that motivate me to teach. This invariably inspires at least a few participants to think about me, and by extension librarians, in a different light. Your instructional persona is about tone, confidence, and authority, all of which impact motivation and influence how learners benefit through the opportunities you provide for involvement and interaction. In my own teaching experience, a curious thing happens as my persona emerges: some aspects of my personality recede almost entirely, while others are blown way out of proportion. I get a lot louder, my posture improves, I become considerably more sarcastic, and I tend to jump around a little frantically (still working on that one).

Whether it comes through live or in a fixed learning object, your *persona* is not unlike acting a part. In her guest post on *In the Library with the Lead Pipe,* however, Carrie Donovan recommends that we not simply play fictional roles in the classroom; rather, that we use authenticity to guide our personas. As I have noted at several points throughout this book, your teacher identity is rooted in a productive sense of self. Connecting who you are to what you teach creates a more positive instructional experience —whether you are training, narrating, or presenting, coming across as authentic and at ease inspires learner attention. Students find personal, real connections with teachers to be one of the most meaningful aspects of education, and I guarantee that you will have a lot more eyes on you if you come across as a human being.[16]

That said, not every learner perceives humanity in the same way. Experienced educators are likely familiar with the sensation of being interpreted differently by distinct groups; reflecting on how you come across to a given audience can help you craft a useful persona, which should be highly dependent on the audience of instruction. This is not to say you should subsume potentially challenging aspects of your identity in order to "hide" from those who might reject you; rather, you modulate certain aspects of your language, familiarity, and pacing to have more targeted impact in communication. Similar to the instructional pitch, effective instructors develop modified versions of their personas that reflect the characteristics of a given learner community. Presenting live to colleagues should feel different than presenting to undergraduates or primary school students; one often wants to appear savvy/capable to one's peers, knowledgeable/in-touch to undergraduates, and unintimidating/approachable to younger learners.

HUMOR: FINDING THE SHARPER EDGE

Humor in instructional delivery is an extremely useful way to capture and sustain attention. The second rule of the SUCCESs model is *unexpected*: seriously, who expects a funny librarian? Using humor whenever possible—cracking jokes, playing off my audience, using weird examples—is one of my own tried-and-true techniques in a live interaction, primarily because it works wonders in establishing lightning-fast rapport between a presenter and the audience.[17] In addition to helping you regain your footing in the event of a

disaster (a technique I discuss in chapter 1) humor can be an excellent method of varying the pace of a potentially monotonous delivery.

Humor is also a double-edged sword: one side cuts through tension and with beautiful precision, but the other bludgeons if a joke falls flat or offends. Ill-placed brevity might come off as insincere, defensive, offensive, sophomoric, evasive, or even a cover for lack of knowledge. Ask yourself: *Am I funny, really?* Record yourself presenting and note audience reaction, or ask a colleague you feel very comfortable with for constructive criticism on whether your attempts at drollery are misguided or effective. If feedback or reflection implies the former, I'd suggest toning it down, trying a new approach, or getting a second opinion. Humor in instructional delivery is an area in which you will receive quite different perspectives depending on the values and personality of the feedback source: Some people cannot support any attempt at comedic pedagogy, so take input in this area with a grain of salt.

FINDING YOUR MOXIE

A final, cautionary note on live instructional delivery: Every so often you will have to deal with a supremely unpleasant participant. This could be a nasty commenter in a webinar, a talker or mocker in a presentation, or a disgruntled staff member in a training session who is bent on making your life unpleasant for one reason or another. This can be avoided or at least predicted by interacting with learners before instruction if you have time to establish some sort of rapport. Talk or chat with people as they enter the space or sign on, and read their textual voice or body language, the rare but potential behavioral red flag. If you lead staff trainings, encourage sanguine interactions by cultivating good working relationships, which seems like a no-brainer but is definitely worth noting. If you create a positive environment and present yourself with confidence, it is more difficult for a potential disruptor to walk all over you.

A pivotal moment in the formation of my own teacher identity was the one and only time I ever eighty-sixed someone from a class. An attendee at a one-shot session started out minorly disruptive and quickly became truly annoying, listening to audible music and being openly condescending. I made the somewhat terrifying decision to call him out on the carpet in front of the group, explaining in no uncertain terms that it is extremely bad form to disrespect a librarian (along the lines of tripping a nun) and asked him to leave. I could instantly tell that other students appreciated the gesture; they all paid more attention after his departure, and the instructor thanked me after class for taking him down a notch (he apparently often challenged her in the same way). Even if your environment of learning is absolutely discovery-focused, don't be afraid to use your authority to assert a tone of equitable and on-task behavior.

PHASE 3: ENGAGE SUMMARY

- In *Engage* you **design the materials of learning** and **deliver the instructional product**.
- **Prototyping** involves creating and revising draft instructional materials.
- **Instructional messages** consist of **pitch** and **persona**.
- **Visual literacy** and principles of effective graphics can be used to enhance instructional impact.
- The PAT (principles, actions, and tools) method can be used to design effective instructional visuals. **Principles** are the cognitive functions that guide how we process and make use of instructional visuals: selection, organization, and integration. **Actions** are steps you can take to streamline learning object design: repetition, proximity, alignment, and contrast. **Tools** are the most basic aesthetic elements, such as typeface/font, color, shape, depth, and space.
- **Multimedia instruction** is the combination of text, sounds, and images to stimulate attention and recall in learners.
- An **implementation** plan can help to stimulate interest in instruction through marketing, or prepare learners for the interaction using advance communication.
- Gagné's **Events of Instruction** are a series of steps that describe the effective progression of instructional delivery.

REFLECTION POINTS

1. Take a handout, presentation, or other visual learning object you have designed and evaluate it using each element in the PAT framework. Identify at least one area of potential design improvement.

2. Think about a typical lesson or topic you deal with during instruction. First, identify the core of the instructional message, then list examples of how you might make delivery more compelling or memorable using the elements of the SUCCESs model (Simple, Unexpected, Concrete, Credible, Emotional, Stories).

3. Do you consider pitch and persona when crafting your instructional message?

NOTES

1. Steven Bell and John Shank, *Academic Librarianship by Design: A Blended Librarian's Guide to the Tools and Techniques* (Chicago: American Library Association, 2007), 49.
2. Ralph Lengler and Martin Eppler, "Towards a Periodic Table of Visualization Methods for Management," IASTED Proceedings of the Conference on Graphics and Visualization in Engineering, Clearwater, FL.
3. Roberts Braden, "Visual Literacy," in D. H. Jonassen (ed.), *Handbook of Research for Educational Communications and Technology* (New York: Simon and Schuster, 1996), 491–520.
4. Sam Wang, *Talk of The Nation*, July 22, 2009, National Public Radio.
5. Richard Mayer, *Multi-media Learning*, 2nd ed. (Cambridge: Cambridge University Press, 2009), 24.
6. Linda Lohr, *Creating Graphics for Learning and Performance: Lessons in Visual Literacy* (Upper Saddle River, NJ: Pearson/Merrill/Prentice Hall, 2008), 60–63.
7. Ibid., 102.
8. Mayer, *Multi-media Learning*, 3.
9. Seyed Mousavi, Renae Low, and John Sweller, "Reducing Cognitive Load by Mixing Auditory and Visual Presentation Modes," *Journal of Educational Psychology* 87, no. 2 (1995): 319–334.
10. Mayer, *Multi-media Learning*, 274.
11. Ibid., 218.
12. Ibid., 87.
13. William Lidwell, Kritina Holden, Jill Butler, and Kimberly Elam, *Universal Principles of Design: 125 Ways to Enhance Usability, Influence Perception, Increase Appeal, Make Better Design Decisions, and Teach Through Design*, 2nd ed. (Beverly, Mass: Rockport, 2010); Ruth Clark and Chopeta Lyons, *Graphics for Learning: Proven Guidelines for Planning, Designing, and Evaluating Visuals in Training Materials* (San Francisco: Pfeiffer, 2004); Lohr, *Creating Graphics*14. By Edward Tufte: *Beautiful Evidence* (Cheshire, CT: Graphics Press, 2006); *Envisioning Information* (Cheshire, CT: Graphics Press, 1990); *The Visual Display of Quantitative Information* (Cheshire, CT: Graphics Press, 1983).
15. Robert Gagné, Walter Wager, Katherine Golas, and John Keller, *Principles of Instructional Design*, 5th ed. (Belmont, CA: Thomson/Wadsworth, 2005), 185.
16. James Stronge, *Qualities of Effective Teachers*, 2nd ed. (Alexandria, VA: Association for Supervision and Curriculum Development, 2007), 22–28.
17. Ibid., 27.

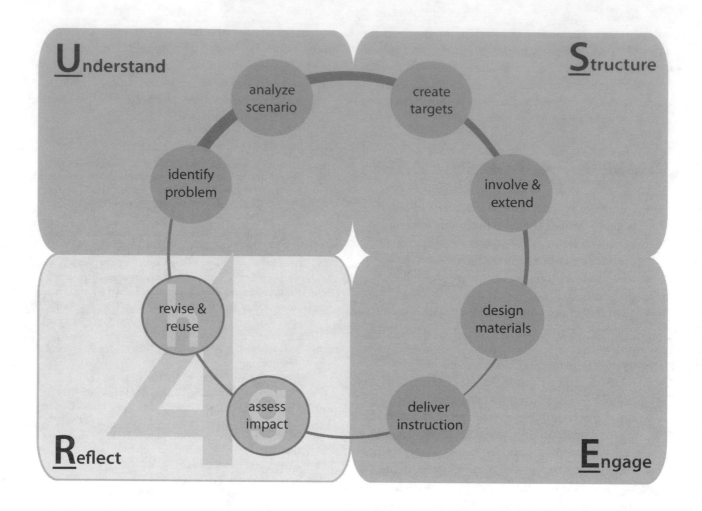

12

Reflect

IN THE FINAL phase of USER, *Reflect,* you evaluate aspects of the learner and instructor experience by **assessing the impact** of the interaction from different perspectives, **revising** your approach, and **reusing** instructional materials to support subsequent projects.

Phase 4: Reflect. Examine whether learning that has occurred and how you might improve and reuse your instructional products.	
g. Assess Impact	**Assess your impact** by determining whether participants have met the desired targets.
h. Revise and Reuse	Evaluate how you might **revise** and **reuse** your content and instructional materials in the future.

USER 4g: ASSESS IMPACT

Evaluation, reflection, and revision are ongoing throughout each phase of USER, but this step concentrates on assessing learning that occurs during instructional delivery, and establishing if additional support is needed. Assessment of this kind is based in the evaluation of learning objectives, which for some is a challenging or relatively uninteresting component of instruction. Because of the many positive learning dynamics it facilitates, meaningful assessment can go far beyond this simplistic definition and become an essential and malleable component of effective instruction. At its best, assessment is reflective (a way of attuning to a learning scenario and adjusting the impact of your teaching). It can also be communicative (a means of demonstrating your investment in the learning process); interactive (a method for engaging activity and connecting with learners); structural (a way of transitioning between activities); nuanced (a strategy for bringing the unique qualities of a learning interaction to the fore); and didactic (an opportunity to facilitate learner self-evaluation and reinforce content).

Assessment Types and Strategies

The rationale for focusing on assessment in library instruction is simple: because of our limited learning interactions, it is important to open as many windows of evaluation as possible to determine if actionable insight is being built. Without a great deal of effort, you can transform low-impact assessments (e.g., yes/no comprehension questions) into something significantly more relevant. There are so many methods of assessing learners that a foundation in research methods can provide insight into how best to align evaluation strategies with a given scenario; refer to table 9.2 and the discussion of user research in *Understand*. Within educational contexts, James McMillan lists four types of assessment strategies:[1]

Selected response: Assessment instruments that present learners with two or more options from which to choose (e.g., multiple choice surveys, Likert scale questionnaires, matching quizzes, classroom response system polls)

Constructed response: Evaluation techniques that require students to create their own response to a given task or scenario (e.g., short-answer essay, one-minute paper, informal questioning, think-aloud exercises)

Teacher observation: Formal and informal methods of observing student progress during a learning interaction. Also, information gathered from a requesting instructor (e.g., assessment of on-task behavior, observation of nonverbal communication)

Student self-assessment: Metacognitive or reflective evaluations conducted by students (e.g., one-minute paper, attitude survey, self-reflection, peer evaluation)

We might do well to add another type, now made possible by collaboration and participatory media tools like Facebook, Twitter, and Flickr: *Social, Backchannel,* or *Collective Assessment.* Each assessment type can judge simple knowledge, complex understanding, skills, affects/attitudes, or products, depending on how they are arrayed. According to McMillan,

effective assessments of all types are guided by a series of principles:[2]

Appropriateness: Evaluation strategies should be based on targets and provide insight into the content areas specified by those targets.

Validity: To ensure that your assessment methods make accurate insights about students, vary investigation methods and use multiple sources of input to increase validity.

Reliability: Assessment strategies should produce consistent results and reduce error with pre-testing and critical consideration of results.

Fairness: To reflect the learning experience of all participants fairly, assessment strategies should give an equal voice to all and not privilege more forthcoming learners over others.

Positive consequences: Evaluation methods should be weighed for their ability to create positive consequences for learners. Assessment should result in productive action.

Alignment: Assessment methods should align with the skill levels and competencies of learners.

Practicality/Efficiency: Assessment methods should be time efficient and practical to the situation.

Consistent and reliable assessment deserves lengthy treatment and is a topic of particular emphasis in instructional design, which tends to feature continuous and diverse instructor and learner evaluation strategies throughout the planning and instruction process. For more detailed insight into strategies and methodologies in this area, consult the list of library-oriented and general works in the Recommended Reading section.

The Feedback Loop

It is as important to differentiate assessment as it is to differentiate pedagogy. As I mentioned previously, it is best to gather multiple kinds of input in order to produce a comprehensive understanding of the learner experience. Evaluating a learning scenario or object holistically from conception to conclusion (and beyond) requires different methods deployed at different points along the instructional cycle. In chapter

2, I introduced the idea of creating a feedback loop to better understand and respond to learners through a process of iterative evaluation. This is the essence of productive assessment: building consistent and multiple opportunities to gauge comprehension and engagement based on predefined targets as well as in-the-moment observation, then revising or supplementing your approach if necessary. Four stages of assessment work together to create an instructional feedback loop:

1. *Pre-assessment* is conducted before instruction to establish prior knowledge and analyze the scenario.

2. *Formative assessment* evaluates materials during design and gives insight into the quality and character of an in-progress interaction.

3. *Summative assessment* occurs at the conclusion of an interaction and judges its overall effectiveness.

4. *Confirmative assessment* occurs well after an interaction and tracks retention and recall of actionable knowledge in authentic settings.

Figure 12.1 pinpoints where along the USER method each of these stages tend to occur.

Pre-assessment begins in the *Understand* phase and carries through *Structure*. Formative assessment occurs during *Engage* as the instructional product is designed and delivered, then summative assessment occurs at the immediate conclusion of the interaction during *Reflect*. If it is pursued, confirmative assessment happens post-interaction in order to gauge effects over the long term. The current USER step is most concerned with formative and summative evaluation.

In the last chapter I discussed how the USER method underwent substantial evaluation and revision before reaching its current version. In addition to the initial research (*macro-level preassessment*) and librarian surveys (*micro-level preassessment*) I conducted prior to writing this book, I invited colleagues in the UC Berkeley Library Instructor Development Program described in chapter 3 to read a working draft of chapter 8 and critique USER in a discussion group (*formative assessment*), which provided an opportunity to assess the design model within in my own community of practice. I also invited participants to submit anonymous feedback via a web form, so that they might share more candid opinions than they may have felt comfortable offering face-to-face (*formative assessment*). In combination with input from my editors (*formative assessment*), these evaluations were a critical piece of USER's overall assessment picture, extremely helpful in identifying inconsistencies and

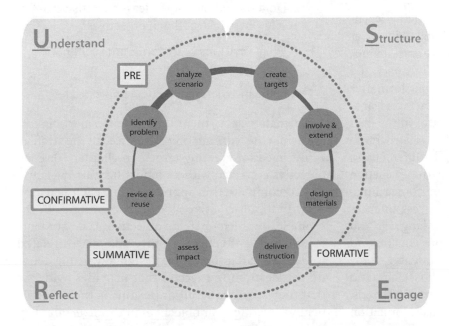

Figure 12.1
Assessment stages along the USER cycle

shaping the method to work more flexibly within different instructional contexts.

PRE-ASSESSMENT

Pre-assessment is how you learn about participants before instruction, a topic I have already covered in some depth. The first and second phases of USER are full of pre-assessment strategies: in *Understand* and *Structure*, needs assessment and learner analysis identifies instructional problems and produces insight into the learning scenario upon which targets and activities are based (table 9.2). Pre-assessment methods shed light on either macro-level characteristics of a large group or class of learners (e.g., adult learners tend to x, y, and z), or micro-level characteristics of a specific learning interaction (e.g., this first-year composition class has x, y, and z qualities). National and regional macro data should be supplemented by local micro research into the specific needs, aptitudes, and expectations of your own users; research reports such as the 2005 OCLC *Perceptions of Libraries* study, or the annual ECAR *Study of Undergraduate Students and Information Technology* provide a wide overview of library learners, but they also blur distinctions between them. The power of micro-level research is illustrated by case studies such as the University of Rochester *Studying Students* project.[3] Together, they build foundational knowledge of your learning community as a whole, and then add nuance to that foundation by identifying unique trends within that community.

FORMATIVE ASSESSMENT

Formative assessment focuses on improving learning during prototyping and instructional delivery, as opposed to summative and confirmative assessments, which provide evidence of the overall impact of a learning interaction. During instruction, formative assessment helps you understand and react to a learning dynamic as you teach.[4] This is useful in the next step, *revise* and *reuse*; it indicates what you might do better next time or what you need to do differently in the moment. The simplest type of formative evaluation is one of the most fundamental instincts of teaching: observing learners during an in-progress interaction. Educators constantly watch body language and facial expressions to check for comprehension and engagement. As you train or teach, think about how often you notice yawns, fluttering eyelids, sighs, and slouches, or signs of interest like eye contact and nods.

It is important not only to notice this information but to respond to it in a way that recaptures learner attention and indicates your investment in the interaction. If your audience seems bored or frustrated, even a subtle shift in delivery method can increase motivation and recapture attention. This can be as simple as walking around the room, asking a question, introducing a small activity, showing a video clip, or something to that effect. You can also choose to take more drastic measures: In chapter 1, I mentioned an old professor of mine who would jump on the table and sing show tunes in falsetto when people weren't responsive enough during seminar. Needless to say, this worked like a charm. Gary Morrison and colleagues recommend asking a series of questions to guide formative assessments:[5]

1. Given the objectives for the unit or lesson, is the level of learning acceptable? What weaknesses are apparent?

2. Are learners able to use the knowledge or perform the skills at an acceptable level? Are any weaknesses indicated?

3. How much time did the instruction and learning require? Is this acceptable?

4. Did the activities seem appropriate and manageable to the instructor and learners?

5. Were the materials convenient and easy to locate, use, and file?

6. What were the learners' reactions to the method of study, activities, materials, and evaluation methods?

7. Do tests and outcome measures satisfactorily assess instructional objectives?

8. What revisions in the program seem necessary (content, format, etc.)?

9. Is the instructional context appropriate?

Formative assessment tests whether participants are achieving learning objectives. Recall the strategy I described for creating targets in chapter 10: Each objective is created with a supporting learning activity. To complete this approach, link each learning activity to a formative assessment method. If, for example, one of your stated objectives is for students to find relevant articles in three databases related to their research topic, you design a learning activity or questioning exercise that provides evidence that they are making progress. This is the rationale behind creating clear objectives in the *Structure* step: if they are specific enough, they outline the evidence to look for in formative and summative assessments (table 12.1).

The objective-activity-assessment cycle is also an excellent way to break a learning interaction into segments, as in Gagne's Events of Instruction from chapter 11. In a one- or two-hour class or workshop, I can define three concrete learning objectives; build individual or group learning activity for each objective prefaced by direct instruction and demonstration; then, use formative assessments such as a worksheet activity, think-aloud exercise, or questioning technique to determine whether students seem to be making progress toward each objective. In this sense, formative assessment becomes punctuation within a learning interaction; it shows you if there is a period, question mark, or ellipsis on the end of a complete instructional sentence. In *Classroom Assessment Techniques,* Thomas Angelo and Patricia Cross list fifty formative assessment methods that can be used in real-time interactions.6 The following are library-specific interpretations of a few of their approaches that I have found personally useful in synchronous online and face-to-face scenarios:

One-Minute Paper. Stop an interaction a few minutes before it concludes and ask learners to note on index cards, half-sheets, or an online form the most important thing they learned and one question that remains unanswered. Follow up with learners via e-mail or other means to address unanswered questions. For a variation on this technique, ask students at the beginning of an interaction to specify one question that they want answered during the session using a course blog or online form. Read these aloud and try to address useful questions raised during the session (see figure 12.2 and visit www.tinyurl.com/libquestion for two examples of this in action).

Muddiest Point. At the end of an interaction or activity, ask learners to quickly write a response to the question, "What was the muddiest point in [this particular lesson or module]?" Read selected responses aloud and follow up on identified areas of missed comprehension.

Table 12.1 Objective-Activity-Assessment Cycle

OBJECTIVE	ACTIVITY	ASSESSMENT
Scenario 1: After defining a preliminary paper topic, students will successfully identify 2–3 core research elements within it and list two alternate keywords or search terms for each.	• model example using questioning and discussion methods • pair and share activity using visual thesaurus to identify keywords; half of class uses Visual Thesaurus, half uses Wordnik	• listen for comprehension among participants during questioning • observe pairs during activity periods • consider and respond to questions that come up during reporting
Scenario 2: Given access to bSpace and their personal computer or laptop, the faculty member will successfully upload ADA-accessible files to the Resources area of their course site.	• some navigation and sound interaction • graphic design elements to capture attention • invite viewer to open bSpace and follow outlined steps at their own pace	• gather feedback from colleagues on tutorial design • self-evaluation questions suggested on final slide • allow viewers to assess tutorial using an interactive star rating system
Scenario 3: Based on their assignment specifications, students will accurately create in-text citations and works cited lists formatted according to a specific citation style.	• animated graphics and on-screen response elements throughout • evaluation questions at end of each module assess learning and progress tutorial	• self-evaluation questions at end of each module assess learning and progress tutorial only when completed correctly • enable rating and commenting system for open-ended feedback

Misconception/Preconception Check. Before a learning interaction, hand out a worksheet or send a survey, message, or forum thread that asks students to respond to a potentially misleading open-ended question or statement about libraries or information as a way of discovering what pre/misconceptions among students might spark productive discussion.

Pro-and-Con Grid. After an activity, use a questioning method or self-directed reflection to ask students to evaluate a resource or scenario using a pro-and-con grid, such as listing specific benefits and drawbacks of each. Discuss pros and cons with the entire group.

Concept Maps. Have learners visualize their understanding of a topic by asking them to draw connections between major ideas and concepts covered in the session or module.

Classroom Opinion Polls. Use simple questioning, classroom response devices, social media tools, or online polls to evaluate learner responses to quick comprehension or evaluation questions during or at the end of a module to stimulate discussion.

Course-Related Self-Confidence Surveys. At the beginning of an interaction ask learners to rate their level of confidence or expertise in the skills or topics you will be covering in class. Review these and make adjustments in skill levels that may be above or below what you anticipated.

It is important to use formative assessments as an opportunity to additional instruction. When built into an asynchronous learning tool such as a guide or tutorial, formative assessments provide reflective markers for learners to evaluate their own progress. For example, figure 12.3 shows a selected-response formative assessment item embedded at the end of a module in the scenario 3 Flash-based citation tutorial. Students complete a similar item at the end of each of the five modules in order to progress. In this example, if students choose the wrong options, they are informed of their error and asked to try again. If they chose the correct answers, their choices are reinforced to enhance retention.

SUMMATIVE ASSESSMENT

Summative (or post-instructional) assessment is similar to formative assessment in terms of its information-gathering methodology, but its focus is on evaluating the learning experience after instruction has concluded. Also like formative evaluation, summative assessments can be constructed to review overall progress toward learning objectives for the instructor's benefit, or structured into a digital or other self-guided learning object to provide learners insight into their own independent progress (such as the Reflection Points at the end of each *RTEL* chapter). Summative evaluation should gauge knowledge acquisition as well as the overall impact of the learning experience. I try to collect summative learner

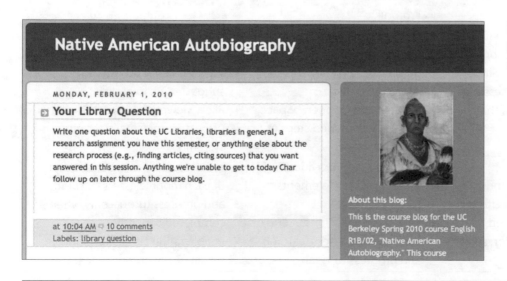

Figure 12.2

One-minute paper variation on a course blog

feedback at the end of every class, presentation, or workshop I give and build final assessments into digital learning objects that prompt users to reflect on their own learning experience. If there are requesting or attending instructors, I ask them for a separate evaluation, which invariably results in thoughtful and useful commentary into my methods.

Many methods for conducting summative assessment have already been listed—surveys, questionnaires, reflections, and so forth. In more involved learning interactions, you can also employ other types of assessment techniques, such as rubrics, which display a grid of subjective, scaled performance ratings, or portfolios, which demonstrate compiled learner output over time. One best practice for summative evaluation is to leverage instructional and productivity technologies to make the results useful over the long term. For example, consider one summative assessment method from my own experience that I often use in teaching and training contexts such as scenarios 1 and 2. In chapter 6, I briefly mentioned using technology to solve long-running problems associated with summative paper assessments in brief workshops. For several years, my approach was to hand out three-question surveys at the end of each workshop that asked students to rate and reflect on their experience and identify anything unclear in the content. When I prepared to move to a new job in 2008, I discovered that I had an entire filing cabinet full of useful, tree-murdering insights that I wanted to retain as a part of my teaching portfolio, but that were prohibitively expensive to move.

This problem motivated me to find a cloud-based solution. Experimenting with Google Docs at the time, I had learned that there was a simple way of creating a web-based questionnaire that would automatically populate an ongoing online spreadsheet. I walked myself through the process of developing an online form to replace my print survey, created a series of summative assessments for each type of workshop I delivered (undergrad, grad, library staff, and faculty), then assigned a memorable TinyURL to each that I could share easily in the last few minutes of class or push electronically to participants after an interaction. I also created a similar survey to link to and embed in digital learning objects, and another to distribute to requesting faculty and graduate students to gather their summative feedback, as well.

I have found that switching to web-based surveys instead of paper questionnaires allows me to better track my instructional effectiveness of over the long term, and also makes it far easier to use varied question types such as association and Likert scales in quick evaluations. I rely heavily on this method and versions of it for summative evaluation as well as pre-assessment in varied learning scenarios. Responses submitted through each form are tallied in the same spreadsheet over time, which allows me to keep a running digital

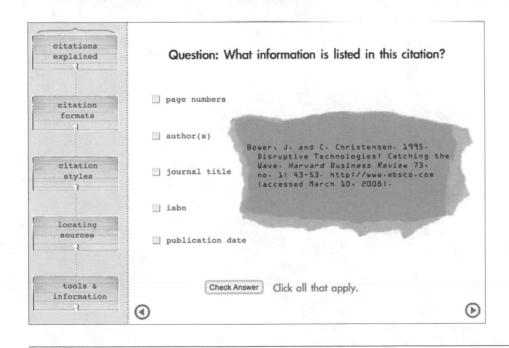

Figure 12.3

Embedded formative assessment item in citation tutorial

record of student, faculty, and staff learner feedback as I tweak my approach to specific workshops. Forms and other online survey tools often also automatically produce a response summary, which visualizes data and makes it easier to interpret without in-depth analysis (figure 12.4). To see examples of these summative web assessment forms live, visit www.tinyurl.com/classeval and www.tinyurl.com/instructoreval.

An example of an approach that mixes pre- and summative assessment methods as well as a creative mix of analog and digital collection and analysis methods: Pat Maughan, a recently retired UCB colleague, used a hybrid micro-level pre-assessment and summative assessment activity in her one-shot sessions, which she called "A Penny for Your Thoughts." At the beginning of a session, Pat would hand out a small pink card and ask students to write down the first three things that came into their minds when they thought of libraries or librarians. At the session's conclusion, she distributed an identical card in green and asked students complete the same exercise. She then compared pre- and post- terms in the moment as a reflective method of considering if she was able to shift student perceptions during the session, and later transferred the before and after cards into a spreadsheet. At the end of a year's time, she was able to visualize the hundreds of responses she received in wordclouds using www.Wordle.net. Figure 12.5 shows her pre- and post-clouds from 2009: In a persuasive demonstration of the power of even short interactions to change opinions, "helpful" was the constant throughout, whereas perceptions of "quiet" and "overwhelming" tended to diminish over her sessions as "knowledgeable" and "informative" gained positive ground.

CONFIRMATIVE ASSESSMENT

Formative and summative evaluation focus on the immediate and cumulative progress made towards objectives in an interaction, but it is also is important to examine the long-term realization of the other two types of targets set in the *Structure* phase—goals and

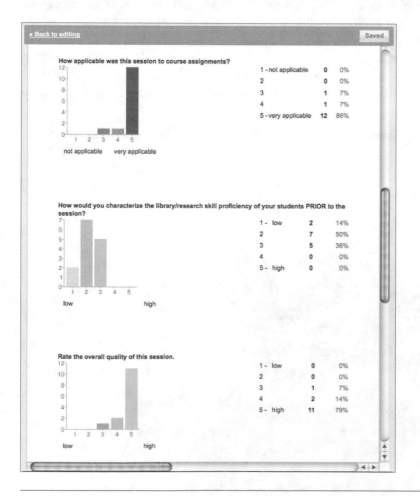

Figure 12.4

Google Form class evaluation summary

outcomes. Because it charts learning effectiveness over the long term, confirmative assessment can be the most difficult type of evaluation for library educators to conduct for a variety of reasons, many of which relate to maintaining ongoing access to participants. In the scenario 1 workshop, confirmative evaluation might require extended contact and coordination with the requesting instructor or postsemester access to the course roster, thus entailing more work for them at an already busy time. In scenario 2 staff trainings, asking participants to engage in another survey or test after the original interaction could be a similarly difficult sell. In digital learning contexts, confirmative assessment can be complicated by privacy concerns.

There are other creative ways to judge the depth of your impact beyond a learning interaction, such as observing the actionable skills, outcomes, and products in their authentic contexts. This may still require collaboration, but can often be less intrusive or onerous. One such approach in course-related workshops similar to scenario 1 entails arranging with a requesting instructor or student to review the final student essays or annotated bibliographies in order to evaluate the quality of their research. Confirmative insight in one-shots can also be achieved by interviewing or surveying requesting instructors at the end of the semester for their opinion of the impact of the library learning on student work. A similar approach can apply when a course guide, online tutorial, or other digital learning object is required of a specific group of learners as a supplement to a formal instruction.

It is a helpful strategy to build confirmative evaluation into the measures you design to extend the learning interaction in the second half of the *Structure* phase; in trainings on specific technology topics such as in scenario 2, it is possible to follow up with participants several months after a training or webinar to suggest additional resources and offer to observe and triage authentic applications of instructional skills. Despite the difficulties it might present, pursuing some confirmative assessment can be crucially important to demonstrating the long-range effectiveness of both digital and face-to-face instruction, even if only in the most general of terms. There are some formal information literacy evaluation instruments, such as the Standardized Assessment of Information Literacy Skills (Project SAILS, www.projectsails.org), that test students' knowledge at the beginning and end of their higher education experience. Similar pre- and

Figure 12.5

Pre- (above) and post-instruction (below) "Penny for Your Thoughts" responses post-testing models can be used to determine staff learning effectiveness after technology skills training programs.

An instructional object should not be fixed in amber, nor should its impact go unexamined. This book is a practical labor of love, and as such I recognize its flaws, celebrate its strengths, and commit myself to working on both in perpetuity. To continue the summative and confirmative assessment process, I enthusiastically invite you to submit comments, challenges, questions, and reflections on your experience with the USER method and other instructional strategies I outline in this book at www.tinyurl.com/rtelfeedback. I will regularly review and respond to these comments (with permission) at my blog, info-mational (www.infomational.com), and www.alaeditions.org/web extras/ or directly via email according to preference.

USER 4h: REVISE AND REUSE

In the last step of USER, you look critically at the learning interaction to determine how you might *revise* the experience to improve its impact, and consider *reuse* strategies that can save planning time and maintain consistency in subsequent learning designs. In this way USER becomes its own prototyping cycle, inviting you to consider how the culmination of one learning interaction might dovetail with, inspire, or support another.

Revise

Reflective teaching is a commitment to continuous change based on meaningful experience and learner insight, and considering concrete ways to revise a learning scenario or object allows even rote learning interactions to become more dynamic. A consistent message of this book is that to educate effectively you must be responsive to your learners, meaning that when summative feedback has been gathered it should be used to adjust your approach. This is the first element of revising a learning interaction: If participants express frustration with an aspect of instruction, brainstorm ways to improve the experience immediately or with supplementary learning materials.

By inviting learner feedback, you are committing yourself to reacting to the information you receive— for a feedback loop to be meaningful, it must generate a productive response at different points along the cycle. This can occur whenever input is received, whether during pre-assessment (participants indicate expertise in an unexpected area, causing you to revise your planning approach), formative assessment (in questioning exercises you ascertain that learners are not grasping a particular search technique as well as you would like, so you provide another example), summative assessment (after performing poorly on an online quiz in a web-based credit class, a learner automatically receives an opportunity to revisit the content with additional reading and write a response for extra credit), or confirmative assessment (instructor feedback on your embedded librarian experiment over the course of the semester indicates that you should create more instructional videos, which were appreciated by students).

Maintaining a manageable feedback loop can be harder than it sounds, because inviting users to tell you what they think is rarely as simple as in receiving the proverbial five out of five stars. For example, at UC Berkeley, I collaborated with my systems department to customize an open-source Ajax star rating tool for each of our existing tutorials. Much like ratings bars in Netflix and YouTube (figure 12.6), the tool allowed users to rate their experience with each tutorial on a simple scale.

We hoped the rater would allow us to gauge effectiveness and inform our revision efforts, thus fostering a more responsive feedback loop in our approach to digital learning objects. Interestingly enough, once the system had been operational for some time, we found that while our tutorials were being accessed frequently, average user rating was quite low—about two to three stars out of five. This is a perfect example of an unexpected challenge created by a feedback loop: the necessity of triaging an apparent widespread perception of tutorial ineffectiveness. It also identified a problem with the rating method: it did not allow users to explain the rationale behind their vote or offer suggestions for improvement. Without contextualization, the loop was therefore only half as productive as it could have been, indicating that both a revised approach to tutorial design and richer commenting methods were required. This example raises an important point. Maintaining a productive feedback loop also requires the ability to accept constructive criticism. While assessments are reasonable and kind 99 percent of the time, it's the 1 percent of unduly harsh criticism that can be truly memorable.

Building instructional literacy increases confidence, which contributes to a growing awareness of the value and sincerity of the external input you receive.

Reuse

The final aspect of the USER method is about thinking ahead. One of the affordances of teaching technologies is their modularity, or their potential to be repurposed into different formats and contexts in order to extend the impact of learning objects and be reused in other planning scenarios. Instead of existing as one-off lessons that require sequential pacing at a certain point in time, *modular learning objects* in the form of reusable tutorials, games, videos, podcasts, and activities can integrate within and supplement the objects around them. Similar to the other aspects in the *Reflect* phase (assess and revise), this step cannot be isolated to one point along the cycle. Reuse is a mentality that it involves cultivating the foresight and knowledge to produce "flexibly adaptive" designs throughout the entire USER process. By considering the delivery format, shareability, and portability of your instructional materials and interactions as you create them, you increase your ability to assemble, reorganize and nest learning objects in other contexts as needed.

Reusability can benefit the designer as much as the end user as a behind-the-scenes method of saving time and avoiding reinventing the wheel.[7] I have provided many cases of reusability throughout this book, such as recording an interaction for later streaming via video or audio or uploading presentation slides to a blog or website. Another familiar example might be the series of print handouts many departments keep on hand that explain common processes such as searching and evaluating materials, which instructors use depending on the situation. These can be digitized, enhanced, made interactive, and plugged into any number of contexts, rather than existing in only one form.

Reuse Profiles. Every technology-assisted or analog learning object has its own *reuse profile*, which can be examined and expanded for greater modularity. In web-based learning, every technology strategy has limitations and characteristics that lend themselves to different types of reusability. Consider the reuse profile of the type of Flash tutorials highlighted in scenario 3. Flash learning objects created with Captivate, Camtasia, or Flash provide a strong platform for asynchronous, interactive instruction, but their output format (.swf) produces files that are large, undesirable to download, and incompatible with YouTube and many other popular streaming media sites. Moreover, if the tutorials involve interface interactivity (user-controlled progression, click here to see your answer, etc.), they become largely unusable by learners

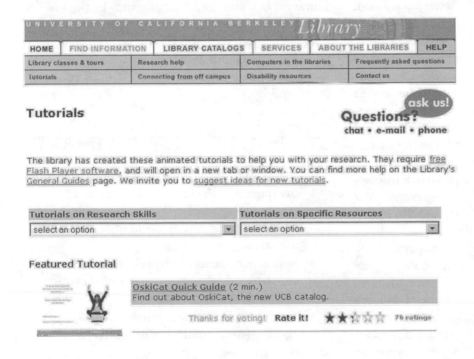

Figure 12.6
Tutorials star rater

accessing them on mobile devices, which have limited interactive capability and arc largely Flash-unfriendly. Learners with visual disabilities also have difficulties using Flash tutorials, which feature on-screen text that cannot be deciphered with screen-reading software. Finally, if the tutorials themselves are long, involved, and not comprised of independent units, their internal content becomes sequestered and difficult to navigate to at a time of learning need.

All of these factors limit the usable range of Flash-based tutorials, but the modularity solution in this case is not to get rid of them entirely (although security is a growing concern with Flash). Instead, you supplement the originals by converting them to a more reuse-friendly video format such as .avi or .mpeg with free or fee-based software, then upload each to a media sharing site such as YouTube or Vimeo in order to generate embeddable source code. This may require returning to your source files and creating less interactive versions or resizing the original to a different screen resolution, but in so doing you will be equipped to integrate tutorials far more easily into mobile and web platforms built for modular learning design, such as Library a la Carte and LibGuides. An excellent example of tutorial modularity in action is Wake Forest University's public "Toolkit" of instructional videos, all of which can be personalized, embedded, and applied in different instructional contexts by faculty and library users (www.zsr.wfu.edu/toolkit/).

Reuse Repositories. In addition to creating modular objects that lend themselves to being substituted, changed, and plugged in and out of different online and analog formats, instructors can create planning templates that they can quickly adapt to new learning scenarios to save time and maintain design consistency. This aspect of reuse is more behind-the-scenes: Maintaining a collection of learning objects that you can modify and combine to form new instructional materials, first mentioned in chapter 2. Having a series of template guides, pages, scripts, or assignments at your disposal makes it easier to adapt to each instructional scenario. Reusable instructional templates allow you to develop pedagogical flexibility, but it is essential to avoid simply grafting an old approach wholesale onto a situation for which it is not particularly suited; a one-size-fits-all mindset is the quickest way to diminish a learning experience. The point of a personal, departmental, or organizational *reuse repository* is to provide yourself and your peers with a reliable and adaptable foundation to streamline planning. Consider the instructor portfolios I mentioned in chapter 2, which provide "tangible evidence of the wide range of knowledge, dispositions, and skills you possess as a growing professional" that can aid in setting goals and evaluating progress.[8] They also double as personal recycle bins that come in handy when you need to adapt a course outline or worksheet fast. Not only does compiling this type of repository speed design, it allows you to observe how your approach to instruction, communication, and assessment develops over time.

The methods you can draw on to collect and access reusable instructional materials vary. Some repositories are vast and collectively maintained: The open education movement discussed in chapter 6 has created many publicly searchable collections of learning materials, such as the Open Educational Commons at www.oercommons.org/ (there are several library-oriented repositories outlined in chapter 3). Other collections are consortial but smaller scale. My personal reuse portfolio is an amalgamation of template and previously used physical and digital objects—handouts, e-mail prompts, assessment forms, images, outlines, links, PowerPoint and Prezi files, notes, syllabi, reflections, and evaluations—that constitute a working record of the presentations, classes, and trainings I develop as well as the feedback they generate. Portfolios can be centralized or decentralized: Mine spans filing cabinets, my hard drive, virtual storage via Google Docs (www.docs.google.com) and Dropbox (www.getdropbox.com), live and archived guides in Library a la Carte, and training sites in the LMS. It doesn't matter how you assemble your repository, so long as the materials you have produced to support your educational practice are flexible, relatively organized, and easily accessible the next time you begin the planning cycle.

STAGE 4: REFLECT SUMMARY

- In the final USER stage, **Reflect**, you **assess** the **impact** of the scenario by evaluating targets and considering how you might **revise** and **reuse** your methods and instructional materials.
- Assessment items can be **selected response**, **constructed response**, **teacher observation**, and **student self-assessment**.
- The four stages of assessment are **pre-assessment**, **formative**, **summative**, and **confirmative**.

- Using **multiple** types of evaluation gives better insight into the learner experience.
- Revising the interaction relies on creating and responding to a productive **feedback loop**.
- **Modular learning objects** are flexible and embeddable in varied instructional contexts.
- Each modular technology type has its own **reuse profile**.
- **Reuse repositories** can save time and create a consistent foundation of learning materials.

REFLECTION POINTS

1. Think about the different types of assessment you use in your teaching practice. Can you identify each of the four assessment types: pre-assessment, formative assessment, summative assessment, and confirmative assessment?

2. Now, think about how you actually apply the data you gather from these assessment methods. In your estimation, is your learner feedback put to productive use? If not, how might you change your strategies to make evaluation more meaningful?

3. Are there elements of your instructional materials that you currently reuse and recycle? Can you imagine strategies that would help you keep track of the reusable elements more consistently?

NOTES

1. James McMillan, *Classroom Assessment: Principles and Practice for Effective Standards-Based Instruction* (Boston: Pearson/Allyn and Bacon, 2007), 59.
2. Ibid., 57.
3. Nancy Fried Foster and Susan Gibbons, *Studying Students: The Undergraduate Research Project at the University of Rochester* (Chicago: Association of College and Research Libraries, 2007).
4. Thomas Angelo and Patricia Cross, *Classroom Assessment Techniques: A Handbook for College Teachers* (San Francisco: Jossey-Bass, 1993), 5–6.
5. Gary Morrison, Steven Ross, and Jerrold Kemp, *Designing Effective Instruction*, 5th ed. (Hoboken, NJ: Wiley, 2007), 239
6. Angelo and Cross, *Classroom Assessment*.
7. Daniel Schwartz, Xiaodong Lin, Sean Brophy, and John Bransford, "Toward the Development of Flexibly Adaptive Instructional Designs," in C. Reigeluth (ed.), *Instructional Design Theories and Models: A New Paradigm of Instructional Theory* (Mahwah, NJ: Lawrence Erlbaum, 1999), 183–213.
8. Robert Slavin, *Educational Psychology: Theory and Practice*, 8th ed. (Boston: Pearson, 2006), 525.

Conclusion

AFTER ALL IS said and done, the message of this book is simple: reflective and design-minded teaching leads to effective, learner-centered instruction. Librarians are redefining our value in a changing information paradigm, and it is essential that we perceive the role of education in this process: Building user knowledge as well as our own. No matter whether they are public, academic, school, or special, libraries are and will remain communities of independent and collaborative learning. As some of the most visible representatives of these communities, library educators are instrumental in shaping the way information is perceived and used in the ongoing "digital transition."[1] Throughout the twelve chapters of this book, I have presented strategies to confront this challenge with a combination of experience, confidence, and conviction, all rooted in learning from your own practice. When we cultivate stronger, more grounded relationships to teaching and learning, we sharpen our ability to advocate as well as educate.

Some think of teaching as an art consisting of flair, ability, and passion.[2] Others perceive it as a set of skills learned through study and experience. The most effective educators balance the two, relying on both inspiration and method to develop a craft-based orientation to education that challenges and engages them personally. Though some may be (or feel) more naturally gifted than others, all can sharpen their skills. As I have tried to explain through the USER method, melding proven techniques and a strong planning foundation to the needs of a scenario helps you come to understand and hopefully enjoy facilitating actionable knowledge among your learners. The more you approach instruction and learning design with an engaged attitude, the more you will come to know the simple, undeniable foundations of effective education: adaptability and personal investment.

Instructional literacy is a framework for developing these traits in yourself: reflective practice is an attitude of constructive self-awareness; educational theory brings evidence to instructional practice; teaching technologies solve instructional problems and help you adapt to shifting expectations; and instructional design is a systematic method for creating effective learning experiences. Developing instructional literacy is about bridging the distance between the motivation to teach and the motivation to learn, an ongoing challenge that moves you steadily toward greater instructional effectiveness.

NOTES

1. Joint Information Systems Committee and Centre for Information Behaviour and the Evaluation of Research, *Information Behaviour of the Researcher of the Future*, www.jisc.ac.uk/whatwedo/programmes/resourcediscovery/googlegen.aspx.
2. Gilbert Highet, *The Art of Teaching* (New York: Knopf, 1950); Burrhus Skinner, "The Science of Learning and the Art of Teaching," *Harvard Educational Review* 24 (1954): 86–97.

Recommended Reading

Assessment

Angelo, Thomas, and Patricia Cross. *Classroom Assessment Techniques: A Handbook for College Teachers*. San Francisco: Jossey-Bass, 1993.

Radcliff, Carolyn. *A Practical Guide to Information Literacy Assessment for Academic Librarians*. Westport, Conn: Libraries Unlimited, 2007.

McMillan, James. *Classroom Assessment: Principles and Practice for Effective Standards-Based Instruction*. Boston: Pearson/Allyn and Bacon, 2007.

Walter, Scott. *The Teaching Library: Approaches to Assessing Information Literacy Instruction*. Binghamton, NY: Haworth Information Press, 2007.

Information Literacy Instruction

Accardi, Maria, Emily Drabinski, and Alana Kumbier. *Critical Library Instruction: Theories and Methods*. Duluth, Minn: Library Juice Press, 2010.

Cook, David, and Ryan Sittler (eds.). *Practical Pedagogy for Library Instructors: 17 Innovative Strategies to Improve Student Learning*. Chicago: Association of College and Research Libraries, 2008.

Grassian, Esther, and Joan Kaplowitz. *Information Literacy Instruction: Theory and Practice*. New York: Neal-Schulman, 2009.

Sittler, Ryan, and Douglas Cook. *The Library Instruction Cookbook*. Chicago: Association of College and Research Libraries, 2009.

Instructional Design

Anderson, Lorin, and David Krathwohl (eds.). *A Taxonomy for Learning, Teaching and Assessing: A Revision of Bloom's Taxonomy of Educational Objectives*. New York: Longman, 2001.

Robert Gagné, Walter Wager, Katherine Golas, and John Keller. *Principles of Instructional Design, 5th Ed*. Belmont, CA: Thomson/Wadsworth, 2005.

Morrison, Gary, Steven Ross, Jerrold Kemp, and Howard Kalman. *Designing Effective Instruction.* 6th ed. Hoboken, NJ: Wiley, 2010.

Library Instructional Design

Bell, Steven, and John Shank. *Academic Librarianship by Design: A Blended Librarian's Guide to the Tools and Techniques.* Chicago: American Library Association, 2007.

Brandt, D. Scott. *Teaching Technology: A How-to-Do-It Manual for Librarians.* New York: Neal-Schuman, 2002.

Dent-Goodman, Valeda. *Keeping the User in Mind: Instructional Design and the Modern Library.* Oxford, UK: Chandos, 2009.

Smith, Susan Sharpless. *Web-Based Instruction: A Guide for Libraries.* Chicago: American Library Association, 2010.

Dupuis, Elizabeth. *Developing Web-Based Instruction: Planning, Designing, Managing, and Evaluating for Results.* The new library series, no. 7. New York: Neal-Schuman Publishers, 2003.

Veldof, Jacqueline. *Creating the One-Shot Library Workshop: A Step-by-Step Guide.* Chicago: American Library Association, 2006.

Information and Graphic Design

Clark, Ruth, and Chopeta Lyons. *Graphics for Learning: Proven Guidelines for Planning, Designing, and Evaluating Visuals in Training Materials.* San Francisco: Pfeiffer, 2004.

Lidwell, William, Kritina Holden, Jill Butler, and Kimberly Elam. *Universal Principles of Design: 125 Ways to Enhance Usability, Influence Perception, Increase Appeal, Make Better Design Decisions, and Teach Through Design,* 2nd ed. Beverly, MA: Rockport Publishers, 2010.

Lohr, Linda. *Creating Graphics for Learning and Performance: Lessons in Visual Literacy.* Upper Saddle River, NJ: Pearson/Merrill/Prentice Hall, 2008.

Mayer, Richard. *Multi-media Learning,* 2nd ed. Cambridge: Cambridge University Press, 2009.

Tufte, Edward. *Beautiful Evidence.* Cheshire, CT: Graphics Press, 2006.

Tufte, Edward. *Envisioning Information.* Cheshire, CT: Graphics Press, 1990.

Tufte, Edward. *The Visual Display of Quantitative Information.* Cheshire, CT: Graphics Press, 1983.

Marketing and Communication

Heath, Chip, and Dan Heath. *Made to Stick: Why Some Ideas Survive and Others Die.* New York: Random House, 2007.

Mathews, Brian. *Marketing Today's Academic Library: A Bold New Approach to Communicating with Students.* Chicago: American Library Association, 2009.

Interaction and Experience Design

Cooper, Alan, Robert Reimann, and Dave Cronin. *About Face 3: The Essentials of Interaction Design.* Indianapolis, IN: Wiley Pub, 2007.

Goodwin, Kim. *Designing for the Digital Age: How to Create Human-Centered Products and Services.* Indianapolis, IN: Wiley Pub, 2009.

King, David Lee. *Designing the Digital Experience: How to Use Experience Design Tools and Techniques to Build Websites Customers Love.* Medford, NJ: CyberAge Books/Information Today, 2008.

Reflective Practice and Metacognition

Hacker, Douglas, John Dunlosky, and Arthur Graesser. *Handbook of Metacognition in Education.* New York: Routledge, 2009.

Hartman, Hope (ed.). *Metacognition in Learning and Instruction: Theory, Research, and Practice.* Neuropsychology and Cognition 19. Dordrecht: Kluwer Academic, 2001.

Schon, Donald. *Educating the Reflective Practitioner: Toward a New Design for Teaching and Learning in the Professions.* San Francisco: Jossey-Bass, 1996.

Educational Theory

Bransford, John, Ann Brown, and Rodney Cocking. *How People Learn: Brain, Mind, Experience, and School.* Washington, DC: National Academy Press, 1999.

McInerney, D. M., and Shawn Van Etten. *Big Theories Revisited.* Research on sociocultural influences on motivation and learning, v. 4. Greenwich, CT: Information Age Publishers, 2004.

Phillips, D. C., and Jonas F. Soltis. *Perspectives on Learning, 5th ed.* New York: Teachers College Press, 2009.

Sawyer, R. Keith. *The Cambridge Handbook of the Learning Sciences.* Cambridge: Cambridge University Press, 2006.

Schunk, Dale. *Learning Theories: An Educational Perspective.* Upper Saddle River, NJ: Pearson/Merrill/Prentice Hall, 2008.

Critical Pedagogy and Educational Philosophy

Britzman, Deborah. *Practice Makes Practice: A Critical Study of Learning to Teach.* Albany: State University of New York Press, 2003.

Dewey, John. *Democracy and Education: An Introduction to the Philosophy of Education.* New York: The Free Press, 1966.

Freire, Paolo. *Pedagogy of the Oppressed.* (M. B. Ramos, Trans.). New York: Continuum, 2006.

Kumashiro, Kevin. *Against Common Sense: Teaching and Learning toward Social Justice.* Reconstructing the Public Sphere in Curriculum Studies. New York: RoutledgeFalmer, 2004.

Postman, Neil. *The End of Education: Redefining the Value of School.* New York: Knopf, 1995.

Sedgwick, Eve. "Buddhism and Pedagogy." In Sedgwick, Eve Kosofsky, and Adam Frank. *Touching Feeling: Affect, Pedagogy, Performativity,* pp. 153–181. Durham, NC: Duke University Press, 2003.

Shor, Ira. *Empowering Education: Critical Teaching for Social Change.* Chicago: University of Chicago Press, 1992.

Instructional Technology

Blogs

Engadget, www.engadget.com

Jane's Learning Pick of the Day, janeknight.type pad.com

LifeHacker, www.lifehacker.com

ProfHacker, www.chronicle.com/blogs/profhacker

Slashdot, www.slashdot.org

The Distant Librarian, www.engadget.comdistlib .blogs.com

The Unquiet Librarian, www.theunquietlibrarian .wordpress.com

Websites

ALA TechSource, www.alatechsource.org/ltr/index

Centre for Learning and Performance Technologies (UK), www.c4lpt.co.uk

Center for Next-Generation Teaching and Learning (UC Berkeley), http://ngtl.ischool.berkeley.edu/

EDUCAUSE Learning Initiative, www.educause .edu/eli

ILT: Institute for Learning Technologies (Columbia University), www.ilt.columbia.edu

ISTE NETS Standards, www.iste.org

JISC Techdis (UK), http://techdis.ac.uk

LITRE at NCSU, www.litre.ncsu.edu

MacArthur Foundation, Building the Field of Digital Media and Learning, http://digitallearning .macfound.org

Pew Internet/American Life Project, www .pewinternet.org

Technological Horizons in Education, www .thejournal.com

W3Schools, www.w3schools.com

WebJunction, www.webjunction.org

Books

Bonk, Curtis. *The World Is Open: How Web Technology Is Revolutionizing Education.* San Francisco: Jossey-Bass, 2009.

Bonk, Curtis Jay, and Charles Ray Graham. *The Handbook of Blended Learning: Global Perspectives, Local Designs.* Pfeiffer Essential Resources for Training and HR Professionals. San Francisco: Pfeiffer, 2006.

Kamenetz, Anya. *DIY U. Edupunks, Edupreneurs, and the Coming Transformation of Higher Education.* White River Junction, VT: Chelsea Green Pub, 2010.

Mackey, Thomas, and Trudi Jacobson. *Using Technology to Teach Information Literacy.* New York: Neal-Schuman Publishers, 2008.

Williams, Joe, and Susan Goodwin. *Teaching with Technology: An Academic Librarian's Guide.* Chandos Information Professional Series. Oxford: Chandos, 2007.

Collaboration and Communities of Practice

Lave, Jean, and Etienne Wenger. *Situated Learning: Legitimate Peripheral Participation.* Cambridge: Cambridge University Press, 1999.

Mezirow, Jack, and Edward Taylor. *Transformative Learning in Practice: Insights from Community, Workplace, and Higher Education.* San Francisco, CA: Jossey-Bass, 2009.

Wenger, Etienne, Richard A. McDermott, and William Snyder. *Cultivating Communities of Practice: A Guide to Managing Knowledge.* Boston, MA: Harvard Business School Press, 2002.

Templates and Planning Documents

The USER Method

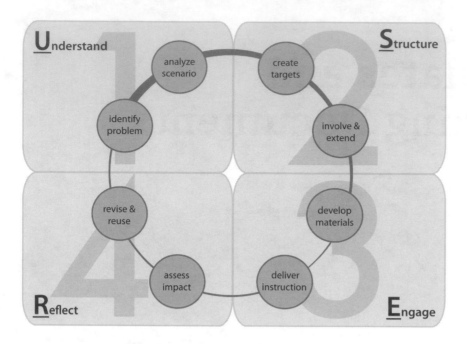

1. **Understand**. In the first phase, investigate the learning scenario.

   a. Start by **identifying the problem** that instruction can solve by asking, *What is the challenge learners face, and how can I help them meet it?*

   b. Follow up by **analyzing the scenario,** or characterizing the qualities and confronting the challenges of each element of instruction: *learner, content, context,* and *educator.* Listing these specifics provides insight into the learning community and how the instructional environment can be shaped to facilitate a positive experience.

2. **Structure**. In the second phase, define what you want participants to accomplish and outline the strategies you will use to facilitate learning.

   c. Begin by **creating targets**—*goals, objectives,* and *outcomes*—that help you organize content and interaction and evaluate the impact of instruction.

   d. Identify methods to **involve** learners using delivery techniques, technologies, and activities, and **extend** the interaction by supporting students along the continuum of learning.

3. **Engage**. In the third phase, create your instructional products and implement the learning interaction.

   e. **Develop the materials** of instruction. This involves developing an instructional message, then creating and revising learning objects using a prototyping process.

   f. **Deliver instruction** by developing an implementation plan, then capturing and sustaining learner attention throughout the interaction.

4. **Reflect**. In the fourth phase, consider whether targets have been met and how you might improve and repurpose your instructional product.

   g. **Assess the impact** of instruction by investigating the evidence of learning.

   h. Finally, consider how you can **revise and reuse** content, materials, and strategies in the future.

USER Planning/Reflection Template

Use this template to structure your approach and reflect on the USER method during instructional planning.

USER METHOD PLANNING TEMPLATE		
1. UNDERSTAND		
a. Identify Problem		
b. Analyze Scenario:		
Learner	*Characterize:*	
	Confront:	
Context	*Characterize:*	
	Confront:	
Content	*Characterize:*	
	Confront:	
Educator	*Characterize:*	
	Confront:	
2. STRUCTURE		
c. Create Targets	*Goal(s):*	
	Objective(s):	
	Outcome(s):	
d. Involve and Extend	*Involve:*	
	Extend:	
3. ENGAGE		
e. Develop Materials	*Object(s):*	
	Message:	
f. Deliver Instruction	*Implement:*	
	Capture & Sustain:	
4. REFLECT		
g. Assess Impact	*Formative:*	
	Summative:	
h. Revise and Reuse	*Revise:*	
	Reuse:	

Technology Toolkit Evaluation Template

Use this template to record characteristics, outcomes, caveats, and instructional affordances of tools for incorporation into your technology toolkit.

TOOL:														
Characteristics	Outcomes	Caveats	Instructional Affordances	Customization	Communication	Collaboration	Visualization	Sharing	Productivity	Portability	Documentation	Assessment	Play	
			Learner											
			Instructor											

Instructor Development Survey Responses

This appendix presents an excerpt of the verbatim responses I received to three short-answer survey items in an anonymous research project conducted in association with this book. Close to four hundred self-identified instruction librarians from different institutions, experience levels, and disciplinary affiliations provided an amazing range of collective wisdom that was instrumental in supporting my planning and writing process. The Google Form survey was distributed via several library education e-mail discussion lists such as ILI-L in the late summer of 2009; it contained the following three open-ended questions:

A. Required: In terms of your own instructor development, in what way would you most like to improve? (386 responses)
B. Optional: If you could offer one piece of advice to new instruction librarians, what would it be? (278 responses)
C. Optional: What is your greatest challenge related to teaching and/or training? Have you tried to confront this challenge, and if so, how? (219 responses)

For the sake of brevity, we list only the first fifty responses to each question; a full survey report can be found at www.alaeditions.org/webextras/. Respondents share a diversity of experiences, perceptions, challenges, and attitudes that I believe keenly represent the contemporary climate of library education. I continue to find it instructive and thought provoking to reflect on their insights.

A. In terms of your own instructor development, in what way would you most like to improve?

1. I'd like to better know how to reach the students, and how to collaborate more with the faculty so that research and the library are integrated.
2. Increased understanding of pedagogy

3. Just a basic understanding of pedagogy as it relates to higher education. I would really like to have had more formal instruction on assessment and course planning.

4. I would like to have a better foundation in curriculum development and pedagogy. Since most librarians are not trained as teachers, we tend to lack the pedagogical knowledge base, which I think would probably be incredibly helpful.

5. I would like to see some type of course ware for Blackboard that we could adapt to our university's library program.

6. Become more creative in what I teach

7. Confidence, presentation skills

8. How to assess workshops

9. The ability to design an engaging online course.

10. Public speaking aspect of the gig, making it interesting/fun/engaging while maintaining relevancy.

11. Length of session.

12. I want to know more about learning theory. I would also like to know how we might have more impact on our curriculum, because let's face it, if we are "allowed" only one or two quick sessions with students in other people's courses, we can be the best teachers in the world and it isn't going to make enough of an impact.

13. Coordination with teaching faculty.

14. Engaging the students more.

15. Presentation skills.

16. Organization & focus AND getting more comfortable with technology I don't use regularly or have no training on.

17. Ability to communicate within organization the impact of instructional activities

18. Working more student participation into my instruction. Teaching to the appropriate cognitive developmental level.

19. Getting the students actively involved with the presentations.

20. Incorporating more assessment into my workshops. I do formative assessment, but rarely do summative.

21. Better design of coursework, better assessment.

22. I would like to integrate principles of learning theory into my teaching, would like to include more interactive components, and create online tutorials.

23. More involvement with classes and instructors other than English.

24. I'd like to work on continued development of solid instruction sessions and determining some type of feedback to know if any aspects were more successful than others.

25. Framing library research instruction and tools within the larger conversations taking place in higher education.

26. I'd like to feel more confident in creating lesson plans with goals and objectives.

27. I would really like to develop more hands-on activities for "one-shot" classes. The standard lecture with three resources gets a little stale for me.

28. Easier way to include assessment as it is related to course learning outcomes.

29. Curriculum planning.

30. I would like to add assessment tools to my instruction. I would like to learn more theory of instructional design.

31. I'd like to be able to see my colleagues doing orientations.

32. I would like to keep my lessons evolving and not stagnate at what worked the first time.

33. Integration of information literacy theory into instruction sessions, tutorials, etc.

34. I would like to learn more about learning theory and how it can be applied in one-shot workshops. I would also like to find ways to include more activities in my instruction sessions.

35. Pacing.

36. Creating better rapport with students and inspiring them to care about Information Lit.

37. Engaging students, making material interesting, making useful assignments that can be graded and challenge the students enough.

38. I've made up my own information literacy instruction program completely on my own because I had no education (and I don't think my MLIS institution even offered courses), mentorship or on-the-job training in this area. I keep working on it and think I do OK, but could use more resources and advice.

39. More interactive, perhaps problem-based learning scenarios, with students teaching students.

40. I would like to be able to move from lecture to hands-on mode easily.

41. I'd like to be better at designing effective active learning exercises, as well as ways to integrate

assessment into my classes without detracting from precious class time.

42. I'd like to find more ways to engage students in a 50 minute one-shot session where the professor really wants the tools taught, rather than having me teach skills.

43. More inclusion of emerging technologies, better time management during instruction sessions, consistent implementation of measurable assessment.

44. Keeping it fresh,

45. Integrating assessment into instruction. Thinking of new and exciting ways to present materials that will engage students. Finding ways to get faculty buy-in so they want and understand the value of library instruction. And practice . . . I've only been doing instruction for about nine months and just today had my first "non-intro" class.

46. Getting attention and creating student motivation.

47. I'd like to get over being nervous (it has gotten better with time) and I'd like to be better at engaging the students/getting them involved instead of just lecturing/showing. However since I never have more than 30 minutes, it's really difficult.

48. LOL—reduce anxiety.

49. Get to a point where there is a rhythm to it.

50. At my full-time job—I would like to consistently teach one class to further develop my teaching skills rather than pick up a class here and there from "real librarians" who have scheduling conflicts.

B. Optional: If you could offer one piece of advice to new instruction librarians, what would it be?

1. Tie the library lesson to a for-credit assignment.
2. Learn as much as you can about education and take ownership of your educational agenda for your students.
3. Don't be afraid to leave your classes somewhat unstructured—talking heads are kind of boring. Allow for give and take and interaction with each class, since every class is unique.
4. Teaching and training are two different things.
5. Observe a kick-ass instructor.
6. Observe a wide-range of professors to learn different classroom management styles.

7. Take a course in the education program at the college you are getting your MLIS from on instructional design.

8. Don't assume all classes are eager beavers and to be prepared with contingency plans that can be implemented right away during classes that don't go the way the instructor anticipated.

9. Adapt and expect change.

10. Learn to do a course outline. Create one. After it is done, go through and CUT three quarters of your content. That is probably what you will be able to get through in one course-period. You can't do EVERYTHING, so focus on smaller "chunks" of information and get the learning right (i.e., show them, tell them, make them demonstrate it).

11. Accept that students will not remember most of what you tell them; focus on making a good impression and 3-4 crucial points.

12. Don't get defensive, and try not to feel ownership about your teaching methods or style. Everyone has at least some room for improvement, and people rarely improve by walling themselves off and avoiding criticism.

13. You're not going to be able to fit everything you want to into an instruction session (especially a one-shot session), so make sure that you keep the information at a manageable level for you and the students.

14. Know your own learning style and use it to learn about teaching and learning. I'm a visual learner and learn through experience, so it helps me to observe others teach and to be observed teaching. Others will learn better by reading about teaching and learning. If that works for them, then that's where they should put their energy. However, at some point, one needs to recognize that presenting to a class is a necessity and that class will be full of people who don't necessarily share your learning style. Be prepared to plan activities that will include other learning styles, even if they're not your own.

15. Make it engaging for the students! Instruction is our opportunity to show that we can be great teachers, that information literacy skills are important, and that the library is the most relevant source of information. We must engage the students—and the faculty, too!

16. Be honest about who you are. In other words, don't try to be someone that you're not. We all

have our own gifts and students get that. They can tell a fraud a mile away. Be truthful to yourself and students will respect that about you.

17. Enroll in teacher training courses. Explore online learning systems outside of libraries. Learn from outside the profession.

18. Instruction is a work in progress. You're always trying something new or a different way to get your point across. You're never "done" with instruction.

19. Teach as if you were the student—what you would want out of this particular class, if you were taking it.

20. Take courses related to pedagogical development and learn web 2.0 and classroom software application.

21. Practice teaching as much as possible in as many different situations as possible to get comfortable with the process.

22. Know your material, don't try to wing it. Know your audience; don't tell them what you want them to hear. Give them what they want to know.

23. The only way to learn how to teach is to do it.

24. Become involved with your local and regional library association, which probably has an instruction section or group.

25. Plan on being flexible. Sometimes the equipment doesn't work or maybe you discover that the lesson you created is way too simple or complex for the students. Be ready to improvise!

26. Make sure you get internship training in teaching if you intend on becoming an academic librarian.

27. Observe others teaching and get as much practical teaching experience as possible

28. If you're doing outreach or scheduling your own instruction, get instructors to pin dates down because they will run out of time/blow you off if you don't. Do active learning or some kind of activity. Assess stuff every time you can.

29. If your academic program offers classes in how to teach, take them!

30. I believe that observing good instructors is very useful.

31. Get experience in the classroom outside of a library. Work as a part time college-level instructor for a few years before moving to library instruction, either as a graduate assistant or as a lecturer. After teaching semester-

long courses for a while, library instruction becomes much easier to do effectively.

32. If you are a newly hired instruction librarian without previous teaching experience, take a public speaking class. Learn to present with energy and confidence.

33. Take chances. If you have what you think is a good idea for engaging students, run with it. The worst that can happen is that you'll learn from it and make it better.

34. Read as much theory as possible, watch some professionals in action, then take all you've learned and shape it to fit your own individual personality and develop your own style. In other words, Be yourself. Employ methods to engage many types of learners but recognize that you will naturally connect with some better than others. That's just the way it is.

35. Observe. Observe. Observe. Watch as many different people teach as you can. You'll learn just as much from the people that are not great at it as from one the one's that are.

36. Don't let anyone make you think teaching is easy—it is difficult and requires training, preparation, and support!

37. I think to watch your peers and attend as many as possible. That's what I'd like to do.

38. Watch other instruction librarians. The best way—without experience—you will learn is by example. Find a mentor that will let you sit in their classes.

39. Volunteer to teach some classes on anything anywhere—even knitting at the local public library.

40. While it is nice to observe other librarians, I would encourage new librarians to design and lead their first instruction session without having observed any of their colleagues. I think it's very important that each librarian be able to find his or her own "voice" or "style" when it comes to library instruction.

41. Jump in. Experiment. If something doesn't work (or work well), learn from it, tweak it, and move onward.

42. I like to think of instruction as a conversation. It keeps me relaxed and also keeps me from getting overly concerned with following my lesson plan word for word.

43. Keep it simple.

44. My library school experience was useless for instruction; everything I learned about being

an instruction librarian, I learned by working in my universities library as a grad assistant in the reference & instruction department. I was able to learn how to teach classes, watch librarians teach classes, participate in the department community to share instruction techniques, and actually plan and teach classes myself. This was INVALUABLE experience that I'm quite sure is the only reason I got a job as instruction librarian. So my advice to new librarians (I guess I should say, grad students in library school) is to get real-life experience in the classroom while you're in grad school. It's priceless.

45. Take any Instruction courses offered before you graduate or as many workshops as possible.

46. Observe other librarians, even librarians who you wouldn't necessarily consider good teachers. Learning what not to do is as important as learning what to do.

47. Do it. The more you do, the more you learn. Take one class at a time . . . have one bad class, don't dwell on it.

48. Do an internship. Get some experience and coaching before you have to go it alone.

49. Even if it's not part of your job description, ask to do it. And volunteer whenever you can.

50. Keep learning. Library school is only the beginning . . .

C. Optional: What is your greatest challenge related to teaching and/or training? Have you tried to confront this challenge, and if so, how?

1. Despite "traditional" teacher training and training specifically for library instruction and experience, I still get anxious before every instruction session and tend to talk too fast. Speaking with my mentor, an excellent instructor, leads me to believe this may never go away, but I know it can cause problems for the students. I've taken speech classes, video-taped my teaching, been observed, and am still struggling.

2. Greatest challenge is getting into the teaching/lecturing mindset, which to me is quite different than being at the reference desk working one-on-one with students or providing online library services. I confront it with practice, reflection, and reading about best teaching practices.

3. Just understanding the basics and having the confidence to lead a course. To remedy my anxiety I am pursuing another master's degree in education.

4. I tend to try, often at the behest of a professor, to cram way too much information into an hour-long session. I think this is a very common problem and I try to be honest about how long it will take to cover various topics. But I still end up trying to fit it all in.

5. We don't have rooms for instructional labs in the library. I wrote a grant for the equipment we needed but we had to place it out in the middle of the room.

6. Lack of classroom space.

7. Endlessly. We simple do not have the time in our curriculum. We've managed our first year student program rather well, but in doing so I'm SWAMPED. We need to do more to integrate along our majors, but I can't take any more classes and most of the other librarians are at their capacities too. Very difficult.

8. Profession's obsession with big, overblown, poorly designed information literacy tutorials, and the negative mental image they have left behind with the senior administrators who need to get behind current, better work. IL librarian dogma.

9. Organizing a session and making sure that students see something new each time I teach. If a student things that they've already been through this before, then they won't pay attention and not learn anything. Mostly I've tried to confront this challenge through trial and error during the sessions, and trying to tie each session to a specific project.

10. Librarians who are resistant to teaching is my biggest challenge. Some people go to library school because they "want to be near the books" or they "enjoy reading." But they end up working in higher ed where they are expected to participate in the teaching/learning community and they don't really want to. Or, they don't like undergrads/students. Why are they working at a college or university library? This baffles, frustrates, and saddens me. I have tried confronting this in many ways, but I don't have much to show for my efforts.

11. My greatest challenge is trying to keep the students engaged and integrating active components into the lesson. I use humor (sometimes successfully, other times not so much), and

group activity to combat boredom. I think we can always do more to keep them interested. I'd probably give you the same answer in 20 years because it is my mission to keep working on this.

12. I'm a new instruction librarian, so I haven't had a lot of experience yet in this setting. I did teach History as an adjunct for a few years and that experience has helped me tremendously. I think the greatest challenge in this environment will be devising ways of keeping the "one-shot" sessions fresh—especially when some of our classes overlap and we see the same students. When you don't get a semester to develop relationships with your class, it's tougher to introduce material and get students engaged. Plus, with mostly one-shot sessions, as a teacher you never know if the students "got it."

13. Assessment issues. I have administered pre- and post-tests in selective classes, but feel that meaningful assessment can only happen over a period of years and we have no way of doing this easily nor is there a campus framework for conducting this kind of assessment. Hi, Char! Guess who?

14. Students tuning the class session out because "they've had this stuff a million times." I start every class with how unique each session is with varying degrees of success. Also, faculty seem to think that students know how to research because they IM/text/use Google/use Facebook etc.

15. Being capable of teaching research to a wide array of disciplines in a meaningful, insightful manner. the amount of prep work I do is amazing, especially when it is about providing library support to new online graduate programs, or science-intensive undergraduate programs.

16. I always attempt to immerse myself in the course content and also work with the curriculum creators to supplement and provide unique and valuable instruction content.

17. I strive to keep the material fresh and interesting to me so I can convey my enthusiasm to the students.

18. We are all assigned to do orientations based on the time of our ref desk assignment, not based on our background or interest. I have been unsuccessful in changing this, because our administrator would have to leave.

19. Dealing with the fall semester flood of instruction sessions. Most of the time I feel like I'm treading water. You just have to accept that things are going to be crazy busy and ride it out. Realize you're not going to get much else done and focus on staying on top of planning and conducting instruction sessions.

20. Other librarians unwilling to make the jump to teaching-based librarianship. I've held plenty of professional development workshops. The intrinsically motivated ones show, the ones who need the most help, don't. Library schools aren't doing their job in translating the needs of today's academic librarians to curriculum.

21. Creating better rapport with students and inspiring them to care about Information Lit.

22. Outreach to faculty. Surveys, talking to them, trying to get a good sales pitch without seeming like I'm harassing them. Getting a real campus buy-in to information literacy.

23. Lack of knowing what to do! I observe others and read books (there are a lot of books out there on information literacy instruction), and assess how our library tutorials go so as to try and improve my performance.

24. Lack of public speaking experience (and fear of it)! I found that just by doing these classes over and over again I got more and more comfortable with the public speaking part!

25. My greatest challenge is holding the students' attention. My best instruction is when there is a clear assignment so that I can show them immediately how to find resources that apply directly to the assignment. Once I have captured their interest, things proceed a lot better.

26. Not burning out. Teaching can occupy so much time that nothing else can get done during high volume times. Self-care can be a problem when teaching requires 12 hour days.

27. I learned that I have to say no when providing instruction will mean more than 10 hours on campus. I have had middling success.

28. Forcing myself to teach skills rather than tools. I have to confront it on a semester by semester basis. It's far too easy to take a day off and just cruise on through teaching interfaces rather than getting students to think about the information they're accessing (and why they're accessing it).

29. Convincing the faculty that it's necessary.
30. I work in a situation where we are severely understaffed (10,000 students on 2 campuses; 6.5 reference positions of which one is paraprofessional) so finding time to prepare for classes is difficult.
31. We simply don't have the technological resources we really need. We only have one computer/instruction lab and it only seats 15. Plus, as far as I can tell there is no desire to offer a for-credit library course. This is something that many students have expressed interest in to me during reference transactions or instruction sessions.
32. I think every librarian should be required to take some version of a Secondary Methods class. I use what I learned in that class every day.
33. Time to develop my skills is in short supply. I stay up on what people are discussing concerning info lit and I watch webinars, but it is few and far between. I feel that my organization does not make training a priority. I have to carve out my own time for individual training for the most part. I have suggested that I train other staff members in a more formal setting. The idea was well-received but then nothing happened.
34. I enjoy public speaking, so sometimes I can be too calm about teaching/training and fail to adequately prepare. I try to confront this by scheduling prep time specifically into my calendar.
35. Maintaining control of the scheduling of the Library Computer Classroom. I have agreed to allow administration to schedule classes other than library instruction in the room because of pressure from the president. Related to this is convincing some faculty and administrators of the worth of instruction.
36. Finding time and money to stay up on trends in the field and improve my instruction by participating in professional development activities.
37. Putting into practice what I learn.
38. Expanding the one-shot class. Am working with an instructor to create a more integrated lesson plan within her course
39. I always feel like I'm winging it, so I read everything I can about improving information literacy problems and I try to get involved with

opportunities to learn more about best practices.
40. I talk really fast when I get nervous. I'm still working on it. I've started asking the class, do y'all get this? Should we stay? Should we move on? Which has helped.
41. Lack of support for development. I've been on my own in learning how to teach.
42. Teaching/training enough. We as librarians don't tend to get enough "face time" with the students.
43. No formal education in teaching/training. See above. In addition to the knowledge and skills I want to learn, I hope this program will also help boost my credibility with faculty, academic technology staff, etc.
44. Two: Feeling confident about the effectiveness of assessment tools and finding a more equal relationship with faculty. I've worked on both, and while they're improving, it's a challenge.
45. Finding/making time to adequately prepare. When you're fairly new in the profession, preparing to teach takes a lot of time, effort, and concentration, so I have to do things like put a "do not disturb" sign on my door, block out whole or half days on my calendar, etc. It's worth it, though, because I find that when I am well-prepared, the sessions tend to go smoothly and students learn a lot.
46. Making it interesting. None of it is interesting to me so it's beyond me to some degree. Boolean? Yawn. Wish there was more out there that we could just take and run with that I wanted to use.
47. Keeping things interesting and balancing instruction with a chance for students to try out what I've been demonstrating (not always possible given the time and technical constraints of some classes).
48. Trying not to be nervous. Still not sure how to deal with nerves . . .
49. Convincing faculty that it is necessary and that the students do not already have these skills. We are working to confront it by making inroads wherever we can as word of mouth is often the best marketing. We also make ourselves very visible on campus by serving on Committees and participating in workshops and training.
50. I took a new position as the education librarian, and while I get to design and create all of

the instructional materials for our website, I miss the interaction and learning opportunities involved with teaching large classes. Our liaisons handle all the requested classes, and our drop in classes are attended less and less.

Glossary

Parenthetical numbers indicate the chapters where these concepts are discussed.

active learning. Instructional theories and approaches based on the premise that there is a strong link between engaged activity and meaningful learning. (4, 5, 6)

ADDIE. Acronym that stands for Analyze, Design, Develop, Implement, and Evaluate, a five-step cycle that represents the core of design thinking and methodology. (7)

advance organizer. Outline provided at the beginning of a learning interaction that links new content with familiar concepts or experiences and previews of what will be covered in the interaction. (4, 5)

affective technique. Instructional and assessment technique that focuses on emotional aspects of the learning experience. (4, 5)

alignment. Positioning of an object or graphic in relation to another. (11)

andragogy. Theory and practice of adult education. (4)

ARCS. Instructional motivation model built on designing learning experiences that maximize learner Attention, Relevance, Confidence, and Satisfaction. (10)

asynchronous interaction. Learning interaction, typically online, that does not occur in real-time (e.g., screencast tutorial). (5, 11, 12)

behaviorism. School of theory that focuses on the stimulus-response model of instruction, wherein positive feedback reinforces accurate knowledge. (4, 5)

blended learning. Learning environment that mixes media and delivery methods, such as a hybrid online and in-person class. (6, 7)

Bloom's taxonomy. Set of successive levels for classifying and describing learning objectives into three domains: cognitive, affective, and psychomotor. (10)

chunking. Separating instructional material into discrete units that function on the principles of cognitive load management. (4, 5)

classical conditioning. Commonly associated with Ivan Pavlov, a form of associative learning that presents stimuli in order to create conditioned responses. (4)

cognitive load. Stress placed on short-term memory during a learning interaction as information is processed. (4, 5, 10)

cognitivism. School of theory based on the premise that learning consists of predictable mental processes and is facilitated by structured information organization. (4, 5)

community of practice. Group of practitioners who collectively provide support and resources relating to shared professional endeavors and goals. (3)

confirmative assessment. Evaluation that takes place some time after a learning interaction in order to test the retention and application of learned content in an authentic setting. (12)

connectivism. School of theory based on the premise that networked information and pervasive technology have changed the learning process. (6)

constructivism. School of theory that views learning as a process of translating experience into knowledge via social processes and cultural contexts. (4, 5)

contextual variables. Environmental factors that can affect a learning interaction. (4)

contrast. Juxtaposition of color, shade, and hue within an image. (11)

Curse of Knowledge. State of knowing so much about a subject that one cannot communicate about it succinctly or perceive it from the perspective of a novice. (1, 5)

design thinking. Application of systematic and outcome-oriented mentality toward the creation of objects and interactions. (7, 8)

differentiated instruction. Instruction that incorporates diverse methods and strategies in order to appeal to learners of different styles and intelligences. (9, 10)

elaboration. Building on prior knowledge in order to create increasingly complex memory structures. (4)

elements of instruction. The four components of a learning interaction: learner, context, content, and educator. (2, 9)

empiricism. Classical philosophical position (Aristotelian) that all knowledge derives from experience. (4)

engagement continuum. Alternative model to the learning pyramid in which "activity" is defined by a balance between experience/motivation and pedagogical strategy. (4, 5)

experience design. Design approach that focuses on the quality of the end user experience. (7)

extrinsic motivation. Motivation that arises from factors external to a learner, such as grades or other incentives. (4, 5)

factors of learning. Four factors that guide an individual's learning process: motivation, prior knowledge, memory, and environment. (4, 5)

feedback loop. Cycle of gathering information from learners and responding productively by revising or adjusting an instructional approach. (2, 12)

figure/ground. Aesthetic concept that distinguishes between what an individual pays attention to (figure) and doesn't pay attention to (ground). (11)

formative assessment. Assessment undertaken during an instructional interaction in order to gauge learning and determine the effectiveness of teaching. (12)

Gestalt theory. Psychological theory that describes the mind's tendency to perceive the whole rather than individual parts. (5)

gleaning. Gathering inspiration and ideas from your environment and community of practice. (3)

goals. Broad, overall aspirations for a learning interaction. (10)

higher-order thought. Top three levels of Bloom's cognitive taxonomy of intellectual activity: analysis, synthesis, and evaluation. (10)

information processing theory. Cognitivist theory based on the premise that the mind is a structured system that processes information according to logical principles. (4, 5)

instructional design. Systematic and outcome-focused approach to planning and delivering educational objects and materials. (7, 8, 9, 10, 11, 12)

instructional literacy. Concept in instructor development that stresses equivalent awareness of four factors: reflective practice, educational theory, instructional design, and teaching technologies. (1, 2, 3, 4, 5, 6)

instructional message. Core of a learning object or interaction that appeals to a learner's self-interest. (1, 11)

instructional technology. Tools, techniques, and products that enable technology-facilitated education. (6)

intrinsic motivation. Motivation that arises from factors internal to a learner, such as self-motivation or personal investment in the content of instruction. (4, 5)

Law of Effect. Behaviorist stimulus-and-response learning model in which a subject learns to make associations between actions and outcomes. (4)

learner-centered instruction. Student-centered learning; education that focuses on the effectiveness of learning and the student experience rather than the effectiveness of teaching and the instructor experience. (4, 5, 9)

learning object. Unit, module, tutorial, or other instructional tool deployed in a learning scenario. (1, 11, 12)

learning scenario. Context in which a learning interaction takes place. (1, 2, 9)

lower-order thought. First three levels of Bloom's taxonomy, which encompass "simple recall"; knowledge, comprehension, and application. (10)

metacognition. Thinking about thinking, or cognition about one's own intellectual abilities and processes. (2, 4, 5)

mnemonic. Aid to memory, such as an acronym. (4, 7)

multiple intelligences. Theory that describes a range of human capacities beyond cognitive ability. (9)

objectives. Performance target that explicitly defines the context and application of learning given a set of specific criteria. (10)

operant conditioning. Behaviorist process of voluntary behavior modification using stimulus and consequence. (4)

outcomes. Performance target that describes the real-world application of learning objectives. (10)

pedagogy. Theory and study of instructional techniques and methods. (5)

personal learning environment (PLE). Combination of digital, physical, and environmental tools that make up an individual's preferred or most effective learning context. (1, 6)

praxis. Practical application of pedagogical theory. (4)

pre-assessment. Assessment strategy deployed before a learning interaction as an information-gathering technique. (12)

prior knowledge. Previous knowledge and experience that a learner brings to an instructional scenario. (4, 5, 9)

prototyping. Iterative design strategy that develops and tests successive revised versions of a product or object. (7, 11)

proximity. Distance between objects that indicates their relationship to one another. (11)

psychomotor. The third of Bloom's learning domains; deals with the physical and kinesthetic. (10)

questioning technique. Reflective and participatory method for assessing students and creating an engaging learning dynamic. (2, 5)

rationalism. Classical philosophical position (Platonic) that knowledge derives from reason rather than experience. (4)

readiness. Degree to which instruction is matched to the developmental level of the learner. (4)

reflective practice. Instructor development strategies that observe and consider one's own teaching effectiveness with the goal of improving the learner experience. (2)

reliability. Consistency of performance of an assessment measure. (12)

repetition. Consistent or recurring elements within a design. (11)

schema. Mental construction that reflects a relationship between objects or concepts. (4, 5)

sensory registers. Perceptual senses that gather information from the environment. (4)

situated learning. Theory based on the premise that meaningful learning occurs in authentic, real-world contexts. (4, 5)

summative assessment. Assessment conducted at the conclusion of a learning interaction in order to gauge the achievement of learning targets and evaluate instructor performance. (12)

synchronous. In real time; as in a learning interaction, usually digital. (5, 11, 12)

tabula rasa. Empiricist (Lockean) notion of the "blank slate," in which one enters the world wholly ignorant and derives all knowledge from direct experience. (4)

targets. Goals, objectives, and outcomes defined before an interaction that guide content, delivery, and learning activities. (10)

task analysis. Methodical breakdown of every step and substep involved in a task; used to define targets and create learning activities. (10)

teacher identity. Personality, beliefs, and conviction a teacher brings to instruction. (1)

three-question reflection. Reflective and summative exercise in which an instructor notes the most positive experience, least positive experience, and one insight gained in a learning interaction. (2)

usability. Accessibility or ease a user experiences with a product or service. (6, 7)

USER. Four-stage instructional design method: Understand, Structure, Engage, Reflect. (8, 9, 10, 11, 12)

validity. Degree to which an assessment measure judges the content or concept that it is meant to judge. (12)

visual literacy. Ability to perceive, interpret, and process graphic information. (11)

visualization. Translation of data or information into visual form. (6, 11)

WIIFM. "What's in it for me?"—a mnemonic and motivational strategy to help instructors remember to speak to learner self-interest in a learning interaction. (1, 5, 14)

working memory. Short-term memory; devoted to processing information and selecting elements that are transferred to long-term memory. (4, 5)

zone of proximal development (ZPD). Extent of learning achievable by an individual in a given learning scenario. (4)

Index

You may also be interested in

TEACHING INFORMATION LITERACY:
50 Standards-Based Exercises for
College Students, Second Edition

Joanna M. Burkhardt and Mary C. MacDonald
with Andrée J. Rathemacher

Perfect for a full-semester course or a single, focused seminar
or workshop, these 50 standards-based exercises show how
to engage students with electronic and print information
resources alike.

PRINT ISBN: 978-0-8389-1053-5
E-BOOK: 7400-0535
PRINT/E-BOOK BUNDLE: 7700-0535
152 PGS / 8.5" × 11"

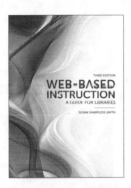

WEB-BASED INSTRUCTION,
THIRD EDITION
SUSAN SHARPLESS SMITH
ISBN: 978-0-8389-1056-6

NO SHELF REQUIRED
EDITED BY SUE POLANKA
ISBN: 978-0-8389-1054-2

MARKETING ACADEMIC
LIBRARIES ECOURSE
BRIAN MATHEWS
ISBN: 978-0-8389-9077-3

MARKETING TODAY'S
ACADEMIC LIBRARY
BRIAN MATHEWS
ISBN: 978-0-8389-0984-3

CREATING THE CUSTOMER-
DRIVEN ACADEMIC LIBRARY
JEANNETTE WOODWARD
ISBN: 978-0-8389-0976-8

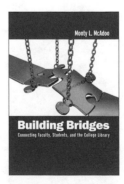

BUILDING BRIDGES
MONTY L. McADOO
ISBN: 978-0-8389-1019-1

Order today at **alastore.ala.org** or **866-746-7252!**

ALA Store purchases fund advocacy, awareness, and accreditation programs for library professionals worldwide.